AFTER THE RAJ

David Rubin

AFTER THE RAJ
British Novels of India
Since 1947

UNIVERSITY PRESS OF NEW ENGLAND
Hanover and London, 1986

University Press of New England

Brandeis University
Brown University
Clark University
University of Connecticut
Dartmouth College
University of New Hampshire
University of Rhode Island
Tufts University
University of Vermont

Printed in the United States of America

LIBRARY OF CONGRESS CATALOGING-IN-PUBLICATION DATA

Rubin, David, date
    After the Raj.

    Bibliography: p.
    Includes index.
    1. English fiction—20th century—History and criticism.   2. India in literature.   3. British—India—Fiction.   I. Title.
PR830.I6R8   1986   823'.914'093254   86-40115
ISBN 0-87451-383-9

In Memory of James Matthew Zito

Contents

Preface

And what is a novel if not a conviction of our fellow-men's existence strong enough to take upon itself a form of imagined life clearer than reality and whose accumulated verisimilitude of selected episodes puts to shame the pride of documentary history?

JOSEPH CONRAD[1]

For more than a century now, a great deal of attention has been devoted to studying problems of East-West understanding, focusing especially on England and India as most richly representative of the complexity of these problems and the fundamental tensions and polarities of outlook of Europe and Asia. The last three decades have been particularly prolific in provocative and controversial works on the nature of the differences between India and the West by such diversified writers as V. S. Naipaul, N. C. Chaudhuri, Jeffrey Masson, Arthur Koestler, Sudhir Kakar, and David Selbourne. Indian commentators like Naipaul and Chaudhuri, it should be noted, are probably the fiercest in their negative criticism of Indian culture. But Naipaul, though ethnically Indian, was born outside India, has never lived there, and is English by education; while Chaudhuri, who now lives in England, has long identified himself with a European point of view. India has always been alien to Naipaul, and Chaudhuri seems to suggest that, once an Indian has been Europeanized in his outlook, it is no longer possible for him to sympathize with, or even understand, the India he has left behind.

Politics, psychoanalysis, philosophy, linguistics, religion, and sociology have been employed as typical prisms through which to examine the sources of incompatibility with Western ideas and ideals and even to question the very possibility of any genuine understanding of one culture by the other—the inexorability of what Shamsul Islam terms Kipling's Law, the familiar line that "East is East and West is West, and never the twain shall meet."

Following the lead of earlier writers (e.g., Katherine Mayo and Albert Schweitzer), Naipaul and Masson, for instance, have attempted to demonstrate the elemental differences in the personality structures, modes of thought, and, as it were, genetically predetermined, irreconcilably separate characters of Europeans and Indians. These analyses—one thinks especially of Naipaul and Chaudhuri—have often been not so much dispassionately objective as hostile and vindictive, motivated by prejudices and a subtle personal malaise possibly not always recognized by the authors themselves, a characteristic that will be discovered also in some of the novelists to be discussed later in this book. Are East and West never to meet? At the end of his poem Kipling allows an exception: "But there is neither East nor West, Border, nor Breed, nor Birth,/When two strong men stand face to face, though they come from the ends of the Earth!" Such conjunctions continue to be rare, it appears, not only among those who theorize about the troubled relationship of Britain and India but among the writers of fiction as well.

In the attempts at analysis cited above, little attention has been paid to the imaginative literature that explores and comments on Indo-British relations since Forster's *Passage to India* (1924) and, in particular, most surprisingly, since Indian Independence in 1947. Yet it seems obvious to me—and I believe it is more than a question of the bias of my own discipline—that it is above all in the imaginative literature of peoples that one can find the most basic, characteristic, and dependable exemplifications of intercultural tensions and misconceptions, and sometimes, at least, their resolution. When fiction has been studied in connection with these problems, more often than not it has been only from a sociological point of view, with no attention to the literary value of the work at hand. Now, since the "meaning" of a work of art cannot be neatly divided into categories of "ideas" and esthetic values, such an approach can provide at best only a limited and superficial insight into the nature of the cultural problems being studied. Furthermore, it seems demonstrable that, more often than not, a direct ratio exists between the degree of the novelist's depth of understanding of the underlying causes of cultural and racial conflict on the one hand and his literary powers on the other.

By means of a thorough scrutiny of Anglo-Indian fiction since 1947 (which will inevitably require looking at some very bad as well as first-rate novels) I want to explore the nature and origins of the elaborate and, I believe, frequently delusional mythology that still dominates British attitudes toward India even forty years after the end of the Raj, and to offer a new evaluation of the most important novels devoted to problems of Indo-British under-standing. I have classified the novelists I study as British because, though all of them reflect English points of view and the English concern with India, some of them are from the Commonwealth, though usually, like Halls and Markandaya, they are longtime residents of Britain. I will often refer to their work as Anglo-Indian, a term used until recently to refer to English people domiciled in India, their way of life, and their literature. Since the fifties this term has been used in India chiefly to refer to Indians of mixed English and Indian origin. Paul Scott, like Forster, uses it in its earlier sense, as do most writers on British literature dealing with India, and the following pages will conform to this usage.

I was tempted to deal with American fiction about India, but by now such writing constitutes a full subject for study in its own right; I have, however, discussed one American novel by Louis Bromfield because, unlike most American fiction set in India, its story evolves from a concern with Indo-British relations on the eve of Independence.

For the generous grant that made it possible for me to complete this undertaking I am indebted to the Social Science Research Council. I would also like to express my appreciation to Ainslie Embree, Robin Lewis, Frances Pritchett, and John DeWind for reading all or parts of the manuscript and for their many valuable suggestions, to Irma Garlick for her intelligent and sympathetic editing, and to Stella Sandahl, William Park, and David Beams for their constant support and encouragement while I was writing *After the Raj*.

New York   D.R.
February 1986

AFTER THE RAJ

Introduction

"Move the population of a lively Colorado town to Rhatore, set up a good local paper, organize a board of trade, and let the world know what there is here, and we'd have a boom in six months that would shake the empire. But what's the use? They're dead. They're mummies. They're wooden images. There isn't enough real, old-fashioned downright rustle and razzle-dazzle and 'git up and git' in Gokral Seetarun to run a milk-cart." . . .

"Because they are not like us," she answered. . . . "If they were clever, if they were wise, what could we do for them? It is because they are lost, stumbling, foolish creatures that they need us."

RUDYARD KIPLING AND WOLCOTT BALESTIER[1]

Nigel grinned and said you had half to believe him, didn't you? It was what attracted him about this country, he explained, this odd mixture of the real and the unreal.

Craddock said, "There is only the real."

PAUL SCOTT[2]

Literature reflecting the British involvement in India did not of course end with the Raj—nor indeed, for that matter, did the involvement. There is an abundance of novels presenting post-mortem views of the Raj, its successes and failures; others, such as those of J. G. Farrell, use India primarily as a stage for the critical examination of British society in the last century; and still others, such as the historical romances of Kaye and Fitzgerald, provide a nostalgic retrospect of an India that never was. Perhaps the largest grouping could be made of those novels, such as the later books of Ruth Jhabvala, in which India, remaining unchangingly extrinsic and aloof, yet somehow magically intensifies the experiences, usually neurotic, of visiting Westerners; in these novels India sharpens the awareness, often with destructive results, all the while it looms as utterly inaccessible.[3]

After so many centuries of British experience in India, there is nothing surprising in the British writer's continuing fascination with the former colony. Unexpected, however, is the survival of so many of the delusions and illusions, mostly negative, about

1

India that had characterized earlier fiction. Particular Anglo-Saxon mythologies about the subcontinent—its mystery, its spirituality, its powers to liberate and to destroy, its dangers, its subtly seductive and threatening sexuality—continue to furnish the material for a number of novels that either take as a given or finally accept the difficulty (and often the impossibility) of genuine understanding between Westerner and Indian. The insidiously implicit, and sometimes explicit, basis underlying these beliefs is the conviction that Indians are somehow inferior as human beings and their culture seriously defective—a view, incidentally, fervently espoused by some Indian intellectuals, usually born overseas, such as V. S. Naipaul, or living there in self-imposed exile, such as N. C. Chaudhuri.

The British attitude toward India and Indians before Independence is obviously easier to understand, if not necessarily to forgive. Some sort of myth of British superiority helped wonderfully in sustaining the Raj, a process in which the role of fiction did not go unnoticed by critical British eyes. In 1926, in *A Book of South India*, J. Chartres Molony wrote:

> As between English officials and educated Indians, relations were embittered by a widely read school of "imperialist" fiction writers, whose method was to depict the Indian as *necessarily* incapable, and as *necessarily* inferior to the Englishman in qualities of energy, decision, and straightforwardness. Such writers were wont to join to a general depreciation of Indians a tactless exaltation of the "fighting" at the expense of the "educated" classes. Moreover, the "martyr" attitude of the European was overdone. I have little patience with the pretence that the Englishman saves India every morning from plague, pestilence, battle and anarchy; or that immolated on the altar of humanitarianism, he spends body and soul in a thankless and ill-requited service.[4]

One of the earliest scholarly studies of "imperialist" fiction is Susanne Howe's *Novels of Empire* (1949),[5] an inquiry into understanding and misunderstandings of the cultures and peoples of India and other colonies through an analysis of the English, French, and German fiction that described them, works written mostly in the nineteenth century.

Two valuable later studies, Allen Greenberger's *British Image of India: A Study in the Literature of Imperialism, 1880–1960*[6] (1969) and Benita Parry's *Delusions and Discoveries: Studies on India in the British Imagination 1880–1930* (1972), have closely examined the nature of Indo-British relations largely by means of a careful reading of British fiction of the Victorian era and the first half of the present century. Greenberger surveys an enormous number of novels and tales thematically, under the general subdivisions of "The Era of Confidence, 1880–1910," "The Era of Doubt, 1910–1935," and "The Era of Melancholy, 1935–1960." Kipling, Flora Annie Steel, and Maud Diver figure among the typical novelists of the first period; Forster, Edmund Candler and E. J. Thompson of the second; the Godden sisters and John Masters of the third. Parry proceeds through a consideration of a much more limited number of writers, each in greater detail and with more attention to their literary qualities than is the case with Greenberger. Since Parry concludes with Forster, and Greenberger, ignoring the early work of Scott and Jhabvala, with Masters, both scholars stop short of what is quite the most interesting (and, I believe, literarily rewarding) period of Anglo-Indian fiction thus far, the period beginning in the fifties and continuing through the seventies.

It will be useful here to summarize Parry's conclusions, since so much of what she finds characteristic of Anglo-Indian fiction before 1930 continues to underlie the attitudes of more recent writers. In dozens of late nineteenth-century and early twentieth-century writers, she finds a near universal acceptance of the absolute incompatibility of English and Indians. The latter are characterized by every form of wickedness and perversion; they are incapable of logical thought or honorable behavior. Although unattractive in themselves, Indians, as though magically abetted by the Indian atmosphere, exert a dangerous sexual seductiveness. Their perversity derives in part from their reprehensible failure to separate the erotic from the divine. The British, on the other hand, are justified in their occupation of the country because they have a Messianic role to save the Indians from anarchy since they will clearly never be capable of governing themselves. The British consistently judge Indians on the basis of their own Western standards, convinced that these standards are uniquely good and universally applicable. The "good" Indians are generally simple, represented by loyal servants and certain martial types—Sikhs, Rajputs, or essentially non-Indian border people, such as the Pathans and Gurkhas, while the worst Indians are the priests and, most noxious, the educated, particularly if they are Bengali.

This summation of the views Parry has found prevalent in Anglo-Indian fiction up through the early part of this century is necessarily a simplification, but it is clear that racist prejudice was fundamental in shaping the attitudes of most novelists toward their material. Their crudity and simple-mindedness shock the more pious sensibility of the present age, but this does not mean that they no longer exist. Rather, they have gone underground, where they are still able to determine the outlook of many contemporary novelists on their Indian characters and setting.

Greenberger points out, "Probably the major source of ideas concerning India came from fiction set in that country."[7] To this we might add that today, film and the reports of increasing numbers of tourists (both frequently fictive) also contribute source material for popular concepts of foreign lands. But filmmakers and novelists themselves have already imbibed prejudices and misconceptions about India even before going there. Greenberger rightly says, "It is events in England, and in the West in general, which determine the image held of India at any particular time. From this it follows that the images were not changed by the Indian reality. It is far more likely that the images have influenced the way in which the reality was seen."[8] The circular process—preconception, failure to alter the preconception in the light of actual experience, and the subsequent regeneration and dissemination of the preconceived image—explains in part the vitality and near-ineradicability of the popular prejudices and myths about India. To divest oneself of all the racially founded paraphernalia of one's background, the inevitable source of such prejudice, and look objectively at India, is apparently too threatening, too potentially self-destructive, to be risked. Those newcomers to India who jettison all the baggage of their preconceptions and automatic responses to both the good and bad that India may offer them, as we shall observe in some of Ruth Jhabvala's fiction, are more often than not without a personality of their own, apathetic to the point of abnormality, and disposed to self-destruction; paradoxically, they remain ultimately quite as remote from the realities of India as the Turtons and Callendars of *A Passage to India*.

Greenberger and Parry are most interested in showing the relationship of the literature to a specific historical framework. My emphasis will be on the literary significance of the works discussed, a significance of which naturally historical elements will form a part. Following Parry rather than Greenberger, I intend, after a preliminary survey of the general background and chapters on contemporary Anglo-Indian novelists in general in terms of the modes of romance they embody in their work, to examine in detail the oeuvre of only a few novelists.

The fiction that concerns me, fiction written mostly since Indian Independence in 1947, is so voluminous that it would be impossible to discuss it all, even superficially, in one volume. Many of the novels in any case are of little literary value, although some of these too must be examined because of what they so plainly represent. Only one major English novelist since Forster, Paul Scott, has been inspired by the drama of Indo-British relations. Despite a somewhat limited personal experience of India, Scott shows a sure grasp of Indians as human beings first of all; they are not regarded as special, a peculiar, separate species requiring greater sympathy or greater censure than other people (Forster sins in both directions, as I shall show later) but are portrayed with the same sympathetic and critical eye he directs at his European characters. To go to the other extreme, in *The Cats of Benares*, Geraldine Halls concentrates on describing what she considers the difficulties—for Europeans—of living in India, the aggravating silliness and venality of Indian men and women, and the general ugliness of daily life: a view all in all so shallow and negative that, even understood as caricature, it repels.

There are a great many novels along the order of *The Cats of Benares* where a kind of perverted classical concept of tragedy is revived, in which only people of royal and noble birth (the Europeans) are considered worthy of serious treatment, while the Indian population (servants, merchants, policemen, bureaucrats, and clowns) are allowed only brief comic appearances as fantastic objects for the author's derision or disgust. In her early work, Ruth Jhabvala promises a fair and serious treatment of the Indian society she knows, but, as her work becomes progressively obsessed with the theme of Westerners in India, it relies more and more on caricature and veers ever closer (no matter how much greater the literary skill) toward the world of Halls. Jhabvala has been criticized by Indians for confining her subject matter to middle-class Delhi society, the deposed princes, hippies, and the Bombay film world (already a vast *matière!*); the charge is of course absurd; a writer is free to write about anything he both can and wants to. The basis for any criticism of Jhabvala must be the depth and humanity with which she is able to imagine her fictional world, and to this subject I shall return in the chapter devoted to her.

There are other worthwhile novelists besides Scott and Jhabvala who have written about India in the post-Raj era: Rumer Godden, for instance, and J. G. Farrell, whose career ended tragically when he was halfway through a second brilliant comic novel about the British in nineteenth-century India. Although they will be discussed in various connections, for the general scheme of the book it has seemed more useful to concentrate on Scott and Jhabvala, with the addition of Kamala Markandaya, who is British by adoption and the most original among her contemporaries in her treatment of the great theme of love, hatred, and misunderstanding provoked—endlessly, it would seem—by every contact between India and Britain. In this triune division of the field, Jhabvala may be said to represent a sort of Inferno, Scott Purgatorio, and Markandaya, in her most recent novels, a near-Paradiso of reconciliation and ultimate harmony.

Much of the material in the next chapter is covered in greater detail, though not always with the same conclusions, in Parry and Greenberger; however, a quick survey of the earlier Anglo-Indian novel's chief characteristics is necessary for understanding the significance of the changes it underwent and the myths that persisted in the decades following Independence.

1

Anglo-Indian Fiction
Before 1947

"You'll never understand the dark and tortuous minds of the natives," she
said; "and if you do I shan't like you—you won't be healthy."

J. R. ACKERLEY[1]

It came to Armin with electric force that people so wonderfully complicated
as this could become the object of a great love, that he could never come
to the end of them. A continuing inability to fit in, to conform, to find a
place by the hearth, which had worried young Armin almost as much as
his schoolmasters, was all of a sudden illuminated. Before, he had been a
foreigner in his own world; in this foreign world he might well find himself
at home.

WILLIAM BUCHAN[2]

The two passages quoted above offer good examples of British
attitudes toward India before and after Independence in 1947.
Writing in 1955, William Buchan would have scant sympathy with
the lady Ackerley is quoting in his 1932 book; Ackerley himself,
for that matter, regards her as absurd. How representative Buchan
is of a genuine transformation of the British view of India and
Indians will become clearer in the following chapters.

It is difficult today, particularly for Americans, to grasp the intensity and rawness of the hostility that characterized British feelings toward Indians not only in the nineteenth century but also
in the very recent past. To sharpen awareness of this animus one
need go back no further than 1944, to take an example at random,
and glance at Beverley Nichols' *Verdict on India*—written on the
eve of Independence—an indictment of everything Indian so vir-
ulent as to leave one breathless. It repeats the well-known charges
made by the American writer Katherine Mayo in 1927 in *Mother
India* regarding the general horror of life in India, and it adds to
it the special offense of derision, a failing Miss Mayo was spared
by her aggressive earnestness. Nichols, for example, dismisses

Indian classical music as a "tale told by an idiot,"[3] and "all the sounds of the slaughter house."[4] Gandhi is not only compared to but equated with Hitler in a chapter titled "Heil Hindu!" Despite Gandhi's well-known attempts to halt communal strife and promote communal harmony, Nichols says that the majority of the one hundred million Muslims of India regard Gandhi "quite rightly, as their most dangerous enemy."[5] In quick succession Nichols derides Indian art, poetry, medicine, politics, and manners, concluding wrongly that Indian languages have no real word for "thank you." "It was the Princess of Berar who first told me the word for 'thank-you.' However, she was not an Indian at all; she was the daughter of the ex-Caliph, and she had royal manners as well as royal blood."[6] As for Hinduism: "Of the many fine, truthful, unselfish Indians I met, hardly one was a sincere Hindu. Almost all had shaken themselves free from the influence of the drug . . . for drug it is."[7] It is interesting to note that Nichols is careful to affect a freedom from prejudice by evoking all the Indians he does like, but he must follow this up by showing them as atypical, liberated from the terrible religion of most of their countrymen—the old case again of "some of my best friends," a smokescreen technique that is still practiced by writers on India, including some of the novelists to be considered in later chapters, as well as journalists (for example, David Selbourne in *Through the Indian Looking-glass*, 1982).

I have devoted attention to this diatribe only because it is representative of so much journalism concerned with India and, in less explicit form, pervades fiction still being written. Similar views, no matter how much more scholarly and documented the form they take, underlie the criticism of Indian civilization by Albert Schweitzer, Arthur Koestler, N. C. Chaudhuri, and V. S. Naipaul. More than any other country in the world, India has provoked devastatingly intemperate attacks, in recent years from her own children as well as from outsiders.[8] Casual observers with only a brief experience of India, such as Nichols, are apt to be the most vituperative in their outbursts, but even longtime residents with strong personal connections with Indian society, such as Ruth Jhabvala, appear to become, with the years, more and more acerbic in their outlook. Rumer Godden writes, "Europeans in India are like cut flowers; that is why most of them wither and grow sterile: they cannot live without their roots, and so few of them take root."[9]

At this point it may be useful to contrast this international theme—the effect of India on the British character and the British imagination (and only occasionally *their* effect on Indians)—with the other, better-known international theme in fiction—America experiencing England and Europe. Writers such as Hawthorne and Wharton, and especially Henry James, equate America with innocence, the Old World with experience, and show both innocence and experience as potentially good or bad, redemptive or destructive. In the polarity of England and India there is scarcely any possibility of such double potentiality. The racism that underlay the British image of India throughout the nineteenth century and persists, though diminished and muted, into the present makes the equation far simpler and near-absolute: the West is good, the East bad. Exceptions are rare and, at least until Independence in 1947, were apt, like *A Passage to India*, to cause a sensation.

The bitterness and contempt typical of the British view of India in most fiction about that country has no parallel in English literature treating an international theme. The possible exception is Dickens' fierce attack on America in *Martin Chuzzlewit*, where the author's raw hostility and sense of personal affront blunt his humor; the more accurate his satire, the less we laugh. If one imagines a comparable approach envenomed with a candid racism and often wanting in mere factual knowledge and accurate observation, one can form a fairly clear idea of the majority of Anglo-Indian novels in the nineteenth century and not a few in the twentieth.

The writers of such novels—to cite one persistent and particularly glaring example of ignorance of Indian culture—often appear unaware of the extraordinary variety of racial, social, and linguistic realities of India. Apart from their usual praise of the martial Pathans and Rajputs and their contempt for the slippery Bengali, they ignore the vast spectrum of what may be called the genetic treasury of India. Where each of their major British characters (and most of the minor ones as well) will be well defined in terms of region, school, accent, and income, the Indians remain amorphous, with invisible backgrounds held to be, perhaps, too dismal to investigate. Forster will have a Bhattacharya married to a Das, a very unlikely match in 1924, and even today one that would be considered scandalous in Brahmin circles. Even so careful an observer as Paul Scott will invent a name like Gupta Sen, when it is invariably Sen Gupta, and he seems unaware that this name denotes a member of a particular Bengali *kayastha* community; his Gupta Sens, apparently unacquainted with Bengali, are exclusively Hindi-speaking; anyone who knows Bengalis of any community settled in the Uttar Pradesh will recognize at once how unlikely this is. Scott will describe Lily Chatterjee, a Rajput, as marrying beneath her when she marries Nello Chatterjee— "into the Vaisya caste," as Lily says.[10] But Chatterjee is a high-ranked division of Bengali Brahmins, and—unless they were Brahmos—the Chatterjees would never have forgiven Nello for marrying not only a woman of lower caste but one they would also consider a virtual foreigner.

Now, these may seem like trivial considerations, but they are, on the contrary, of considerable importance. One would never (to invent an example), trust a novelist who thought that Jones was an Italian name; if one had an Italian Jones in a story, the circumstances would have to be explained, if only humorously. But such verisimilitude is apparently not required in writing about Indian society. So also in the matter of language, where even those British novelists who possess a knowledge of military or kitchen Hindustani have never acquired a mastery of grammar or even of an Indian alphabet. In most of these cases the carelessness about such matters reveals not only the British writer's contempt but also a deeply rooted, often unconscious racism,[11] and it is only another dreary example of what Nehru complains about. "It is quite extraordinary how ignorant English people, apart from some experts and others, are about India. If facts elude them, how much more is the spirit of India beyond their reach? They seized her body and possessed her, but it was the possession of violence. They did not know her or try to know her. They never looked into her eyes, for theirs were averted and hers downcast through shame and humiliation. After centuries of contact they face each other, strangers still, full of dislike for each other."[12]

In view of the combination of ignorance and hostility, it is most extraordinary to find that the third dominant characteristic of virtually all fiction written with an Indian setting, from Steel to Jhabvala, is the supreme importance of India itself, not just as atmosphere but as an obsessive problem, or complex of problems. The novels' very raison d'être is the power, fascination, and danger that India not simply represents but is. The authors and their characters cannot stop talking about India, describing, interpreting, condemning, rejecting; they cannot love it but they cannot leave it alone. The concern with India is often the only intrinsically interesting element in their novels—surely a unique condition of the Anglo-Indian novel. As Ainslie Embree remarks, "It would be odd to refer to *A Dance to the Music of Time* as interesting because it is about England."[13]

Given the grim earnestness so many of the English novelists of India bring to a frequently unnovelistic task (for often their impulse appears merely journalistic), it is not surprising that humor does not abound in their work. In 1949, Susanne Howe wrote: "Novels about India provide more vicarious discomfort than anyone is entitled to. They are among the unhappiest books in the language. They are long on atmosphere, but short on humor and hope."[14] "One element lacking from the image of India at all times is humour," writes Allen Greenberger. "The British could never paint their picture of India in anything other than the darkest colours."[15] After 1947 the humorless mode still prevails; a notable exception is Paul Scott, who, here as in so many other respects, rises above the limitations of the tradition.

The negative tone is so pervasive that in few of these novels is there ever any expression of a sense of wonder or delight at the obvious beauties of India and the pleasures and excitements of daily life there—inevitable, one imagines, at least occasionally, for even the most disaffected visitor. It would seem that filth and poverty, "heat and dust," have annihilated the first and bureaucratic complications the second, leaving behind only ill temper and bitterness. Among novelists since Kipling and before Scott, E. J. Thompson presents a rare and happy exception to this astonishing insensitivity.[16]

During the eighteenth century the British attitude toward India was by no means as negative as it was to become. In *The Nabobs*, Percival Spear has reproduced the favorable comments of English and other foreign visitors concerning the character of Hindus of various castes (although in general the dim view of Muslims appears to have been current from the start). But by the end of the century, with a growing number of British residents permitting the formation of a self-sufficient European society, the gulf between the newcomers and the local population widened, preparing the ground for the fiercely critical view of India that was to prevail in British fiction.[17]

In her Indian tales at the beginning of the nineteenth century, Mary Martha Sherwood (1775–1851), a widely read novelist in her

day, set the tone for a whole century of fiction in which India
would figure as a land monstrous in itself and desperately in need
of England's civilizing mission. In Sherwood's terms, civilization
was synonymous with Christianity, and much of her fiction, not
only the stories set in India, serves mainly to provide a framework
for sermons. *Little Henry and His Bearer* (1812) and *Lucy and Her
Dhaye* (1822), to cite two of her most popular novellas, are edifying
tales of Indian-born English children whose saintly disposition,
preaching, exemplary lives, and early deaths serve to convert their
loyal Indian servants. These works contain a great many random
observations about India and Indians, with glossaries and foot-
notes to translate Hindustani words and explain such terms as
caste, but one looks in vain for any favorable comments about the
country. For a succinct example of Sherwood's general attitude
toward India, consider the remarks near the beginning of a story
called *Arzoomund* (1828?), which are intended to introduce Indians
to the wide English reading public who can have no acquaintance
with them. The present inhabitants, she writes, "are deplorably
ignorant, idolatrously worshipping images of wood, and stone,
and clay."[18] They are, furthermore, "so besotted by their idolatries
and the delusions of their false religions, that they had no other
cares but the providing themselves with food, and no other pleasures than the enjoyment of that ease of body and indolence of
mind which are considered as the sum of human felicity by the
majority of the natives of India."[19] When he is not quite five years
old, Little Henry, under the influence of the house servants, believes not only that the river Ganges can wash away sins but even
"that the Mussulmauns were as good as Christians; for his mother's *khaunsaumaun* had told him so."[20] Such deplorable mistakes
are soon corrected by the arrival of a clergyman's daughter.

The pernicious effects of India on an English family residing
there is described in one of Sherwood's most popular (and longest)
works, *The Lady of the Manor* (1825–1829), in the section titled "The
Garden of Roses." In a remarkable work called *The Indian Pilgrim*
(1818), Sherwood narrates the spiritual quest of an Indian who
allegorically ascends from the least worthy religion to the only
true one. Predictably, Hinduism is at the bottom, Islam on the
next higher rung, then Judaism, Roman Catholicism, and finally
Sherwood's own Protestant Christianity. Sherwood's shrill intolerance of both Muslims and Catholics is often expressed through-

out her writings, but there is nothing to compare with her violent, one might say hysterical, presentation of Hinduism, which is portrayed in a series of lurid descriptions of torture, widow burning, human sacrifice, infanticide, and charnel houses strewn with "the horrid effluvia of putrid and mangled carcasses."[21] In 1844, *The Indian Pilgrim* was translated into Hindustani; one can only wonder how its Indian readers reacted.

Sherwood was followed by a great many nineteenth-century novelists with equally negative responses to India. The violent uprising of 1857 resulted in an even more extreme view of Indians, reflected in a host of novels glorifying British heroism and castigating the natives for their treachery. Flora Annie Steel termed the Mutiny "the Epic of the Race," and so it was popularly viewed in fiction for another century. It is of course impossible to determine precisely how strongly such writing influenced the British imagination and disposed visitors to India to see only what they may have anticipated from that reading. What is certain is that the bad press for India was sustained by British fiction for over a century and that the old racism, no matter how modified its expression, continues into the present, as I hope to demonstrate in the following chapters.

Throughout the Victorian era the negative spell of India was so strong that it could be evoked in works that fundamentally had little or nothing to do with that country, and by writers who had never been there. Consider Conan Doyle's *Sign of Four* (1890), which so faithfully reflects the image of Indians in the minds of the late Victorian English at home. In this tale, the "Four" are three Sikhs and an Englishman who, during the Mutiny, when "two hundred thousand black devils" are "let loose, and the country was a perfect hell,"[22] murder a merchant and steal his treasure. Though they are murderers, the Indians remain true to their word, the pact they have made with the Englishman; and later the Andaman islander, "the unhallowed dwarf with his hideous face," despite his own intrinsic wickedness, also keeps faith with Small. What is interesting in this is the fusion of various prejudices: the martial Sikhs are loyal, if murderous, and the aboriginal islander, a veritable demon from the underworld, also is capable in his primitive, childish way of loyalty to the one he serves. Doyle, personally unacquainted with India and, at the time of *The Sign of Four*, probably Indians as well, taps the rich reservoir of British images of the subcontinent for the facile interpolation of these exotic elements, perfectly suited to his tale of mystery and terror.

Until Kipling no major British writer was deeply engaged by India. Thackeray, born there, like Dickens and Collins uses the country to send some characters to, bring others from. His India is Jos Sedley's curries and the facetious references to Boggley Wallah. Dickens and Collins borrow from that country the sinister art of thuggee. Even in the twentieth century, major novelists, Scott always excepted, use India in much the same way: Virginia Woolf, Elizabeth Bowen, and Iris Murdoch, for example, have characters go off to or reappear from India, though Murdoch's involvement with Indian philosophy makes her a special case, which will be discussed later.[23]

Of the many nineteenth- and early twentieth-century women novelists who wrote, often prolifically, about India, Flora Annie Steel is the most significant because of the seriousness with which she attempted to come to grips with the country. Unlike most such writers, she read scholarly books about India and also was conversant with some Indian languages. Her best-known work, *On the Face of the Waters* (1897), glorifies English traits. All her novels tend to stress the demonic side of Hinduism, with villainous priests, lurid ceremonies, and the like.[24]

Before *A Passage to India*, Rudyard Kipling's *Kim* (1901) is the only memorable novel inspired by the subcontinent. Although the book is often regarded as a kind of paean of love for India, it is a love so seriously qualified as to be compromised in the end. G. T. Garratt notes that

Kipling allowed himself the most astounding generalizations about Indian duplicity and mendacity, or the physical cowardice of certain races. Even in the two novels which take a wider scope and deal more directly with Indian life—*Kim* and *The Naulakha*—the Indians are all drawn "in the flat," as types, not human beings, whereas the Europeans or the country-bred Kim are so indubitably drawn in the round. The one possible exception, the old Lama, is not really an Indian. Not until he had left India for many years could Kipling rid himself of that obsession, driven into the minds of all Englishmen who went East before the War, that a denial of racial superiority was the one deadly sin.[25]

Kim, when he joins the Great Game, automatically sets himself up as a being superior to the Indians he has cherished and to the seductive life of the Grand Trunk Road, substituting the greater good of Britain for the life of the heart.[26] What Kipling himself had loved, like so many before and since, was not "India" but the happiness of the life he had led there. There is an unconscious irony in Kim's telling Mahbub Ali, "I shall be altogether a Sahib." And, already a typical sahib, Kim has chosen an Afghan Muslim for his closest friend among the natives. Kim could enjoy the low life of the bazaars and the adventures of the Grand Trunk Road precisely because he was a scion of the sahibs, never in danger of sinking to the depths; his happy life, before he becomes involved in the Game, is a fantasy of escape: "slumming," if you will, a lesser game in which he never has to be trapped in the miserable, often desperate situations that are part of the everyday experience of indigent Indians. *Kim* is an endlessly beguiling book, but it should not be taken as in any way a faithful picture of Indian life.

Kipling's racism is most apparent in his Indian tales. In "His Chance in Life" he states the theme of the story: "The Black and the White mix very quaintly in their ways. Sometimes the White shows in spurts of fierce, childish pride—which is Pride of Race run crooked—and sometimes the Black in still fiercer abasement and humility, half heathenish customs and strange, unaccountable impulses to crime."[27] This is to prepare us to understand the character of Michele D'Cruze, a telegraph signaler, who "looked down on natives as only a man with seven-eighths native blood in his veins can."[28] In a riot Michele, his heart "big and white in his breast, because of his love for Miss Vezzis,"[29] handles himself courageously. The Police Inspector, "afraid, but obeying the old race-instinct which recognizes a drop of White blood as far it can be diluted,"[30] takes orders from him. But when the English Assistant Collector arrives, "Michele felt himself slipping back more and more into the native, and the tale of the Tibasu Riots ended, with the strain on the teller, in an hysterical outburst of tears, bred by sorrow, shame that he could not feel as uplifted as he had felt through the night, and childish anger that his tongue could not do justice to his great deeds. It was the White drop in Michele's veins dying out, though he did not know it."[31] The quaintly scientific pretension of the story, with its emphasis on precise proportions, the one drop and dilution, is rendered somehow more ludicrous by Kipling's capitalization of what he considers the key words, *white* and *black*.

In a few stories an Indian will show some character, but in such cases he will be one of the border peoples the British favored. In " 'Yoked with an Unbeliever,' " Dunmaya marries an Englishman who has very little character at all. But Dunmaya is a "Hill-girl," and this apparently is meant to justify her making "a decent man of him; and he will ultimately be saved from perdition through her training."[32]

In "Without Benefit of Clergy" (from *Life's Handicap*), one of Kipling's best stories, both Indian lover and her Eurasian child die. Kipling portrays his lovers, English Holden and Indian Ameera, with respect, but his imagination, restricted by the prejudices of his time, could not conceive of a future for them together, and of course the child of such a union would be an anomaly, unacceptable in British society. For all his genuine affection for India, Kipling is unwilling to challenge the fundamental racial prejudice of that British society any more than he will conceive of Holden and Ameera passing over into an Indian world where they and their child would be acceptable. As measured against the profoundly ingrained British racism of that time, Ameera and her baby would ultimately prove to be embarrassments; but since Holden's love for Ameera is genuine (and Kipling portrays it touchingly) the writer's conflict between the particular situation and his general conviction can be resolved only by removing Holden's beloved and child from the scene. When, after Ameera's death, Holden "put his hands before his eyes and muttered, 'Oh you brute! You utter brute!' "[33] his imprecation could be for the perversity of his situation—or simply for India itself.

In many of the stories of *Plain Tales from the Hills* (1887), Kipling had cast a sharply satirical eye on the Anglo-Indian population of Simla, the summer capital—the redoubtable Mrs. Hauksbee and her world. But his criticism of British manners is limited significantly to the pettiness, the follies, and the general shoddy morality of the British among themselves; he is not concerned with, or apparently conscious of, the general shabbiness of these people in their dealings with Indians. It remained for Forster, in *A Passage to India* (1924), to focus on British manners and morality, their implications and failures, as illuminated directly by his compatriots' behavior toward the subject race. An enormous amount of critical analysis has been devoted to *A Passage to India*, and it is not my intention to discuss the novel here except to point out that not enough attention has been given to the question of Forster's own attitude toward Indians and the degree of his freedom from the traditional stereotyped views. The best-known Indian consideration of this question is doubtless N. C. Chaudhuri's essay "Passage to and from India,"[34] but Chaudhuri's critique, disguised as dispassionate analysis, is, like so much of that writer's work, a vehicle for the expression of his own violent prejudices and eccentric opinions.

Forster, for all his real sympathy for Indians and his censure of the ignorance and heartlessness of colonial Englishmen, is not free from certain common prejudices. Consider first his Indian characters (there are not many, except for those who swell a progress, start a scene): Aziz, both childlike and childish, sentimental, prone to tears (like Michele D'Cruze), helpless in a crisis, capable of great vindictiveness and the most astonishing fantasies and lies, such as telling Adela that his wife is alive; mediocre, cowardly and silly Dr. Panna Lal; the fatuous Nawab; and Professor Godbole, who is not so much profoundly spiritual as merely absurdly irrational. In the long run, their India remains true to the convention of muddle and what the author himself terms "the celebrated Oriental confusion." Mrs. Moore may be taken for a goddess by the populace of Chandrapore, but the vision India has given her is one of the bleakest despair. When Professor Godbole remembers her in association with a wasp, the rational reader must be at a loss: since the professor cannot know of Mrs. Moore's affection for the wasp she glimpses in her closet ("pretty dear") we must assume a remarkable coincidence or some powerful spiritual or, better, supernatural element. Or is this, like Mrs. Moore's intuition of the ghost on the road, merely mystification? *A Passage to India* is a brilliant novel, but its absolute seriousness, and its author's control, must be viewed in a somewhat dimmed light because of these indications of, first, the acceptance of a superficially glimpsed set of Indian characters and, second, the indulgence in something very close to psychic phenomena. On the other hand, these strictures also help us to realize that the central concern of the novel is only accidentally, as it were, India. Its ultimate value stems not so much from presenting a radically new vision of India (which it does not do) but rather from the vivid dramatization of the failure of the English public school to produce human beings capable of love; India is its most appropriate stage, in part because cultured Indians (unlike natives of many other

colonies) can meet and be compared with the English on at least
a few common terms; and—perhaps—in part because India seems
to have been so very difficult to love.

Forster, though a first-rate novelist and, something equally rare
in the desert of Anglo-Indian fiction of his time, a splendid stylist,
had no comprehensive knowledge of India, and his experience
of the country on both visits was extremely narrow. His grasp of
specifically Indian questions is vague, and even his conception of
general human problems unlimited by race or culture, for all his
wit and grace, is at times shallow and frivolous. To say that "one
touch of regret—not the canny substitute but the true regret from
the heart—would have made [Ronny] a different man, and the
British Empire a different institution"[35] is mere sentimentality; it
would have changed nothing important and not even sent Ronny
back to his viola.

Forster was not a philosopher (and it is not his fault that he
has been taken for one by enthusiastic readers of *Passage*).[36] The
cult of human relationships, the Arnoldian longing for mutual
loving and kindness, may be considered a respectable principle
but not precisely a philosophical system, and the principle itself
did not prevent Forster in his indignation from being extremely
unkind, not to say unfair, to the Anglo-Indians of Chandrapore.
Paul Scott rightly takes him to task for caricaturing them.[37] For
Scott a man's vocation was an essential element in his character,
and this provides a continuing theme throughout his work. Forster, "without evidence for the accused being admitted," in Scott's
phrase, completely ignores the actual work done by his Turtons
and Callendars so that they appear as cartoon figures, residing
incomprehensibly in India and doing nothing at all except being
unfair to the Indians unlucky enough to be under their domination. Scott himself was later to contradict this simplification,
revealing the Anglo-Indian's involvement with India as poignant
as often as it was contemptible, sometimes humanly fulfilling,
sometimes tragic, and always complex with a complexity not
amenable to satire but demanding rather a Tolstoyan scope and
seriousness for its successful dramatization. Forster's "good"
British, though far more interesting than most of the Chandrapore
civil station, are disposed of somehow too neatly, too easily: Mrs.
Moore is overwhelmed by nihilism and begins her return to England; Fielding, saddened and at a loss, unable to sustain a friendship with an Indian, returns to England; and Miss Quested finds

that the "real India" she has so earnestly desired to discover is as hostile and painful as the cactus spines that Miss Derek and Mrs. McBryde extract from her flesh after her hysterical dash from the cave.

What of India and the Indians themselves in Forster's novel? Between the time he began *Passage* in 1912 and its completion in 1924, the political awareness of the educated Indian had emerged with a vengeance. But nowhere in the novel is there the slightest reference to the continuing political upheaval, the phenomenon of Gandhi, Jallianwallah Bagh, the Rowlatt Acts, the Khilafat movement, the Muslim League or the Congress—all of which must have figured significantly in the twenties in the consciousness of an educated Indian like Aziz. Forster, obviously, was under no obligation to write a political novel, but his story, in the event, is a story with a basic political dimension that he leaves completely unexplored. Perhaps after his experience with Dewas Senior he found it impossible to conceive of an Indian as a political reality. Instead we have Aziz, charming but ineffectual ("whose emotions never seem in proportion to their objects"[38]), with his languid Muslim friends, and the comic Hindu Panna Lal and the mystifying Godbole. They come as no surprise when we read some of Forster's comments on India, and Hinduism in particular, in *The Hill of Devi*.[39] No matter how subtle and educated, Forster's Indians are childlike—a Romantic inheritance, perhaps, one shared by many British administrators who saw this as the justification for their continuing rule over the "jewel in the Crown." Because they are children, the Indians can be as emotional, sentimental, crude (remember their jokes about Miss Quested), and vindictive as they like, because children are expected to be like that. Given this outlook, a genuine friendship with an Indian is scarcely possible. This is the reason why, at the end of *Passage*, it is impossible for Aziz and Fielding to "be friends now." Forster's famous melodramatic final paragraph ("But the horses didn't want it—they swerved apart; the earth didn't want it, sending up rocks through which riders must pass single file, . . .") is once more a kind of mystification, an attempt to explain something at one level—a kind of mythic justification—that is really merely whimsical, *fantaisiste*. The fact is far simpler: Fielding and Aziz cannot be friends, not because the nation of one is oppressing the country of the other but because of a perceived but unexpressed racial inequality that probably both unconsciously accept. As its title suggests, the novel throughout employs transportation as a source of recurring metaphor, and the transport always goes wrong. Bicycles are damaged, tongas are appropriated or delayed, boats collide, Mrs. Moore never completes her passage home, and finally, horses must "swerve apart"; even a train leaving untypically on time provokes disaster. So Kipling's Law remains incontrovertible.[40] We must look to E. J. Thompson and, later, Paul Scott for portraits of deep and lasting friendships between English and Indians. Forster is a superb lyric writer, and the most impressive moments in *Passage* are in the wonderfully accurate communication of how it *feels*, emotionally and physically, to be in India, how one apprehends and responds to people, atmosphere, nature. And as a comic commentator on the worst British behavior in India, he has never been surpassed. As a writer about India historically, his value resides not so much in his insights as in the fact that he is the first of the novelists to make so concerted and violent an assault on British prejudice, an assault that, if it did not by itself make the literature that followed possible, certainly influenced it, shaped it, and in the case of Scott inspired a kind of parallel or, better, counter creation that would surpass the original.

Edward Thompson, in the three of his six Indian novels that make up a loosely connected trilogy, presented a pro-Indian view based on knowledge and experience rather than on liberal principle. Thompson was well acquainted with Indian philosophy, languages, and literature, and, if his pen is not so novelistically expert as Forster's, it is more dependable—one is tempted to say more honest—and at its best extremely vivid. In the course of the three novels, *An Indian Day* (1927), *A Farewell to India* (1930), and *An End of the Hours* (1938), he confronts the prevailing British myths regarding India and shatters them. His British and Indians can be genuine friends; the educated Bengali can be a good and decent man, quite up to the British standard in ideals and ethical behavior; the missionaries and teachers are a mixed lot but at their best kinder, more sensitive, and certainly far more sympathetic to India on its own terms than Forster's Fielding; even a British police superintendent may be a normal, decent human being; Indian religion and Indian holy men (quite rational ones!) may have values parallel to and on occasion surpassing Christianity; and even though the memsahibs are, as in so many other Anglo-Indian novels before and since, a destructive force,[41] the group also produces splendid women like Hilda Mannering. When Thompson writes of John Findlay, one of his heroes, "He had learnt to accept whatever happened; he had no generalizations left where Indians were concerned,"[42] he might have been describing his attitude toward his own countrymen as well. It is the attempt to avoid generalization and to come instead to grips with experience in immediate concrete terms that distinguishes Thompson's fiction from that of most of his Anglo-Indian contemporaries.

By way of introduction to the fiction of the post-Independence period, and to Paul Scott in particular, it may be useful to consider here one of Thompson's novels in more detail. Three concurrent and interrelated fables make up the story of *An Indian Day*. In the first, Vincent Hamar, an English district judge, has earned the opprobrium of his more jingoistic countrymen by refusing to convict Indian revolutionaries when the evidence does not warrant a conviction; by the end of the book Hamar, when he has become deeply sympathetic to Indians and learned to prize their friendship, is rejected by them for convicting other suspected terrorists fairly on the basis of the evidence. The second fable is the story of John Findlay, a dedicated missionary, in love with India, who loses his daughter to disease and his wife to suicide and must reproach himself for neglecting his personal, family responsibilities in favor of abstract, theoretically principled service to the Indians of his district; in the end he experiences an ecstatic oneness with all humanity that has nothing to do with taught principle, and he becomes a *sannyasi,* renouncing the world according to the Indian tradition. In the third strand of plot, Neogyi, a pro-British Oxford-educated Bengali magistrate, admirable in his firm idealism and incorruptible ethics, attempts to withstand the vicious maneuvers of Deogharia, the Indian commissioner, a sycophantic, avaricious, utterly corrupt man. Deogharia, triumphant, effects Neogyi's transfer to a remote jungle district and, admired by an ignorant visiting member of Parliament, Sir Spencer Tomlinson, is soon rewarded with a knighthood. Throughout, Thompson does his best to present his characters with objectivity and fairness. Spencer and Deogharia alone are stock figures encountered in other Anglo-Indian fiction. Of his countrymen embarked on careers in India Thompson writes:

As Alden maintained, every one of his countrymen was an able man at his job; the slackers or the bunglers in the Civil Service, or the police, or any other service, could almost be counted on one hand. But intellectually the community was third-rate, and its mind was fed on starch and sawdust. That was why those who were great when in India, sometimes incredibly great and influential, rulers of provinces and heads of huge departments, when they retired to England became stagnant pastures of fat contentment or volcanoes of spouting impotence.[43]

Of the alleged benefits of British civilization in India he writes:

And, if an Indian once was caught in the wide web of intrigue, and left for ever the shallow dishonest folly that we called education and the bitter struggle for the tiny prizes of official service, and if he came to some waste place as the sun was setting—or in the glory of the passionate dawn—how could he help feeling that the landscape was a living creature, appealing to her sons for liberation? Aliens were "civilizing" her beauty, they had brought in mills and factories and heavy, squat, white buildings; they had no homes here, they merely ruled and criticized and had their pleasure and went away. They did not care to understand, they did not love or praise or feel happiness.[44]

No other novelists, not even Forster or Rumer Godden, can match Thompson in the near-ecstatic evocation of Indian nature; but he is even more interesting for the ways in which he anticipates Scott in the sympathetic but objective contemplation of the waning Raj, his respect for the work done by the British even while he sees its shortcomings, and still more his sense of the passionate, almost mystical feeling that marks certain men's commitment to their vocation.

Forster and Thompson are clearly the most distinguished of the English novelists who tried to come to grips with India in the period between Steel and the post-Independence era. Part of their distinction resides, obviously, in their questioning of the basic values of the Raj—an anticipation of what was to become a commonplace in the following years. Through the twenties and thirties most of the fiction writers remain plainly pro-Raj. When we find one who believes the British should leave India, as in the case of Edmund Candler in his novel *Abdication* (1922), the reason given is only that it is no longer possible for them to accomplish anything in the country. There were, to be sure, a few novelists who upheld what they perceived as Indian values against those of the British, but their India was not contemporary or realistic. At the beginning of the century, F. W. Bain had dealt with remote mythological subjects; in the late twenties and thirties, L. H. Myers set his novels in a romantic medieval India.[45] Similarly disposed to the path of escapism, more recent English writers who wish to celebrate the virtues of the Raj have also turned back to a largely chimerical

India, the North India of the Mutiny translated into the flamboyant fantasies of M. M. Kaye and Valerie Fitzgerald.

But with the thirties there are changes anticipating the fiction of the years following the Raj. To think of India as offering spiritual illumination has become a distinct possibility. Thompson is clear about this; and in his memoir, *Bengal Lancer,* written in 1930, Francis Yeats-Brown goes so far as to include an appendix explaining his conception of yoga and suggesting that Christian teaching was derived from an Indian source.[46] These foreshadow the spiritual quest novels of the next decades, such as Maugham's *Razor's Edge* (1944) and Nevil Shute's *Chequer Board* (1947), of which more in the next chapter. Eurasians are now treated with more sympathy, as in Rumer Godden's *The Lady and the Unicorn* (1937), anticipating still later novels in which the Eurasian predicament becomes the main subject—Dennis Gray Stoll's *The Dove Found No Rest* (1947), Jon Godden's *The City and the Wave* (1954), and what is probably the best-known of such works, John Masters' *Bhowani Junction* (1954). Still, in all these novels the emphasis is on the unhappy, even tragic nature of the Eurasian's situation, caught between two worlds. In the matter of interracial marriages, despite all the happy unions between Europeans and Indians (which surely must have been visible to even the most obtuse observer), the novelists have preferred to dwell upon the easily dramatized incidents of conflict and failure.

In one area, curiously, there was to be no change. In a country where violence toward foreigners has been so rare (at least since 1858), even during the Independence movement, almost all writers of Anglo-Indian fiction have depended heavily on such violence for their plots. Leaving aside, naturally, the Mutiny fiction and concentrating on novels with a twentiety-century setting, one finds almost every writer relying on a heavy dose of rape, mob attack, and murder. Many instances of this will be cited in the ensuing discussion of particular novels; here I wish only to draw attention to another aspect of the persistently negative image India presents to the Western imagination.

After the twenties assertions of racial superiority are no longer entirely respectable. Allen Greenberger, quoting a review of Candler's *Abdication* to the effect that "racial arrogance is going. . . . Racial consciousness must also go," comments: "Clearly, this is part of the change. No longer do writers hold forth the idea of racial superiority in the same way that they had once done, but at the same time they cannot get away from a racial consciousness which gives to each race certain values which are quite different from those of other races."[47] But Greenberger's qualification is more important than he concedes, for an implicit racial superiority appears all but ineradicable. Indians and their culture may be regarded more sympathetically, but they remain for the most part too alien, too bizarre, to offer the possibility of friendship and marriage; the myth of transposed racial identities, which I shall discuss later, confirms this interpretation. It is of course hardly surprising if, from the twenties into the forties, British racism should positively flourish. This was, after all, a period when Roy Campbell was taken seriously and writers like T. S. Eliot and Wyndham Lewis found inspiration in Maurras and the Action Française.[48] Anti-Indian racism, as will become clear in the following chapters, has continued up to the present to cast its shadow over Anglo-Indian fiction.

The years immediately preceding Indian Independence, which would become the period portrayed in Scott's tetralogy, were marked by increasing malaise. Yeats-Brown gives one description. "It was a jolly life, yet among these servants and *salaams* I had sometimes a sense of isolation, of being a caged white monkey in a Zoo whose patrons were this incredibly numerous beige race."[49] Several later writers will describe the peculiar sadness of many English at this time as they begin to realize that there will be no place for them in the new India that is coming into being— Scott, Jon Godden in her first novel, *The Peacock* (1950), William Buchan in his first, *Kumari* (1955). In this last we see the heirs of the great administrators and their society in decay, the deepening sympathy of some for the Indians and the exacerbated hatred of others, both indications of the autumn of the Raj. In the thirties, less than a century after the Mutiny and the declaration of Empire, Buchan's British are beset with doubts, anticipatory nostalgia, so to speak, as they foresee their departure. In their private lives, adultery, nymphomania, and homosexuality reinforce the atmosphere of decadence. Paradoxically, it is a character in *Kumari* who, after Independence, can react to India in the way described in the second epigraph to this chapter and find himself more at home there than in England. Such ambivalence, and the tensions it generates, would continue to inspire the best and the worst of the novels after the Raj had ended.

2

Four Modes of Indian Romance

"What is this place called where the treasure is?" Jason asked.
"Coromandel!"
"Coromandel. Coromandel! Where is it?"
"It's in India."

JOHN MASTERS[1]

No land has ever equaled India for the fascination it has exerted over the British imagination. This fascination has led to the evolution of fantasies, which might better be termed mythologies, of considerable complexity in which India, no longer simply a wonderland convenient as the setting for a literature of facile escape (though there is plenty of that), may become an agent, benevolent or evil, of revelation or destruction. No brightness in the world can equal India's for those who quest for illumination, it would seem, and no darkness can match the Indian night—or the Indian spirit when ruled by Shiva and Kali, who redeem only through annihilation.

In earlier Anglo-Indian novels the emphasis tended to be on romantic escape and glorification of the Empire, its mission, and its ideals as represented by heroic action in times of overwhelming danger, the Mutiny of 1857 offering the most popular subject for this approach. Such novels continue to be written and to sell widely not only in Britain and the Commonwealth but around the world. In the decades since the end of World War II, one finds fiction of greater sophistication (at least superficially) attempting to use Indian experience as the basis for symbolic or allegorical tales of spiritual development or personal failure; these too have their seeds in the earlier, more extroverted writings of the late nineteenth and early twentieth century. In classifying the different trends in this literature, for the sake of clarity I have subdivided it into escape into the past, the fable of transposed identities, India as the source of light, and India as destroyer. The associated mythology that has grown up around India as a sexual force, with all its variety of fantasies, prejudices, and delusions, will be treated separately in the next chapter.

Escape into the Past

> Lastly, the Mutiny taught India and the world that the English possessed a courage and national spirit which made light of disaster, which never counted whether the odds against them were two or ten to one; and which marched confident to victory, although the conditions of success appeared all but hopeless.
>
>   SIR LEPEL GRIFFIN[2]

> It has been suggested that all outward signs of the Mutiny should be obliterated, that the monument on the Ridge at Delhi should be levelled, and the picturesque Residency at Lucknow allowed to fall into decay. This view does not commend itself to me. These relics of that tremendous struggle are memorials of heroic services performed by Her Majesty's soldiers, Native as well as British; and by the civilians who shared the duties and dangers of the army.
>
>   LORD ROBERTS OF KANDAHAR[3]

> Then followed a scene of indescribable horror and confusion. The sepoys were joined by the convicts released from jail and other goonda elements, and they all set out to slay the Europeans and burn and plunder the houses. They killed indiscriminately, not sparing even women or children. . . . Howsoever one might apportion the guilt, Mirat set an example which was only too closely imitated, ere long, in numerous localities over a wide area. But, as will be shown later, the British troops were more than a match for their Indian colleagues, not only in military skill, but also in perpetrating such cruel deeds. The sepoys had sown the wind and the Indians reaped the whirlwind.
>
>   THE HISTORY AND CULTURE OF THE INDIAN PEOPLE[4]

The uprising of 1857, sometimes called the Sepoy Rebellion and often, in India, the First War of Independence,[5] was one of the most popular subjects for Anglo-Indian fiction in the late nineteenth century and the first quarter of the twentieth. Something of the hold it exercised over the British imagination can be grasped from this passage from Paul Scott's *Birds of Paradise* (1962), in which William Conway reminisces about his childhood in India in the twenties.

To Mrs. Canterbury the Mutiny was of absorbing interest. There was a time when I thought she had actually been involved in it, then that her mother had been, then her grandmother. She had a special compulsion for the well at Cawnpore. From the stories she told me I built up a childhood picture of it crammed with bodies, so crammed that the limbs of those on the top layer stuck up stiffly at odd angles over the edges. She spoke of a pink satin slipper, a relic of the bodies in the well, that could be seen in a museum in London. I used to imagine that the slipper had belonged to someone in her family. I had nightmares about the well and would wake in the dark, bite my hand to stop myself crying out.[6]

Since the end of British rule, the Mutiny has continued to be a very popular subject for fiction. The novels of both eras have many points in common, among them the lack of literary quality—Farrell's *Siege of Krishnapur* is a notable exception on this count. The historical circumstances of the Mutiny make much of the plotting of such novels predictable, but of course there has been a change in the expression of British attitudes toward the uprising, whether profound or superficial I shall try to discover through consideration of four of the best-known post-Independence Mutiny novels: Kaye's *Shadow of the Moon* (1957), Fitzgerald's *Zemindar* (1981), Masters's *Nightrunners of Bengal* (1951), and Farrell's *Siege of Krishnapur* (1973).

Earlier Mutiny novels, such as those by Steel and Wentworth, were intended to glorify the Raj and those specifically British virtues that sustained it, and of course to vindicate the actions of the British army during and after the struggle. Nevertheless, from early on, as in Prichard's satirical *How To Manage It* (1864), there is strong criticism of British bureaucratic incompetence, the blind faith of the military in the loyalty of their native troops, and the general British lack of understanding of (and disrespect for) Indian religious beliefs; while in *Oakfield* (1854) William Delafield Arnold is highly critical of the frivolous Anglo-Indian life-style in the years preceding the Mutiny. All these themes continue to appear in post-Independence Anglo-Indian fiction.

One theme that will disappear after 1947 is the idea that the British rulers had not been sufficiently stern in confronting Indian unrest. As Greenberger puts it, "particularly in the stories of the Mutiny there is a constant theme that much of the trouble was due to the British failure to realize their own power and use it."[7] Nor is it often suggested in the early Mutiny fiction that one day the Indians ought to (or could) rule themselves; one exception is Arnold's *Oakfield*. Although one finds the inevitable cast of loyal servants, ayahs, and other underlings, until well along in the twentieth century, Indians in general are regarded with scant sympathy. It was obviously not only beyond the imagination of most Anglo-Indian novelists before World War I to conceive of major Indian characters in a favorable light, but also far better copy to concentrate on the allegedly villainous Rani of Jhansi, Nana Sahib, Maulvi Ahmadulla of Faizabad, and those most popular villains, the Thugs. Even when these historical figures did not appear in person, they served as models for the typical Mutiny novel villains, and—more surprising—continue to do so in the recent fiction of writers like Kaye and Masters.

As might be expected, Mutiny fiction written after 1947 will not only take into account the end of the Raj and India's success in governing itself but also reflect the new generally liberal attitude in the Western world where race is concerned. Some sympathy for Indians and their aspirations now becomes a stock feature of post-Independence fiction. The heroes of *Shadow of the Moon* and *Zemindar* both express pro-Indian sentiments, anticipate the Mutiny, and deplore the blindness of the East India Company administrators and military alike, oppose the annexation of Oudh, and forsee justifiable resentment and ultimate violence. Both novels by women support the view that English women and children will be terrible impediments in the coming conflict. Kaye writes, "If there should ever be a rising, then all women would not only be an anxiety but a deadly handicap."[8] Rodney Savage, the hero of Masters's *Nightrunners of Bengal,* goes much further, regarding the post's memsahibs ("a pack of vixens"[9]) as a pernicious influence in the serious business of administering India. Such views were of course unthinkable while the Raj held sway.

M. M. Kaye is Indian born, with a long residence in India behind her, and a member of an old Anglo-Indian military family that included Sir John William Kaye, who wrote one of the first accounts of the Mutiny criticizing British atrocities. Her first Indian novel, *Shadow of the Moon*, received a new life with the great success of *The Far Pavilions* (1978), a generally inferior tale of India after the Mutiny through the period of the Second Afghan War. *Shadow of the Moon* is a long, rambling story, in which suspense is often killed by the author's predilection for the pluperfect tense. Its heroine, Winter de Ballesteros, is Indian born and bred, half-English, a quarter French, and a quarter Spanish. Her closest friendships before she is sent to England at the age of six and a half are Indian. Her Spanish aunt marries a *rais* of Lucknow, so she has half-Indian cousins who are, of course, Muslims. At seventeen, in 1856, Winter returns to India, engaged to the commissioner of Lunjore, a distant cousin named Conway Barton and a dissolute rake, and is trapped into accepting him as her husband, though she has fallen in love with a Captain Alex Randall. Despite the quaint genealogy Kaye has invented for her heroine, Winter is entirely English, and from this point on the plot is predictable. Randall is aware that the Russians are plotting to foment rebellion among the sepoys but is unable to make the British, either civil or military, aware of the impending disaster. Because he is dark and speaks good Urdu, he can circulate among the Indians and gather information. He observes, among other things, the sacrifice of a white child to Kali by Brahmins at a secret meeting. When the rebellion finally begins, Lunjore is swiftly seized by the rebels, and at least half the novel's characters, including Winter's revolting husband, are disposed of once and for all. With Randall's help, Winter and a handful of others eventually make their way to Lucknow to her cousin's house, where they are protected until the British at last raise the siege of the Residency, and all ends happily.

As I have noted above, Kaye, like the other Anglo-Indian novelists of her time, expresses sympathy for the Indians. For one thing, the aspirations of Indians to be free of British rule can, with hindsight, obviously no longer be considered fantastic since the Raj has actually ended. But apart from this, how different from earlier Mutiny fiction is *Shadow of the Moon?* Let us first consider the Indian characters. Few of them are of of any importance in the plot. The half-Indian Ameera, Winter's cousin, is a special case: married to an Indian, she automatically has veered toward the Indian side of her heritage, though she can still speak a little Spanish. She remains a shadowy character, important only as a *ficelle* whose home can be a refuge to the British on the run. Then there is the ''bland, inscrutable'' Kishan Prasad, who is trying to organize an insurrection and whom Randall saves from drowning on the journey out from England; because of this he gives Randall a ring, ''a talisman that may one day save you from much evil,''[10] as quite predictably it does. Later, in his turn he saves Randall's life, and he is heard protesting against the child-sacrifice. Nevertheless, he is portrayed chiefly as disloyal and conniving and altogether iniquitous. As a creature straight out of gaslight melodrama, he cannot be taken seriously—yet he is the least odious of those Indians who fight against the British.

The other Indian characters are for the most part the usual crowd of lowly servants and attendants, distinguished by their simple and touching loyalty to the Sahib-log. Only in Winter does Kaye

attempt to represent a person embodying a more complex relationship to India. Because of her Lucknow childhood and her
knowledge of Urdu, Winter has both a deeper understanding of
the land and a more credible sympathy for it. "There was a fatalism
too about the East that appealed to her, and the filth and squalor
and cruelty that everywhere underlay the beauty did not in any
way lessen her love for the land. The city was ugly and foetid
and full of sights that were unbelievably horrible to Western eyes,
and Winter's eyes did not miss them. But she loved the city too.
The heaped colours of fruits and vegetables and grain in the bazaar. The rich smell of mustard oil and masala, of musk and spices
and ghee."[11] The catalogue of the delights of the land continues
at length, but it is significant that all the images are pictorial. People are seen and enjoyed only as "the drifting, jostling crowds."
Miss Quested had complained about seeing Indians as "picturesque figures" who pass before her "as a frieze,"[12] and this apparently is how Kaye's heroine, completely satisfied, views the
populace: the time-worn stereotypes of loyal retainers, cutthroats,
cringing talukdars, banias, and so forth.

Alex Randall also continues a tradition, the Anglo-Indian who
hates urban India but has a deep love for the land. At one point
he recalls the "capacity for cruelty, the fanatical hatreds and blood-
feuds that obtained in the East."[13] Later, he reflects on "the sight
of filth and disease and the callous indifference to suffering of
man and beast," which, unlike his fellow-countrymen, he cannot
ignore. "The cities spawned as much evil as filth. Murder and
prostitution, theft and trickery, intolerance, hatred and talk: a froth
of talk that went in circles and was seldom concerned with essentials . . . windy poison with which to disturb the hearts and
minds of the credulous."[14] Given all this, one wonders what precisely it was that Randall or Winter could find in India to love so
profoundly.

All in all, we have not progressed very far beyond Flora Annie
Steel's vision. The emphasis on squalor and treachery, the lurid
child-sacrifice, the violence, all hark back to the women novelists
of fifty and sixty years before. In other respects too Kaye is, as it
were, behind the times. Like Steel, she admires, without reser-
vation, such heroes of the Mutiny as Nicholson and Hodson, who
in the light of new historical inquiry are apt to be viewed as ab-
normal personalities.[15]

Although brought up in India, Kaye apparently never learned

much Hindi or Urdu. Like other books of this sort, her novel abounds in grammatical howlers—*Piara Ma* and *Burra Begum*, for example, comparable to something like *cher maman* or *grand dame* in French, which would of course be unthinkable in any English work. The curious spelling of words also suggests that Kaye never learned either Nagari or Persi-Arabic script; she will consistently write *garh* ("fortress") for *ghar* ("house"), for example. This may seem like a minor matter, but because it is so widespread, it suggests that the sort of British who write (and who are described) in such fiction have not learned to have genuine respect for their subject.[16]

Valerie Fitzgerald's *Zemindar* offers a close parallel to *Shadow of the Moon*, although it is better written and historically more believable. Laura Hewitt, the heroine and narrator, accompanies her cousin Emily out from England in 1856 and falls in love with a mysterious zamindar named Oliver Erskine, a man who holds himself aloof from Anglo-Indian society and in general is drawn along the lines of innumerable heroes of Gothic fiction. Trapped in the Mutiny violence, Laura manages to get to Lucknow, only to be caught there in the long siege. Many incidents are almost identical to those in Kaye's novel and are repeated in many other books and screenplays, so that they seem to be obligatory elements of a fixed tradition. Laura, like Winter, assists at the delivery of a baby amidst danger and violence. Oliver, like Randall, has his faithful Pathan companion who will stick with him through thick and thin. Whereas Alex receives a ring for saving the life of an important Indian, Laura is given a bracelet (which will stand her too in good stead) for saving the life of the son of a Lucknow nobleman. Oliver Erskine describes India in much the same terms as does Alex Randall. "It is a cruel country, a cruel and a heartbreaking country. But perhaps you will find the strength to withstand it, as all of us who love it have to learn to withstand it."[17] Like Randall, Oliver also foresees the coming storm and rails in vain against the blindness and insensitivity of the British and, also being dark and fluent in Urdu, he can pass for a "native."[18]

Now, why any of these people, in either novel, love India is never made clear. The emphasis is always negative. Laura describes the "fetid streets, lined with crazily constructed open-fronted booths, and strewn with decaying vegetable matter and accumulations of ancient ordure nauseous to both nose and eyes, crowded with shabby, shoving, shouting humanity."[19] Both Ran-

dall and Erskine, despite the atrocities of the Mutiny, are un-
swerving in their love for the land and its people—a most unconvincing reaction, and one without historical precedent for those
who had personally suffered agonies and losses in that unhappy
time. Again, as in Kaye, Fitzgerald's Indian characters play minor
roles and are quite without even the limited depth and resonance
of her Europeans. The assertion of affection for India seems ultimately merely sentimental—that is, the gushing of a willed
emotion unsubstantiated by and utterly disproportionate to the
circumstances—and may be considered a mid-twentieth-century
liberal anachronism.

John Masters planned a series of no less than thirty-five novels
in which, through the saga of several generations of the Savage
family, he would recapitulate and dramatize the entire history of
the British in India. Only nine of these were completed, each one
devoted to an important moment of that history. Of these, one
of the best is Masters' first novel, *Nightrunners of Bengal,* his treatment of the events of 1857. This is a terser, more believable tale
than either Kaye's or Fitzgerald's later Mutiny novels. It derives
historically from events in and around Jhansi (Masters's fictional
Bhowani) rather than the better-known and more sensational
events surrounding the siege of the Lucknow Residency. Whereas
Kaye dedicates her book to her distinguished forebearers and "so
many other British families who served, lived in and loved India,"
Masters dedicates his to "the sepoy of India—1885–1947."

Unlike Kaye and Fitzgerald, Masters has a realistic understanding, uncomplicated by sentimentality, of the way a British officer
would almost certainly have felt after the Delhi and Kanpur massacres. Rodney Savage reflects: "Treacherous, murderous swine.
The first and last task now was reconquest. The English were
conquerors here, not friends, and it was a ghastly mistake ever
to forget it. There must be no peace and no quarter until every
last Indian groveled, and stayed groveling. A hundred years hence
the inscriptions must be there to read on the memorials: *Here English children were burned alive in their cots, and English women cut in
pieces by these brown animals you see around you.* DO NOT FORGET.
A hundred years would not be enough to repay the humiliation."[20]
This is clearly not Masters' own view, at least at the conscious
level. In his foreword he writes, "The world cracked, and the
British were running together with the people, burning, shooting,
stabbing, strangling."[21] He goes on to emphasize the compassion

that he feels is the province of historical fiction. Kaye and Fitzgerald are not sufficiently imaginative to reproduce the kind of wildly vindictive response that Masters attributes to Savage, or perhaps they are too self-indulgently British themselves to attribute such violence and cruelty to a British officer.

In other respects as well, Masters, with his own knowledge of cantonment life at a later period, is able to create a far more convincing picture of both military and civil society in the last century. It is largely a negative view, emphasizing the pettiness of the intrigues, the incompetence of the officers, and the general moral decay of Anglo-Indian family life. More believable too is the description of the relationship of English officers to native troops, which derives from Masters's own career as a commander of Gurkhas.

These virtues notwithstanding, *Nightrunners of Bengal* adopts many of the commonplaces of the tradition that preceded it and still continues, even to the bestowal on the hero by an Indian of a ring that will serve him in times of danger. Although Masters (through his foreword and even in the character of Rodney Savage) acknowledges that the British too committed atrocities, it is the crimes of Indians that preoccupy him—indeed obsess him—so that for gore he surpasses all his peers in this genre. Even more significant, the Indian characters are straight out of lurid melodrama: the usual plotting, treacherous Dewan, indolent courtiers, faithful ayahs. The most important of the Indians, Sumitra, the rani-regent of Kishanpur, is beautiful and deceitful, murders her husband (for patriotic reasons), and is a nymphomaniac into the bargain. If, as seems likely, Sumitra was suggested by the Rani of Jhansi, that heroine of the Mutiny is here crudely vilified. The rani would no doubt, far from inviting Savage to her bed, have been inexpressibly shocked at the very idea of his seeing her face or touching her little finger. Here, too, is a rather vulgar racism inherent in the conception of this character and her actions; that is, in keeping with an old pattern in which racism is combined with male chauvinism, the writer accepts as perfectly natural that a maharani will both love and lust for the first British officer she meets. The whole situation is reminiscent of the flirtation of Nick Tarvin and Sitabhai,[22] the wicked gypsy rani, in Kipling and Balestier's *Naulakha*, and, like Tarvin, Savage brutally and cynically exploits the rani's passion for him to advance his own cause in a way that would not even occur to him were the woman European.

Masters is a good storyteller; in *Nightrunners of Bengal* he comes close to a kind of minor classic on the Mutiny, but, although he is far superior both as stylist and narrator to most of the writers in this genre and possessed of deeper insights into the historical circumstances of 1857, he mars his work by descending—as in many of his later novels—to the bathos of improbable romance that, perhaps unconsciously, panders to the commercially advantageous popular prejudices and misconceptions concerning India.

Before discussing Farrell's *Siege of Krishnapur,* the novel that gathers together all the stereotypes of the genre and employs them brilliantly for a completely contrary purpose, I would like to consider the reasons for the continuing popularity of the Mutiny novel. The nostalgia that motivates that popularity is more than a yearning for olden romance. It is a chance to revive a time when, despite all the built-in attempts to disclaim it, one may see British India in terms of black and white (here the literal and the metaphorical coincide), a time when it was possible, even fashionable, to condescend to Indians, when the only Indian characters perforce would be servants and a few moth-eaten rajas and nawabs, transformed for dramatic purposes into inscrutable and villainous foes. Given such a situation, there is no need to agonize over the difficulty, or even the very possibility, of more complex relationships with the subject race. The Mutiny presents an opportunity to dwell on the treachery of lesser breeds and their ultimate defeat by the superior British, despite the vast numerical superiority of the former. Such overt racism is of course not acceptable in the twentieth century except when embedded in the well-known incidents of the Mutiny or similar historical episodes, such as the suppression of thuggee (Masters's *Deceivers*) or the feudal horrors of a backward princely state in the interval between the Mutiny and the Second Afghan War (Kaye's *Far Pavilions*). All the more recent novels cite the incompetence and stupidity of the English in command before the uprising, but this makes the British triumph all the more meritorious.

A related reason for this hankering for the past is that with Independence the Englishman's conception of his bond with India, and indeed its justification—the idea of service—came to an end. The British had been in India only to save the country from anarchy, from famine and disease, from the Russians, from itself.[23] Romantic historical retrospectives allowed writers to resurrect and indulge this immensely popular fantasy even though it had been under attack for over a quarter of a century before 1947 by writers like Forster and Thompson. This delusion and its loss would become the great theme of Scott's *Birds of Paradise* and *Raj Quartet.*

Another element of the spell of the Mutiny novels is the familiarity of the historical framework. Like the Greek audiences for ancient productions of the Oresteia or the Oedipus plays, modern readers know the general outline of what is going to happen in North India in 1857 and can savor all the thrills in anticipation. The succession of events must lead inevitably to the massacre at Mirat (Meerut) on 10 May, to be followed by the others at Delhi and Kanpur (Cawnpore), and, most exciting, the particular fictional location of each novel. Kaye, Masters, and Fitzgerald, for example, all make a point of incorporating the fatal date of 9 May, the very eve of the disaster, as the occasion for a festive visit from old friends (Fitzgerald), a bacchanalian orgy of the most dissolute English (Kaye), or a children's party (Masters). Much as in a murder mystery, one can speculate on which of the important characters will be removed on 10 May or soon thereafter, and in what gory fashion. (Among the first victims there is usually a pretty but vain and foolish young woman whose end is recounted in sadistic detail; this is the case in all three novels just cited.) Only the hero and heroine are guaranteed survival. The customary presence of a protagonist who foresees doom but, Cassandra-like, is helpless to convince anyone else, makes the suspense all the more delightful.

What is wrong with all this? one may ask. Here are, after all, the elements of popular fiction that have assured success for centuries. All that is wrong is that this popular fiction (proliferated through films and teleplays) in this particular instance also assures the perpetuation of prejudice and confusion where India is concerned. It is precisely in this regard, along with its remarkable literary qualities, that Farrell's *Siege of Krishnapur* is unique.

In this novel, in keeping with traditional Mutiny fiction, among the central figures are a man and woman (brother and sister), out to India on a visit, who are trapped there by the rebellion; and an administrator perspicacious enough to be concerned about the possibility of violence and (like Henry Lawrence in Lucknow) to make preparations for a siege that, though laughed at by the other British, prove to be their salvation. Fleury, a young man-about-town with romantic-liberal ideals, and his sister, Miriam, have

come to India to visit their mother's grave; Fleury is also considering writing a book on "the advance of civilization in India."
Hopkins, the Collector at Krishnapur, is an enthusiast for Victorian
civilization and an apostle of science; he has returned from the
Great Exhibition of 1851 full of optimism and equipped with all
the latest books and gadgets from the Crystal Palace. The Residency, where he lives and works, because of his collection may
be said to be a miniature replica of the palace, although it "was
more or less in the shape of a church, that is, if you can imagine
a church which one entered by stepping over the altar."[24]

Among the notables of Krishnapur are two doctors, McNab and
Dunstaple. McNab (who was to be the hero of Farrell's unfinished
novel *The Hill Station*) is a somewhat dour but brilliant physician
who guesses correctly that the source of cholera is water, while
Dunstaple, an incompetent, considers him a quack, and the whole
station is divided into the McNab and Dunstaple camps. Fleury
falls in love with Dunstaple's daughter, Louisa, while Louisa's
brother, Harry, falls in love with a Miss Hughes, a young woman
ostracized by the station because she has been "ruined" by an
affair with an officer who has abandoned her. The station Magistrate, Willoughby, is a total rationalist, a liberal who has lost
faith in and affection for the people and become a cynic. Set in
opposition to him is the Padre, an archetypal representative of
the Victorian Anglican church in its most complacent stance. The
makings of an allegorical structure are, I believe, already clear.

With the outbreak of rebellion some of the characters undergo
profound changes; others, such as the Magistrate and the Padre,
remain unalterable—which is to say, in a sense quite mad. The
horrors of the siege shatter the Collector's faith in science but turn
him into a kind of compassionate savior, an indestructible source
of inspiration to the besieged. All the clutter of the Residency,
that is, the Crystal Palace and all the vaunted accomplishments
of British intellect in the nineteenth century, must be sacrificed
in an unexpected cause, namely, to shore up the fragile ramparts
that are all that stand between the British at Krishnapur and annihilation by the rebels. As a part of their retreat to the Residency
to make a final stand, Harry Dunstaple blows up the Cutcherry
(court building), and the ensuing snowstorm of shredded documents bewilders the Indian attackers and contributes to their failure to take the Residency. In their transformation into a snowstorm, a decidedly British weather phenomenon, the documents

"had certainly proved more useful than most."[25] To reinforce the defenses, the Collector strips the Residency of all the marks of culture: the fine furniture, chesterfields and Louis XVI tables, statues, the shattered grand piano; and finally, "bookcases full of elevating and instructional volumes," samplers, tiger skins, "rowing-oars with names of college eights inscribed in gilt paint" all are sacrificed to shore up the mud ramparts. Among the few objects spared are "the Queen in zinc (for patriotic reasons), a few objects in electro-metal such as *Fame scattering petals on Shakespeare's tomb*, with the heads of certain men of letters, and a few stuffed birds."[26] Giant smiling busts of Plato and Socrates become the two wings of a cannon emplacement. Eventually, even allegories become allegorized: "a stray musket ball ricocheted off *The Spirit of Science Conquers Ignorance and Prejudice* by the window."[27]

The British—many of them, at least—survive the siege, Indian sabers and muskets, cholera, malnutrition, insect invasions, and the demolition (temporary) of their own rigid social order; but, for the Collector, "India itself was now a different place; the fiction of happy natives being led forward along the road to civilization could no longer be sustained."[28] This melancholy realization is beyond the imaginative (or intellectual) powers of the other Mutiny novelists and is one of Farrell's distinctions. His comedy leads to still more melancholy conclusions: the Collector, known as "the hero of Krishnapur," in years to come withdraws more and more from society and the "glorious and interesting life that was awaiting him" in England and is continually haunted by the remembrance of two Indians and two bullocks turning endlessly around a well, drawing water every day of their lives. "Perhaps, by the very end of his life, in 1880, he had come to believe that a people, a nation, does not create itself according to its own best ideas, but is shaped by other forces of which it has little knowledge."[29] Fleury's sensible sister, the closest to a heroine we find in the novel, marries Dr. McNab, while Fleury himself "had grown rather opinionated"[30] and is impatient, when he meets the Collector in Pall Mall, to be on his way to "an appointment with a young lady of passionate disposition." Although he had earlier argued, during the siege, that "civilization is decadence,"[31] he is taken aback by the Collector's remark during this last meeting, " 'Culture is a sham. . . . It's a cosmetic painted on life by rich people to conceal its ugliness.' " He protests that " 'culture gives us an idea of a higher life to which we aspire. . . . No one can say that ideas are

a sham. Our progress depends on them. . . .' " " 'Oh, ideas, . . .'
said the Collector dismissively."[32]

Farrell is not especially fascinated by the typical East-West
problems of understanding that generate the basic stuff of so much
Anglo-Indian fiction. He is aware of them, of course, and alludes
occasionally to the difficulty of knowing India, but not in the grand
manner of those who enjoy being baffled by her philosophies and
mysteries; rather, he sees it in much more mundane terms.
"Looking at the Prime Minister the Collector was overcome by a
feeling of helplessness. He realized that there was a whole way
of life of the people in India which he would never get to know
and which was totally indifferent to him and his concerns. 'The
Company could pack up here tomorrow and this fellow would
never notice. . . .. And not only him. . . . The British could leave
and half India wouldn't notice us leaving just as they didn't notice
us arriving.' "[33] Later, Fleury "too, thought, as the Collector had
thought some weeks earlier in the tiger house, what a lot of Indian
life was unavailable to the Englishman who came equipped with
his own religion and habits. But of course, this was no time to
start worrying about that sort of thing."[34] With similar irony, Farrell refers to one of the officers "who had decided as a pastime
to study the natives."[35] The only Indian characters of some importance, Hari, son of the Maharajah, and the Prime Minister,
are lightly sketched and serve mainly as foils to emphasize some
of the more bizarre characteristics of the British. On a larger scale,
it is clear early in the novel that India and the 1857 Mutiny are
meant to serve chiefly for Farrell's meditation on the fragility of
Victorian (and, by extension, all) civilization.

The Siege of Krishnapur has two heroes: Fleury and the magnificent Collector. Fleury is an Everyman who (like Hans Castorp)
is both an innocent child of life and a kind of genius. Listening
to the Padre extol the perfection of creation (" 'Think how apt
fins are to water, wings to air, how well the earth suits its inhabitants! . . . Everything, from fish's eye, to caterpillar's food,
to bird's wing and gizzard, bears manifest evidence of the Supreme
Design. What other explanation can you find for them in your
darkness?' "), he stumbles casually on the theory of evolution.
"Could it not be, he wondered vaguely, trembling on the brink
of an idea that would have made him famous, that somehow or
other fish designed their own eyes?"[36] Later he conceives of motion
pictures. "Could one have a series of daguerrotypes which would

give the impression of movement? 'I must invent the "moving daguerrotype" later on when I have a moment to spare,' he told himself, but an instant later this important idea had gone out of his mind."[37] But as we have seen, Fleury, after the excitement of the siege and the shedding of his illusions, becomes quite ordinary when he resumes life in London married to the pretty and comfortably ordinary Louisa.

The Collector's greatness is of another kind. Earlier, he had apparently been unaware of the futility of the British mission. " 'The foundations on which the new men will build their lives are Faith, Science, Respectability, Geology, Mechanical Invention, Ventilation and Rotation of Crops!' " he declares, riding in the creaking landau with Miriam, and his "shouts rang emptily over the Indian plain which stretched for hundreds of miles in every direction, and Miriam fell at last into a deep sleep."[38] And later, when he goes up on the roof of the Residency to watch the burning cantonment in a "perfect semi-circle of fire," he imagines it as "some mysterious sign isolating a contagion from the dark countryside."[39] But after his illumination about the vanity and hypocrisy of the British presence on the subcontinent, he still remains a compassionate man—indeed, even more compassionate than before. The foolish Padre distributes tracts to the hard-pressed men defending the Residency and argues fanatically about Protestant truths and the decline of the church in Germany as bullets whiz about him and decapititated bodies plunge earthward. Meanwhile the Collector's concern is with finding shelter for the Christian Indians (whom the others wish to exclude from the Residency) and a fair method of distributing food, all the while he sadly wonders, " 'Can it be that the Indian population will ever enjoy the wealth and ease of the better classes?' "[40]

There are strong satirical tendencies in *The Siege of Krishnapur*, but I believe it would be a mistake to regard the book as a satire. It remains fundamentally a comedy, the ironic distancing of its style tinged with affection, impartial in its view of everybody concerned but tending to compassion rather than distaste. The danger of the satirical impulse is of course that it leads to flat caricature, and at times Farrell does come close. But even here the ironies tend to redeem the obvious and increase our wonderment. The Magistrate, to cite one instance, has been arguing for years with the Hindu priests and landowners about the necessity of building embankments to stop the annual flooding. The Indians reject this, as they always have, and insist on sacrificing a black goat instead. " 'But that doesn't work. You've tried it before. Every year the floods are worse,' " the Magistrate tells them. "The landowners remained silent out of polite amazement that anybody could be so stupid as to doubt the efficacy of a sacrifice when properly performed by Brahmins. They were torn between amusement and distress at such obtuseness."[41] For his part, the Magistrate regrets only that, when the river floods again, not these Indians but only the poor will suffer. But the Collector reflects that " 'Willoughby doesn't understand the natives. He's too rational for them. He can't see things from their point of view because he has no heart. If I had been there they would have listened to me.' "[42] But as things turn out, when the flood begins this time, a couple of goats are sacrificed while the priests and landowners "chuckle nostalgically" as they recall the Magistrate's silliness, and the waters obediently recede "and the worst was over."[43]

In another instance, the "rational" Magistrate's passionate interest in phrenology, as it happens, is paralleled by an identical obsession on the part of the scatterbrained son of the Maharajah. Hari is in many ways a parody of Western culture, with his fanatical but often uncomprehending devotion to photography, European literature, and so on—all this intended not to ridicule Hari but rather to underscore the fragility and relative unimportance of these trappings of the "superior" culture.[44]

Farrell's style is unfailingly resourceful and inventive, serving his irony with a tone that never cloys or turns to archness, and usually suggests some underlying and persisting affection for the object of that irony. The Collector is handsome but suggests "an immense cat" with his great side-whiskers, which, like his spirit, undergo many transformations during the rigors of the long siege. The Magistrate, whose own whiskers are variously described as cinnamon and ginger, is the only man at hand when pious Mr. Bradley is shot through the chest. "And so the poor man had been obliged to die in as Christian a manner as possible in the arms of the atheistical Magistrate who had, of course, listened without the least sympathy to Mr. Bradley's last pious ejaculations, impatiently muttering: 'Yes, yes, to be sure, don't worry about it,' as poor Mr. Bradley, looking up into that last, glaring, free-thinking, diabolical, ginger sunset of the Magistrate's whiskers, commended his soul to God."[45]

Farrell is fiercest about the persistence of British social and religious prejudices during the horrors of the siege: Lucy Hughes is snubbed because she has "fallen"; angry arguments break out over where the line is between the Protestant and Catholic cemeteries and which body is to go into which grave. Even more than class or religion, money remains potent in the very shadow of death. As various defenders are killed off, the question arises as to whether to auction off their provisions and other belongings or simply to distribute them equally among the whole community of survivors. The Collector does not believe that it is right that only those who have money should survive, but the Magistrate, "unable to restrain his sarcasm," says,

"In the outside world people perish or survive depending on whether they have money, so why should they not here?"
"This is a different situation," the Collector had replied, scowling. "We must all help each other and depend on each other."
"And must we not outside?"
"People have more resources in normal times."
"Yet many perish even so, simply because they lack money."[46]

The Siege of Krishnapur is a brilliant performance, a highly original and controlled approach to a hackneyed subject. It breaks the stranglehold of the tradition by adopting it and, with cool intelligence, pushing it to extremes so that at times it approaches satire or black humor. But—ultimately more than the sum of its parts— it remains comedy, a sphere in which illusions are dispelled and lives (at least for a time) redeemed, more compassionate than angry, and, above all, able to evoke laughter. Part of Farrell's success stems from his candid indifference to India as a problem. As we have seen, the Collector becomes aware of the gulf between the British and the people they govern, but this is only an inevitable concomitant of Farrell's main concern with the fragility of civilization, specifically as represented by Victorian England, a civilization whose strength and superiority are smugly and arrogantly assumed by the Collector's contemporaries. The Indian characters in the novel serve mainly to point up this theme, but Farrell is not lured into letting them divert or usurp it. They are primarily human beings for him, not a distinct (and dangerous) species, so he is able to dispense with the cant that persists in the subtly racially prejudiced novels that continue to be written about India by Kaye, Fitzgerald, and so many others. Farrell's unfinished *Hill Station* is concerned with Tractarian and Oxford disputes in the Anglican church in the 1870s; one can only speculate about the role India would have played in it beyond its importance as a setting in which English civilization would once more be presented in isolation for a penetrating critique.

The Fable of Transposed Identities

"When I left England I was in doubt. I could not be sure whether my home, my true home, was there or in Chiltistan. . . . I am no longer in doubt. I am a citizen of no country. I have no place anywhere at all."

A. E. W. MASON[47]

Though he was burned black as any native; though he spoke the vernacular by preference, and his mother-tongue in a clipped uncertain sing-song; though he consorted on terms of perfect equality with the small boys of the bazaar; Kim was white.

RUDYARD KIPLING[48]

Since they began writing fiction about India, novelists have been fascinated with the Anglicized Indian and the Indianized Englishman. In most cases the Englishman, as we have noted in the romantic novels of the Mutiny, passes for Indian only as a means of disguise and self-protection. On the other hand, the Indian who has had an English education and acquired English notions usually turns out to be either a misfit or a villain. The fable that embodies one of these typical cases is in effect a testing of Kipling's Law about the irreconcilable essences of East and West and is based squarely on a clear racial prejudice. Just as George Sand, according to Henry James, might become a man but never a gentleman, the Indian may acquire a Western education and manners but he can never become genuinely English in his viewpoint, fundamental responses to situations, or, for that matter, dependability and ethics. Paul Scott's detailed presentation of an Anglicized Indian, as we shall see later, offers a major exception to this pattern.

The Englishman, on the other hand, seems to pass easily for a "native." The eponymous hero of Kipling's *Kim* (1901) is probably the best-known example, but Kipling had earlier created Police Detective Strickland, the protagonist of several short stories in *Plain Tales from the Hills* (1887) and *Life's Handicap* (1890) ("Miss Youghal's Sais," "The Bronckhorst Divorce Case," "The Mark of the Beast," etc.), who can pass not only for an Indian but for almost any kind of Indian—Muslim or Hindu, with a whole repertory of castes and professions. Like most such remarkable impersonators in later fiction, he is dark and spare with black eyes, as though Nature had cooperated by granting him a physical appearance to accommodate his talent for mimicry. Kipling treats Strickland with some irony, and his adventures are escapades, usually not to be taken too seriously.

Kim is a creation of an altogether different order. He is a child brought up entirely as an Indian with only the dimmest memory of his Irish father and none at all of his mother. In this he is like the heroes of several other novels (e.g., by Henty and Kaye), some of whom are not even aware while children that they are British. Kim, with a healthy child's distaste for tiresome English missionaries and "secretaries of charitable societies," nevertheless never loses sight of his goal: the discovery of the red bull on a green field (his father's regimental flag) that will reveal his fate, which turns out to be returning to his own people. His Indian identity, which is so absolute when he wills it to be that neither British nor Indians can tell that he is European, provides him with a pleasant and adventurous life, free of schooling and preaching. This was a fantasy of Kipling, who himself suffered so intensely from being torn away from his Indian childhood; Kim, indeed, might well have been called Kip. With his restoration to the British, Kim's double background is integrated into a mature self, allowing him to use his Indian persona as a means for him to play the Great Game, that is, to spy for his own people, presumably to protect India (held naturally to be unable to protect itself) from the Russians, but of course also helping to preserve the Raj for both British prestige and business.

G. A. Henty, a contemporary of Kipling, was an immensely popular writer for boys; much of his work, including several novels with Indian settings, glorifies the Empire and the exploits of its military not only in India but in Natal, the Gold Coast, Canada, and so on. Published a year later than *Kim,* his *At the Point of the Bayonet: A Tale of the Mahratta War* is the story of an English boy raised as an Indian who, on discovering his true origin, easily transforms himself into a conventional Imperial soldier.

In more recent times, we have seen that the heroes of *Zemindar* and *Shadow of the Moon* can without difficulty assume the identity of a Pathan or Afghan at will. A more elaborate case is that of the hero of Kaye's *Far Pavilions.* Ashton Hilary Akbar Pelham-Martyn (also called Ashok), like Henty's character, is brought up as an Indian with, at first, no knowledge of his origin, and eventually he is obliged to confront his own inalienable link to that origin

and be reintegrated into it. Unlike the other protagonists cited
above, Pelham-Martyn at the end of the novel rejects, superficially
at least, his English heritage and India too—the India of both the
Great Tradition and Islam—to set out with his wife to look for
some paradisiacal Himalayan valley where people "neither carry
arms nor engage in blood-feuds—or make war upon each other."[49]
" 'Once, many years ago, your father's *Mir Akor*, Koda Dad Khan,
said something to me that I have never forgotten. I had been complaining that because I was tied to this land by affection and to
Belait [England] by blood, I must always be two people in one
skin; and he replied that one day I might discover in myself a
third person—one who was neither Ashok nor Pelham-Sahib, but
someone whole and complete: myself. If he was right then it was
time I found that third person.' "[50] But at heart Pelham-Martyn
has never been anything but English. The wife he chooses is part
Russian, and her Indian lineage is of the sort the British admired:
"There was good Rajput blood in Juli";[51] even her Indian name
is interchangeable with an English one. The ideal life he seeks is
the great romantic goal of the West, the recovery of the Garden,
for which in this case all the descriptive paraphernalia consists of
grossly material familiar Western images ("valleys with streams
running through them that would grind our corn, and where we
could plant fruit trees and keep goats and build a house"[52]). And
his "Indian" friends, with few exceptions, are border people, Pathans, faithful servants, and British military.

In John Masters' *Deceivers*, William Savage, the English hero,
assumes the guise of Gopal the weaver, an Indian believed to be
dead; his original purpose is to keep Gopal's wife from committing
(or, more correctly, becoming) suttee. Later he assumes the role
of Gopal once more in order to infiltrate the society of stranglers.
Savage carries out his masquerade, aided only by a little stain on
his skin and Indian clothing, with astonishing ease. The improb-
ability of this is passed over, or perhaps not even imagined, by
Masters, in part, it would appear, because of his own inability to
see, rather than simply to look at (or through or past) Indians.
Describing one Indian, he writes: "Now he could only lie still,
remember the man's face, and see what happened. He glanced
sideways, and after two minutes pursed his lips and knew he
could not describe his companion at all. Apart from the slight tilt
of his head he was non-descript, indescribably average: brown
skin, dark eyes, slight body; lips, chin, nose, hands—nothing to

say except that he had them."[53] "Indescribably average" must be counted not only as mediocre prose but as an unconscious admission of the way the character, and very likely the writer, is accustomed to imagine Indians. Gopal, an important character (not dead, after all), is portrayed thus: " 'Gopal her husband was no older than Savage-sahib, in the prime of life.' He looked thoughtfully down at William. 'He was very like you, sahib; a broad forehead, short jaw, your height, strongly built. He was rather dark in skin, and not disfigured by smallpox like so many of us. Brown eyes. His hair was blacker, of course—what you could see of it under his turban.' "[54] Here Masters has sacrificed all claims to verisimilitude to advance his plot. Vague and generalized as it is ("your height, strongly built"), the description does not ring true. Indian villagers rarely resemble Westerners in build, they age at an entirely different pace, and so on. Here Masters has carried things even further than Kaye was to do in her novels. Similar farfetched impersonations of Indians by Englishmen are a commonplace of adventure tales, and of course of the cinema as well—we find them, for example, in A. E. W. Mason's screenplay *The Drum* (American title, *Drums*) and the film *Lives of a Bengal Lancer* (which has nothing at all to do with F. Yeats-Brown's memoir). What emerges clearly from all these tales of English metamorphosed into Indians is that the metamorphosis is both succesful and superficial: the essential Englishness of these men (for they are almost always men) is never compromised, never overwhelmed either by an Indian upbringing, which may have kept them for years in ignorance of their origin, or by the assumption of a role that obliges them not only to act but also to think and feel as much as possible like Indians; lapses are temporary and ugly, as when William Savage breaks his vow and in his role of strangler is led to murder. There is never any question of the Englishman being somehow seduced by the charm of Indian ways and adopting them; such would not happen until Jhabvala's unhappy hippies wander on to the scene.

On the other hand, the Indians who aspire to a British identity—indeed, long for it passionately—are always not only unsuccessful but permanently marred by the experience. In Steel's *Hosts of the Lord* (1900), two characters, the Hindu Dya Ram and the Muslim Roshan Khan, are warped and spoiled by their imperfect English educations, while in her story "At a Girls' School" in *From the Five Rivers* (1893), the young woman Hoshiarbibi is portrayed in a way that ridicules the very possibility of any transformation. In Mason's best-known Indian story, *The Broken Road* (1907), Shere Khan is sent to Eton and Oxford and appears to have become thoroughly Anglicized. But on his return to his homeland, he learns that he is an Indian of Chiltistan and is expected to act like one and marry a woman of his people; he finds himself roundly rejected by the Englishwoman he has fallen in love with and who, in England, had seemed to favor him. There is not much subtlety in the presentation; Mason has no qualms in having Shere Ali revert on the spot to the barbarous, English-hating ways of some of the border peoples. (In *Jewel in the Crown*, Scott would show up the crudeness of such a conception of radical, instantaneous transformation with his infinitely more complex and both humanly and logically compelling portrait of Hari Kumar.)

Kumari, in William Buchan's novel of that name, has been brought up in a remote part of India in an entirely English fashion, so that at sixteen she is indistinguishable except in complexion from an English girl. But the marriage with an Englishman planned for her never comes off because Indian revolutionaries interfere, killing her fiancé (who is also her foster parent) and kidnapping her, leaving her fate a mystery. In this way, Buchan avoids testing the success of this interracial Pygmalion-Galatea experiment when it might very well have proved successful—a choice on his part that may point up the distaste for such unions that appears endemic in Anglo-Indian fiction.

Over and over again the irreconcilability of East and West in the minds of British novelists is confirmed in tales of unsuccessful or merely superficial transposition of racial identity. In Christine Weston's *Indigo* (1943) the two principal characters, French Jacques de St. Rémy and Bengali Hardyal Rai, both sympathetically and fairly portrayed, almost succeed in exchanging their cultures and ways of thought. Jacques, born and raised in India, is as completely in harmony with Indian attitudes and feelings as he is with Indian languages, while Hardyal, after his education in England, can pass for English when he returns to his homeland.[55] But their friendship is strained, and the exchange of what might be called racial selves proves, during the independence agitations following World War I, not so profound as each had believed. Earlier the two boys had performed a symbolic exchange that, to a discerning eye, partly presages the future. "Aubery Wall . . . began to laugh. Hardyal and Jacques had exchanged clothing; now

Hardyal wore Jacques' white drill suit which was too tight for him, and Jacques was resplendent in Hardyal's gold embroidered muslins. Wall stared at Ganpat Rai's son. By Jove, he thought, the boy will make a very presentable Englishman when we've done with him. But Hardyal's garments on Jacques seemed to him effeminate and unbecoming."[56]

As usual, the impulse toward Anglicizing an Indian is not questioned: the more English the Indian becomes, the better, the more "civilized" he will be. It is, however, paradoxically taken for granted that such experiments are doomed to failure, but this does not suggest that it may have been a mistake to desire it in the first place. When a character in *The Broken Road* opposes the sending of young Shere Khan to England, it is only on the grounds that to do so is to make a potential enemy even more dangerous. And when the experiment *is* successful, as in the case of Hari Kumar in Scott's *Quartet*, British society in India unequivocally and harshly rejects the Indian who has actually become an Englishman.

Indian writers, for their part, have rarely taken up this theme. The best-known example is probably Tagore's *Gora* (1910), a novel in which the protagonist learns only at the end of the tale that he is an orphan of the Mutiny whose parents were Irish. The effect on him of this knowledge is simply to reinforce his liberal anticaste and anticommunal beliefs and above all to confirm him in his identity, so that he can say finally, "Today I am really an Indian!"[57] a striking contrast indeed to the British resolution. Gora, of course, is a somewhat allegorical hero, representing all the universalist ideals of Tagore's Calcutta Brahmo society. In *Too Long in the West* (1961) Bhalachandra Rajan describes the difficulties and alienation of a young woman educated at Columbia University who returns to her very traditional village in South India, but in this case all ends happily as Nalini, the heroine, fortified with her Western ideas and her very Western sense of her own worth as an individual, makes a successful marriage (though it will prove tumultuous) with a man of low caste and begins to reorganize her village along more modern lines.

If the two peoples are doomed never to acquire more than a superficial understanding of one another, then it follows that to blend the two races, like attempts to mix oil and water, can only be unsuccessful. The Eurasian child was always a reminder of a mixed union, a union that automatically rejected Kipling's Law and was therefore an affront to those who held to it fanatically. For some reason or other it was taken for granted that Eurasians would automatically manifest the presumed "worst" qualities of both races. Michele's brief display of courage in Kipling's "His Chance in Life" is presented as a kind of sport or freak, a rare and all-too-temporary exception that merely points up the rule.

One might have more logically supposed that a Eurasian would have the option of moving toward one culture or the other, or even to fuse them in a new, comprehensive and rich amalgam, but this seems never to be the case. In Masters' *Bhowani Junction* (1954), Eurasian Patrick Taylor says, "The whole point that made it impossible to give way, even to argue, was that we *couldn't* go Home. We couldn't become English, because we were half Indian. We couldn't become Indian because we were half English. We could only stay where we were and be what we were."[58] It is true that after 1947 many Eurasians who chose to go to Britain were unhappy there and some returned to India, while those who remained in India faced problems unknown before Independence, that time when jobs were guaranteed on the railways to those who wanted them and their educational institutions were partly subsidized by provincial governments. On the other hand, just as many, if not more, of these people of mixed background adjusted in both countries without any particular hardship or psychological strain, but the novelists are rarely interested in these humdrum happier endings.

When *Bhowani Junction* was to be filmed in India, Frank Anthony, leader of the Eurasian community there, objected, so the film was shot in Pakistan. Later, when shown in India, it was heavily censored, both in deference to the Eurasian community and because the main thread of the action—a plot to assassinate Gandhi and Nehru—was deemed inflammatory. Indeed, so much was cut that it was scarcely intelligible. The question remains: is Masters fair to his Eurasian characters, or does the book reveal a perhaps unconscious acceptance of the old stereotypes and a prejudice against them? Masters himself in his technique for the novel is oblique: the first and final sections are narrated by Patrick Taylor, the second by Victoria Jones, also Eurasian, and the third by Colonel Rodney Savage, the representative at that moment of the Savage family. Taylor comes through in his own narration as muddled, inept, snobbish, at times dishonest about his Indian background, and insufferably prejudiced against Indians, whom he regularly terms "Wogs." Victoria, more honest, more intelligent, is pulled in both directions, toward the British and Indians alike, although in her culture and attitudes she is British. She tries wearing a sari, and at one point, out of gratitude rather than love, she becomes engaged to a Sikh and begins the process of conversion to his religion but is unable to go through with it. Later she enjoys a brief idyll with Savage on a hunting trip; he is willing to marry her, but finally she rejects him for Patrick Taylor because, though she has no illusions about him, she loves him and feels that as Eurasians they belong together. It is not a convincing solution as Masters presents it; the author wriggles and squirms far less in portraying the parallel romance of Victoria's sister, Rose Mary, who snares George Howland, an English second lieutenant: Rose Mary is the stereotypical morally loose Eurasian girl and Howland incredibly vulgar, crude, and obnoxious—an instance, again, of the worst of each community getting together as they seem always, in fiction, to have done. But for the decent and intelligent representatives of those same communities, Victoria and Savage, it is once more a case of "never the twain shall meet."

The most significant passage in the book is one in which Rodney Savage, very possibly representing a viewpoint close to Masters' own, describes his feelings when he celebrates with simple village people following a leopard hunt. "This was my India, not because of the capering or the drunkenness but because these people had no desire to become like me, nor I like them. There had been a place for me round such fires as this for three hundred years. The Ranjits and Surabhais, who were trying to change themselves, didn't light bonfires and dance round them. They read Paine and Burke and spoke in English because the ideas they were trying to express did not exist in their own language. If I and my sort had an idea, it was to make Indian wood into better wood, not change it into bakelite. In general, though, our great virtue was *not* having an idea."[59] This remarkable statement may be attributed in part to the irrepressible romantic notion of a return to the Golden Age. But as a comment on one man's India, it is astonishing for its simplicity—one is tempted to say simplemindedness. In effect, Savage is implying that a Western idea of progress is not applicable to Indians, that they are better off without Western ideas, and that miscegenation at the cultural level is counterproductive, while at the racial level (and this is confirmed by the rest of the novel) it is at best a sad development that can satisfy only the lowest common denominator and bring nothing but suffering to the highest. The best that can be said for the presentation of Eurasians in *Bhowani Junction* is that Masters has tried to show sympathetically the difficulties and anomalies of their position, their insecurity, snobberies, and paranoia, but in so doing he cannot avoid a tendency to make them appear ridiculous and, worse, beyond hope. As a comment on the fable of transposed identities, the novel appears to suggest that, even when he is half-English, a person cannot become an Englishman.

India as the Source of Light

> "That wonderful day, with the brilliant sunshine, the coloured, noisy crowds, the smell of the East, acrid and aromatic, enchanted me; and like an object, a splash of colour that a painter puts in to pull his composition together, those three enormous heads of Brahma, Vishnu and Siva gave a mysterious significance to it all. My heart began to beat like mad because I'd suddenly become aware of an intense conviction that India had something to give me that I had to have. It seemed to me that a chance was offered to me and I must take it there and then or it would never be offered again."
>
> W. SOMERSET MAUGHAM[60]

From the time of the late Victorians on, novelists have most often seen India as a destructive power, but a few, particularly in recent years, have been attracted by Indian philosophy and religion (which are not precisely distinguished in Indian thought), finding in them a source of enlightenment and consolation superior to anything available in the Western traditions. In a probably unique instance—the fiction of Iris Murdoch—Indian teaching is seen not as opposed to but as consonant with Platonist and Christian mystical thought. A possible precedent—or, better, hint—in this direction is offered by Eliot's *Waste Land* (1922), with its references to Buddhism ("The Fire Sermon") and the Upanishads ("What the Thunder Said").

In Western fiction the guru or swami has been regarded mostly as a comic figure, often fraudulent as well, but there is a precedent in E. J. Thompson's trilogy for the guru who is both saintly and wise. "Findlay saw as satisfactory a Sannyasi as any globe-trotter could have desired to see—sitting upright on a seat of tiger-skin, his naked body gleaming silverly with its smear of ashes. Findlay knew that Jayananda must be forty-five, at least; but there was mark of neither age nor youth upon him, he was impersonal and timeless."[61] This sadhu, as he is usually called, is also worldly-wise, witty, politically shrewd, and endowed with a sense of humor. There will not be many more like him in the decades to follow.

A curious case is the Buddhist astrologer, a very minor character, in Nevil Shute's *Chequer Board* (1947). In this odd tale John Turner, a veteran of the recent war, when he finds that he has only a few months to live, is impelled to try to learn what has happened to three men who were in hospital with him. This impulse is to be understood as a kind of vague and inchoate striving to do good. While he lies ill in Burma, a Buddhist astrologer casts his horoscope and reveals to Turner's friends that the man has attained to a certain level of goodness; he also tells them that Turner is dying and when he will die. By the end of the novel we see Turner, presented originally as a very ordinary, even mediocre human being, growing in sweetness, delicacy, and the desire for good, as well as in the admirable stoicism that has marked him from the time he learned of his approaching death. The most important element in his development, as he himself understands it, is his two-week visit to Burma, which has somehow opened his eyes to the magnitude and variety of the world and the possibilities in it for happiness and success. The influence of the East in this novel is discreetly proffered; the Buddhist character is there only to reveal facts hidden from Western minds, not to teach or illumine, although the very fact of his supernatural powers is evidence of something the East can offer to the West.

The best example of the naïve but successful quest for illumination in India, and a work that also foreshadows the great hippie adventure of the sixties, is the story of Larry Darrell in Maugham's *Razor's Edge* (1944) (its title drawn from an Upanishadic metaphor). World-weary at twenty-two and haunted by the horror and futility of World War I, Larry abandons his wealthy Chicago circle and drifts through Europe, then to India, where he studies, wanders, and finally finds an ashram and a guru in Kerala that lead to a kind of illumination (though Maugham—and this typifies his discretion concerning mystical experience—never confirms it or even attempts to define it precisely). In his quest for God and enlightenment (they are not distinct entities in his mind), Larry has spent some time in a Benedictine monastery, one Western equivalent of the ashram, but leaves it uncommitted, troubled by the Christian preoccupation with sin and the enigma of evil in a world created by an allegedly perfect and all-loving divinity. When he meets Shri Ganesha, the man who is to be his teacher, the swami says, " 'I've been expecting you,' " although no one has told him of Larry's coming. Larry goes on: " 'I've told you what he looked like; what I haven't told you is the serenity that he irradiated, the goodness, the peace, the selflessness. I was hot and tired after my journey, but gradually I began to feel wonderfully rested. Before he'd said another word I knew that this was the man I'd been seeking.' "[62] This swami is not fanatically ascetic, he speaks seldom, and he generally bestows grace by his mere presence, a traditional Indian conception of the saint's role. Larry, when he has reached a peak of joyous awareness, returns to Europe and meets his old circle once more. Among them he performs minor miracles of healing through hypnosis or, more accurately, basic meditational techniques, delivers a long lecture to his friend Maugham on the teachings and significance of Advaita (Non-dualistic) Vedanta, and then disappears, having renounced his inheritance and resolved to work his way back to America, work in a garage, and eventually buy a taxi. Much of the ideology he preaches is an echo of what one finds in Huxley's novels of the thirties (*Eyeless in Gaza* [1936] and *After Many a Summer Dies the Swan* [1939]) as well as the tracts of Gerald Heard (*Pain, Sex and Time* [1939]); and the character of Larry Darrell is probably based to a great extent on Christopher Isherwood, who in the early forties had become a sort of acolyte of Swami Prabhavananda of the Ramakrishna Mission.[63] *The Razor's Edge* is a glib tale, expertly told, philosophically shallow but extremely interesting as the forerunner of the movement of young Westerners toward India after World War II. Part of Maugham's skill in lending at least a little conviction to this story of the possible effect of the mysterious East on an impressionable Western mind comes from his acting as the skeptical narrator, commenting and objecting when Larry reports his extra-ordinary spiritual adventures in India.

A more fulsome (though less convincing) tale of a Westerner's spiritual quest in India is Maggi Lidchi's *Man of Earth* (1968, published in England as *Earth Man*). Searching for enlightenment (which for him equals liberation from his past), Christopher, a forty-year-old alcoholic Englishman, drifts into an ashram in Ceylon run by a lively Irishman who subjects him to an initiatory discipline: walking barefoot, washing at the well, sleeping on a mat, sweeping, and so on. Christopher rises above the need for alcohol, learns to try to tell the truth and to dispense with the rigid categories of Aristotelian logic. From Ceylon he goes to an Indian village, where he finds an exquisite mountainside fresco of six apsaras and a sculpture of the Goddess as Shakti. In his emotional and mystical relationship to these works of art he makes further strides in his progressive liberation from his ego. Later, after various adventures, a young Indian woman doctor helps him to the next step, the discovery of the possibility of a kind of selfless loving that leads to his ultimate freedom, the freedom to go on questioning, uncommitted and genuinely independent of his past, including the fussy discrimination of distinctions and separations into categories that are fundamentally unreal for the Shunyavadin and the Aurobindo integralist alike. (Lidchi has had a long association with the Sri Aurobindo Ashram in Pondicherry.)

Unlike Maugham's book, Lidchi's novel of Indian questing is badly written, philosophically not only shallow but hazy and dull,[64] in which respect it is unfortunately close to the norm for such works. The characters are predictable—the Irish guru and the Indian doctor and her family are basically hollow, while Christopher is not there at all. India and Ceylon seem to have produced a total discontinuity with his past, a discontinuity so complete that one would expect it only in cases of severe mental illness. He bumbles along, dead to all the vigorous and colorful life around him, waking up only to fall in love with the six painted apsaras. His response to the all-too-evident suffering he encounters is so rudimentary that one realizes he has achieved no emancipation from the ego but remains locked in himself, having advanced very little from his starting point, which seems to be a conviction that Eastern illumination is incompatible with Western sanitation. At the end of the story he writes down several pages describing what he considers his final vision and gives them to the girl, who weeps, "It's just that it's so beautiful." But it isn't. It is neither illuminated nor earthy but only earthbound, and it has, after all, nothing much to do with India or anywhere else except that certain characters may be recognized by those familiar with the ashram in Pondicherry.

I have dwelt so long on this work because it is in many ways representative of one new kind of Indian novel that came into being with the legitimizing, so to speak, of Indian philosophies in the sixties. It is as though the writer can get away with all sorts of vagueness and other inadequacies of characterization, inaccuracies of observation, and improbable events, any of which would be enough to prevent publication if the story were located anywhere else. Not everyone who goes to Japan or Mexico or Turkey, say, writes a novel, but it seems that everyone who goes to India does, and *Man of Earth* is typical of the result.

In several of her novels Iris Murdoch—to leap from the ridiculous to the sublime—alludes in various ways to India. In some there are Indian characters (Biscuit in *A Word Child* [1975], Parvati in *Bruno's Dream* [1969]); in others, at the end, characters go off to India either as tourists of a very special kind (Hugh, Mildred, and Felix in *An Unofficial Rose* [1962]) or to do good works (Nigel in *Bruno's Dream*); and in still others, some aspect of Indian philosophy is central to the work's theme—the Katha Upanishad in *The Italian Girl* (1964), Mahayana Buddhism in *The Sea, The Sea* (1978), while the black prince, in the novel of that name (1973), is at times identified as Krishna (Sanskrit *krsna*, "black"). All these novels are extraordinarily complex (far more so than appears at first glance), based apparently on a concealed allegorical structure that has hardly been understood—or indeed suspected—by the majority of critics who have innocently rushed in to analyze them. In these books India itself, as a specific geographical entity, is never important, and the Indian characters are not seen as humanly different from any of the other figures in the novels, which thus differ from what one has come to expect in Anglo-Indian fiction.

What is most interesting in Murdoch's "Indian connection" is her use of Indian philosophy and myth as the basis for her remarkable allegorical structure in *Bruno's Dream*. David Beams has brilliantly and exhaustively analyzed the Indian basis for that allegory;[65] here I will do no more than recapitulate the main points that establish the link with Indian myth and philosophy in this novel, which is probably the outstanding utilization in fiction of India as a redemptive and illuminating power, and also one of the few philosophically soundly grounded examples of this—perhaps the only one.

Bruno's Dream is the story of the drama accompanying the slow dying of an old man who has come to resemble the spiders that have fascinated him all his life, his body now only "the contingent improbably human form, strengthless, emaciated, elongated, smelly."[66] He is a widower, like his son Miles and his son-in-law Danby. Danby's wife has died in an heroic attempt to save a child she thought was drowning, establishing the theme of the bodhisattva, who is represented most clearly by Nigel (who nevertheless remains very frail and human). Miles's Indian wife, Parvati (the spouse of Shiva), has died in an airplane crash in the Alps (an event that confirms her name: Parvati, the woman of the mountains). In her special capacity as "Indian," Parvati enunciates a Vedantic principle that underlies the book's plot: "Parvati's Oriental ability to see that everything was, from a certain point of view, everything else, baffled and charmed Miles's Aristotelian Western mind."[67] But it is Nigel who is at the center of both the action and the allegory. Nigel, who loves everybody[68] and exists to be imposed upon,[69] is both a Shaivite yogi with supernatural powers of observation and "unpersoned,"[70] a bodhisattva, who reconciles Bruno to death ("God is death," he instructs him[71]) and teaches compassion both to him and to Miles's second wife, Diana. Love is death, and the acceptance of death is a liberation from life, which itself is only the imposition of an illusion upon the reality (which must be nondual). "Up any religion a man may climb," Nigel says at various points in the novel, and, by interfering in the duel between his twin brother, Will, and Danby, he symbolically abolishes, for the moment, the delusion of duality that is the source of human suffering. Nigel has been a puzzle to commentators; William Hall, for instance, recognizes that Nigel is a bodhisattva but cannot explain his relationship to his brother or his cousin Adelaide.[72] Beams, finding the Indian key to this puzzle, identifies Nigel, Will, and Adelaide in terms of the Upanishadic (originally Sankhya) concept of the three *gunas*, the strands of matter of which all individuals are held to be composed in varying proportions. Each of the three characters personifies both realistically and emblematically one of the *gunas*—Adelaide is *tamas* (inertia); Will is *rajas* (passion, activity); and *sattva* (harmony, goodness) clearly predominates in Nigel. The other characters may be analyzed in terms of the particular mix of the *gunas* that they exemplify, with Diana, instructed by Nigel, coming closest to the sattvic, accepting love as death and the unreality of the dual. (Her name, *di*, "twofold" in Greek, and *an*, "one" in Anglo-Saxon, already points toward her growth.)

Mythological elements abound. Miles has been taught something of love by Parvati (as was Shiva), and London is Shiva's "Night City."[73] Nigel, who describes himself as "God,"[74] is "many-handed, gentle," and "flutters like a moth, filling the room with a soft powdery susurrus of great wings," and he can smile "the tender forgiving infinitely sad smile of almighty God."[75] The spiders too have an Upanishadic significance.

I have presented the swiftest of surveys of this remarkable work, remarkable not only for its ingenuity in adapting Indian thought to an English environment and for the broad and deep knowledge of Indian religion that it embodies, but also for the fact that in it, East is not set up against West but rather exists in harmony with it, redeems and even in a sense beatifies it. If after all everything is in some way everything else, and consequently everything of this world may also be, in terms of ultimate reality, nothing, so also all contraries and oppositions fade to nothingness for the genuinely enlightened man, and East finally has become recognized as West—or both as nothing.

Murdoch's appreciation of India evolves from a close study uncomplicated by a residence there. Of the novelists whose experience of India was contemporary with the period just before and after Independence and who derive a positive value from that experience, Rumer Godden is perhaps the best. In a series of novels, many closely paralleling events in her own life, she gives us an India that is both destructive and redemptive, or perhaps, to put it better, accepted as intensely real whatever value one attaches to it. Despite the strong autobiographical elements in some of these works, particularly *Breakfast with the Nikolides*, *The River*, and *Kingfishers Catch Fire*, Godden maintains a craftsman's distance from the material that is objective without irony and compassionate without sentimentality. She will often present her material from the point of view of a child, with all the unhampered imaginativeness and hardheaded realism of a child; and even a grown-up, such as the beguiling Sophie of *Kingfishers Catch Fire*, owes both her frequent disasters and her joyousness to the childlike openness of her nature. Although Godden's characters are by definition outsiders in India, they feel at home there—an interesting contrast to some more recent novelists like Jhabvala. Their sorrow comes rather from having to leave India, to give it up, since for them, India, the theater where they come to know of loss, separation, illness, and death, nevertheless remains the Garden for their ideal selves.

India as Destroyer

Only those who have lived through days of endless Indian heat know their effect on one's behavior. . . . My western characters—who of course include myself—have reason to be appalled at the transformation to which they are being subjected. Along with their behavior their most cherished principles and feelings seem to be changing.   RUTH JHABVALA[76]

A country that, for instance, can set an urbane and gentle man like V. S. Naipaul screaming and despairing within a few hours of arrival clearly performs miracles of character transformation.   PAUL SCOTT[77]

From the preceding pages it must by now be very evident how negative much of the fiction dealing with India is about that country. In fact, it is possible to say that India has exerted the greatest appeal to writers who are looking for a means to vent some deep, pent-up hostility and who have a view of the world too dark to be acceptable in a European setting, or perhaps to those who have a need that is both sadistic and masochistic to wallow in filth and disorder and who have a view of the world so desperate that only India is able to justify it. A character in Halls' *Cats of Benares* says: "No wonder Indians are always talking about [God]. You feel His presence. You see Him getting down to things . . . shriveling up deserts, flooding rivers, killing off millions of people. . . . Like a page from Genesis. Because people don't matter to God. It's only to mankind that man matters. So no wonder they haven't any dignity, or any hope. They know that God doesn't care about them; they aren't worth bothering about."[78] Instead of bringing illumination, India undermines, disorients and often completely destroys those whom she fascinates. Many novels of this type are of inferior quality but so consistent as to constitute a kind of minor tradition. Ruth Jhabvala, the best of the recent writers who see India as destructive, is also too complex to be considered in this general survey and will be discussed in a later chapter, as will the role of sex in the process of destruction wrought by India.

In Masters's *Deceivers*, William Savage is aware of the duality in his feelings for India.

As an Englishman he had fallen in love with Madhya, and this central land's pattern of beauty had grown into him—its earthy reds and deep greens, the shading of its still water in old masonry tanks, its rivers that flowed by white and smoky blue villages. Yet always his race had held him back from complete absorption in it. He had been physically unable to see or hear or smell beauty without noticing the dirt and disease that were part of it. Then, when he noticed, his love changed to something else—to reforming zeal, desire to raise up, to alter.[79]

But he may be said to have underestimated India. Here is a description of his feelings when, later, he finds himself impelled to kill:

> All the brightness outside, and the movement, were reflected in black mirrors behind William's eyes, and the rumal was in his hand. A wolf snarled at his feet. It was the evil of Kali, as the harlot girl had been the lust of Kali, and he could strangle it in one motion. It was the evil thing that God made and, having made, strove to destroy. His knuckles sprang up white . . . he heard the double crack.
> He bowed his head and slowly, luxuriously, let his wrists turn down. The rumal unloosed. There was never such power as this in all the world, or such fulfillment.[80]

And later:

> His face was set in the grim and thoughtful mask that the grass fire had scorched onto it the day of the massacre at the Padampur ford. Behind the mask he feared for himself, because he had learned the power of Kali, and his own weakness, and had learned in the spasms of his three murders to love the evil of the goddess. Since Padampur he had not killed with his own hands; he was the great Jemadar, the planner. But the terrible beauty lingered; a warmth at his wrists and heart, and he was afraid of the moment when he must meet Mary's eyes.[81]

India, here personified as Kali, has the power to bring out the potential evil in any man, to make an Englishman kill and enjoy it. This is grandly, melodramatically conceived. At a more modest level, India also produces witches, practitioners of black magic who are to be feared. In Anthony Burgess' *Earthly Powers* (1980), a terrible Tamil—who at his most beneficent bores his guests to death and gives them dinners that make them ill—through black magic brings about the death, a slow and vile wasting away, of an English doctor he wrongly holds responsible for his son's death. The caricaturing is so vicious and inhuman that one cannot be either touched or amused. Though the episode is set in British Malaya, a land richer even than India in traditions of ghosts and witchcraft, Burgess apparently decided that an Indian would be more appropriate as a personification of this potent wickedness.

Masters' lurid passages and Burgess' supernatural destroyer recall the feverish imaginings about Hinduism that haunt the novels of the late Victorians. The more recent tradition is generally less lurid, but the insidiousness and danger of India are just as potent. The more typical Anglo-Indian novel of the last three or four decades, frequently written by a woman or presenting chiefly a woman's point of view, will describe a Westerner or a Western couple in India for an academic year, an engineering project, a search for a guru. Under the ruthless assault of the land, a marriage breaks up, old values are destroyed, a career is derailed, a personality disintegrates. For a representative example, let us consider *The Cats of Benares* (1967) by Australian-born Geraldine Halls.

In this novel, English Richard Mardellis (who narrates the story) falls in love with Helen Siegel, the Australian wife of a United Nations official in New Delhi. The slender plot has actually very little to do with India, except that somehow that country's capacity for bringing out the worst in everybody sets the machinery in motion for a catastrophic ending. The novel is replete with savage comments on India, and all the Indian characters are portrayed as unreliable, illogical, tactless, and, if not venal and corrupt like Krishan (who plays the role of English Giles's lover), then mercenary (Ruplal) or destructive and vindictive like Krishan's brother Shankar. Of one Indian, Mardellis says, "I quite liked Ram Chandra, though he was as unreliable and neurotic as only an Indian can be."[82] And of Alisulman, a servant: "A neat little Moslem with a carefully trimmed, patent black mustache and enormous eyes, stupid with sickness and resignation. Like most of India, he was wearing someone else's clothes."[83]

It is true that the European characters in contrast are not idealized, but at least they do emerge as individuals. Indians, whether rich or poor, neurotic or corrupt, are denied any genuine individuality by Halls, and of course in consequence both our interest and our belief as well. In an attempt, perhaps, to atone for this ungenerous and unrealistic view, Halls has Prasad, an Indian teacher, attempt to explain it to Mardellis. " 'We are all half Westerners now. . . . This has been brought about by such men as Gandhi and Nehru. . . . Gandhi was a great admirer of the Christian Bible, which is full of action and social welfare, and we have come to believe that these activities are necessary to our country. But action, Mr. Mardellis, can be a very dissipating force. We waste ourselves in the violence of movement. In India we have our own strength, and we must not lose it in this sudden frenzy of rushing about that has overtaken us. When there is a great deal to be endured, it is more important to build up powers of endurance.' ''[84]

It may be quite properly argued that this has very little to do with the novel, but then the entire story would have been little different if acted out in Sydney or London, except for the final disaster when Helen Siegel has her arms and legs broken by angry villagers after a car driven by Krishan kills a cow and Krishan is clubbed to death. Mardellis's own view of the country is set forth early in the novel and never changes. "I thought what a mess India was—a greasy, grubby physical mess, and a soggy, sentimental intellectual mess. A land of sugar-coated putrefaction; where two lies are better than one truth, and everything is excessive—or nothing at all. And I thought that in my heaven there would be prizes for restraint and rewards for symmetry."[85]

In the prologue to the novel, Mardellis' wife had tried to feed a horde of stray cats in Varanasi, causing a scandal at her hotel. The cats are slaughtered and Pamela Mardellis leaves India in a state of nervous shock. Her husband, trying to understand what has happened, writes her "on a solemn moral note."

I've been thinking a lot today about what happened to you in Benares. I feel that the whole trouble with India is that she takes hold of our beliefs and stretches them to a point where they become so ludicrous that we can no longer maintain them. And this is frightening. It's always frightening, suddenly, to be stripped of your convictions. India's extravagances, her extreme postulations, are always logical; that's what takes us unawares, because we'll always pursue a logical deduction. Other cultures let us off lightly; we're not used to being subjected to such stringent tests. When we say we won't take life, we usually mean that we won't resort to killing our neighbors, or, if we're really fanatical, we become vegetarian, or refuse to practice birth control. But we don't mean that we'll meekly sit back and allow a plague of monkeys to devour our melon crop, that we'll spare the lives of cockroaches and centipedes, and wear gauze masks over our mouths so that minute particles of life floating in the air won't fall victim to our gastric juices.[86]

This statement, which seems to attribute Jain *ahimsa* to all of India, is not particularly useful for explaining Pamela's nervous breakdown, since it was produced in part by the Indian hotel management's very practical and efficient extirpation of the troublesome cats. When she returns to India, she commits suicide because of her husband's infidelity, but it is made clear that it is the impact of India that has disposed her to this extreme.

Halls lived for two years in Delhi before settling in England. If there is any point to her book, it must be that she is, in a sense, attempting to explain, or understand, her own Indian experience, whatever that may have been. Her observations, when they are objective, are precisely rendered, if limited always to the depressing side of Indian life—heat and dust, flies, filth, and frustration. But her grasp of India goes no further than that, and perhaps she has convinced herself that indeed there is no more.

Another originally Australian novelist (who now lives in Canada), Janette Hospital, has given us in *The Ivory Swing* (1982) a perfect model of the failed passage to India, the story of an academic couple whose compatibility is severely tested by living near Trivandrum, in Kerala. Discontented Juliet and pedantic, sexually suppressed David are mostly passive before the onslaught of Indian impressions. When they, along with Juliet's sister Annie, a free spirit and sexual adventurer, meddle in the lives of the Nairs among whom they live, they bring disaster to the only two Indians they feel any affection for. The Indians are shown as irrationally violent, superstitious, naïve, and fanatical. Their landlord, Shivaraman Nair, is strictly orthodox and, despite stirrings of desire for his widowed cousin-in-law, follows the code of his community with medieval inflexibility. Prem is a Marxist agitator who talks in slogans until he loses his virginity to Annie, after which he becomes virtually mute. Yashoda, the widow, except for one excursion completely concealed in a *burqa*, is so passive as to be scarcely animate. Prabhakaran, the sweeper boy, is an unreal, romantically conceived child who enchants Juliet with his flute music. All the Indians, with the exception of those who mercifully speak no English, discourse almost entirely in the present progressive tense.

"Mrs. David Juliet! My mother is bringing fresh tea. You are not wanting it to be cold, isn't it?"[87]

"When your name is being called . . . you may be coming to the desk and your questions are being answered, isn't it?"[88]

"There are not being many Christian students at this college. They are not affording."[89]

The hostile exaggeration of this imperfectly transcribed speech pattern will be immediately apparent to anyone with Indian experience.

The book is completely humorless, and its prose abstract, gushy, trite, and inaccurate ("peaceful as the earth at springtime"[90]). Curiously, the language seems to sag whenever there is something pleasant about India to record and to be revivified when it becomes a vehicle for the author's anger.

> The woman was like a gazelle, light as air, beautiful as lotus flowers. Though her voice was soft and melodious, there was a sense of urgency about her, a kind of nervousness poised for defence or flight. Her silk sari fluttered like restive wings.[91]

> She was sitting in the Trivandrum office of Air India. The room was crowded, the fan not turning, the ferment of body odors was more pungent than curry, and the clerk at the desk—the sole clerk assigned to this roomful of inquiries—might have been engaged in the tranquil and delicate art of calligraphy. His movements were languid and precise, he leafed lovingly through schedules and timetables, he bestowed upon them his earnest attention, dignifying a select few with a rubber stamp.[92]

The tale really has nothing to do with India in particular, and again the prose gives it away—the few flashbacks to Canada convey a sense of reality missing in the rest of the book. India serves only as a whipping boy for Juliet's frustration and anger, most of which stems from her fatuous refusal to employ a servant, a stand that she attributes to her working-class background and sympathies but of course simply condemns one more Indian to unemployment. The Indian situations are the ones described already in scores of novels, the observation of character and place as generalized and dull as one has come to expect. In Kipling usually and in Forster always, there is a dynamic relationship between a specific India and a specific European individuality, private dilemmas in concrete situations that interact. But in *The Ivory Swing*, as in *The Cats of Benares*, India serves only as a general sort of dummy that has been set up to confirm the Western characters' prejudices, exacerbate their already intense personal problems, and send them home glad the Indian stay is over. They may be challenged by India, confused and disillusioned and even killed, but they are never really involved with the country, illuminated or liberated by it. They can never stop talking about it; that is to say, they can never stop seeing it as alien, the other, the adversary, a kind of inhuman abstraction that effectively precludes any genuine understanding and love. Forster is aware of this, and so, in a way, is his character Fielding, and this provides the principal tragic element in his tragicomedy of mingled Imperial and Hindu muddle.[93] But for Halls and Hospital the abstract vision is unshakable, which in turn leads to caricature and a hate-motivated satire that is the farthest fiction can go from either tragedy or comedy.

3
The Mythology of India and Sex

"The East, at any rate . . . seems to have acted like some kind of hot-house for forcing the women. Gave them all kind of wet dreams."

"This girl didn't dream." Mrs. Tremlett was trembling, as old passions were kindled. She didn't care for such language either. "The poor thing was shamefully—" she shied away from the raw word, and substituted another, "shamefully violated, the whole station knew that. There was no excuse for suggesting anything else whatever."

"Whatsisname put it in a book, didn't he?" said Boyle yawning. He had not read the book. The event was before his time, and anyway had little time for women who put themselves in that position.

"He left it up in the air," said Mrs. Tremlett, somewhat perilously. She had never forgiven whatsisname for it.
                                KAMALA MARKANDAYA[1]

For the Victorian and Edwardian women novelists, India represented a threateningly potent sexual force. Benita Parry has discussed the fantasies that run through the fiction of Flora Annie Steel, Maud Diver, and others,[2] fantasies usually modified or disguised in stories of wicked Indian cult leaders demanding blood sacrifices, particularly of young women. For those novelists, the mystery of India was in reality the fearsome world of sexual taboos and suppressed longings (recognized or not). Though in general unworthy, undependable, and often treacherous, Indian men and women may also be dangerously seductive. "Although the Major was so sympathetic to India, his piece sounds like a warning. He said that one has to be very determined to withstand—to stand up to—India. And the most vulnerable, he said, are always those who love her best. There are many ways of loving India, many things to love her for—the scenery, the history, the poetry, the music, and indeed the physical beauty of her men and women— but all, said the Major, are dangerous for the European who allows himself to love too much. India always, he said, finds the weak spot and presses on it."[3]

The Major, in Ruth Jhabvala's *Heat and Dust* (1975), is supposed to be writing some time in the twenties or thirties. Unlike Dr. Saunders in the same novel, who is convinced that the weak spot is always "something, or someone, rotten," the Major attributes the weak spot to the most refined, sensitive, and gifted people. Now, whatever the Major may think, in this survey of the whole expanse of Anglo-Indian fiction for the last hundred years, one finds few Europeans who like anything at all in India. They are oppressed by the dullness of the scenery (except for the Himalayas); they are not interested in history except to remember, with pride and indignation, the Mutiny of 1857; they rarely learn enough of any vernacular to appreciate (or suspect the existence of) the poetry; they find the music mere caterwauling. But the men and women continue to fascinate, corrupt, and destroy. There is no question that these men and women are out of bounds; the more attractive they are, the more dangerous. As I have shown, novelists from Kipling through Buchan and Masters preach against India's sexual temptations, as it were, by consistently showing that all love affairs and marriages between the two races are doomed not just to fail but to provoke catastrophe.

The Indian sexual myth has persisted past Indian Independence, furnishing thematic substance for the best and worst writers in the field. The myth has been modified—has shed its disguises, so to speak—with the ever greater explicitness in analyzing sexual feelings and activities allowed in recent decades. Instead of human sacrifice, the fundamental material of the myth has been revealed as the way in which India brings awareness of repressed and suppressed sexual drives to characters who, until they have baked a while in the ardent climate of the subcontinent, were fearful, only half-alive, and sexually inert. The majority of these characters, in the work of both men and women writers, continues to be women; while male characters often turn out to be homosexual when wakened by Kāma, the Indian Eros.

This new phase of the sexual myth begins explicitly with Forster. As one expects from so gifted a novelist, his approach to the myth in *A Passage to India* is complex and made to serve a more universal theme. In Miss Quested, unacknowledged racial and sexual fears combine to bring about her hysterical crisis in the Marabar Caves.

She is saved from the stereotype in so much fiction of the withered
virgin or frigid woman whom India brings to frightening awareness by the care Forster expends on rounding her individual character, her sound instincts, her good intentions, untested liberal
sentiments, and unsuspected vulnerability. Nevertheless, her
sexual muddle is at the heart of her catastrophic mistake: her failure to recognize how strongly Aziz ("beloved" in Arabic and Urdu)
has attracted her. Allegorically, Adela is Britain, which has raped
India; the guilt at the base of her wish to know and sympathize
with "the real India" has become distorted into a justifying fantasy
in which Britain is raped by India. For all her generosity and good
will, Adela ("so uglier than the man") cannot admit that an Indian
attracts her so much more than her English fiancé. So race and
sex are ingeniously and convincingly combined in Adela's situation. It is of course no accident that Adela's crisis coincides with
Mrs. Moore's spiritual crisis in a nearby cave—Mrs. Moore driven
to despair over "poor talkative little Christianity" by the annihilating experience of India. *Her* passage to India precludes the possibility of a passage back to an England still comfortable in its
shallow faith and its delusions about the Imperial mission.

One wonders how Forster, so reticent about his homosexuality,
would have developed his story (in the Jamesian sense) had he
written two or three decades later. In his novel he allows no reference to a kind of sexual experience he might have shared, re-
placing sexual taboo with Adela's sexual hysteria. Writing a few
years later, his friend J. R. Ackerley is more candid. *Hindoo Holiday*
(1932), a memoir posing as a novel in the form of a memoir, is
one of those rare works, a book that describes, with enjoyment,
the comic side of Indian life. Rather unexpectedly in such a book,
the author is casually candid about the pleasure he takes in the
fine appearance of various servant boys. But he is not undone by
this, and there is no melodrama; he enjoys his few months in an
Indian princely state and then returns, with some regret, to England.

In the thirties the most striking embodiment of every aspect of
the Indian sexual myth is Louis Bromfield's *The Rains Came*, sub-
titled *A Novel of Modern India* (1937). (This is one of the few works
of fiction dealing with India that became a best-seller in the twentieth century; it was twice lavishly filmed.) Although it is not my
intention to consider American fiction that deals with India, the
Bromfield novel presents an interesting case of a work whose

theme, the bridging of national and racial divisions, is obviously influenced by Forster, while its obsession with sex seems to show some effect of D. H. Lawrence along with the traditional mythology of erotic India. *The Rains Came* differs from the generality of British novels about India in the prominence of the Indian characters and in the way they are viewed. That is to say, they are drawn as indistinguishable in basic human terms from the culturally different English and American characters in the book; Bromfield has much less difficulty than his British contemporaries in showing that Europeans and Indians of good will can understand one another quickly and spontaneously.

Nevertheless, the central relationship in the novel, the love affair of Lady Esketh with Dr. Safti, is not allowed to reach a happy conclusion. Lady Esketh, whose sexual appetite is close to nymphomania, finally achieves a satisfying, even ideal, love relationship with Dr. Safti but, understanding that his commitment to India is more important to him than any personal bond can be, drinks unpurified water and dies of typhoid. But India has done its work, awakening in her not a dormant sexuality (for it was never dormant) but on the contrary a capacity for profounder feeling—at the cost of her life. Here, then, several different mythologized clichés converge: India illuminates, India destroys, India brings sexual fulfillment to those who have never found it elsewhere. Virtually all the other characters in the book are feverish with sexual longing: the "bad" American missionary wife (there is a good missionary couple to counterbalance her and her husband), Nurse MacDaid, lesbian Miss Dirks and her friend Miss Hodge, who has fantasies about the Sikh guards at the palace, Maria Lishinskaia and Harry Bauer, adolescent Fern—all Europeans, for the Indians are apparently too sexually sophisticated to suffer from frustrated or misunderstood desires. As Lady Esketh sees it: " 'No,' she thought, 'even my own slut's life is more normal, is better than that. Even Shiva and his dingus is better than the chastity and barrenness of the Christian Church.' "[4]

Here is an instance of India vindicated, freedom as opposed to outmoded prudish conventions. This is not often the case; to conceive of India in such terms may have been in any case easier for an American than for an Englishman. The latter is apt to see the "liberation" offered by India as only the beginning of the downward path to corruption and damnation. A typical case in point is found in *The Cats of Benares*, where an English homosexual named Giles likes India's "climate of unrestrained individualism and permitted excesses."[5] "It suited him to live in a country where virtue has never been organized into a social force and where eccentricity can blossom without reproof."[6] This of course is Giles's (and apparently Halls's) conception of India—a curious one when one considers the quasi-Victorian outlook on sexual matters that continues to prevail in Indian society today. In his relationship with Krishan, his Indian lover, a student and "rotten little whore," Giles feels no love but regards him with "expectant and unaffectionate lust."[7]

In Han Suyin's *The Mountain Is Young* (1958), once again, as in Bromfield, the characters are obsessed with sex. Anne, the heroine, an Englishwoman who had wondered if she was frigid, abandons her gross and egocentric English husband for a South Indian engineer in Nepal. Whereas her husband is crude, infantile, bullying, and unaware of her as a person, Unni is subtle, graceful, all-understanding, suave, and effortless, and most important, a perfect lover "with the dexterity of his people." Isobel Maupratt, an English schoolteacher, loves Unni too, but she is repressed, because of her Christian beliefs, to such a degree that she is driven to drink and finally madness. Despite Han Suyin's intelligence and gift for journalistic description, the book is shallow, the prose often purple, and the division between good and bad, Eastern and Western, all too simplistic. The Europeans are brought to either salvation or destruction by the effect of Nepal, most commonly through the medium of sexual awakening or sexual degeneration. The "bad" Europeans are aghast at the erotic woodcarving and sculpture so common in the Valley; the "good" ones take it in stride. For people who knew Kathmandu in the fifties and later, *The Mountain Is Young* is also a shameless roman à clef—Vassili = Boris, Hilde = Inger, Father MacCullough = Father Moran, Ranchit = Prince Vasundhara, and so on; this merely confirms the fundamentally journalistic inspiration of the novel.

In Deborah Moggach's *Hot Water Man* (1982), two of the three protagonists have unexpected and unbelievable sexual experiences. The first case is that of Duke Hanson, an American entrepreneur in Karachi to negotiate a site for a new hotel; he is seduced by Shamime, a Western-educated freewheeling Pakistani siren. Duke is old-fashioned and rather puritanical, and has never been unfaithful to his wife of a quarter-century, but he is no match for seductive Shamime in her beach hut. The affair is unbelievable first of all because Duke is a caricature, one of those embarrassing "Aw Gee Heck" Americans who pop up in British fiction, and then Shamime is another kind of caricature, the unscrupulous and shallow—but irresistible—Oriental woman. The end of the affair, unprepared, unmotivated, and arbitrary, is the most unbelievable part of all: Shamime concludes that Duke has been using her only because her uncle is an important minister, although in fact she has used this same uncle all along to tighten her hold on Duke. The case of Christine Waley is more fantastic. Moggach writes of Christine, a young English wife, "*A Passage to India*—that book haunted her, it was written for her."[8] Like Adela Quested, Christine wants to get to know the real country; she has also wanted to become pregnant after many unsuccessful tries. When she visits a shrine where Muslim women go to pray for children, she accidentally, as it were, allows Sultan Rahim, a man she scarcely knows and who remains literally more than half-asleep throughout the encounter (he has been having a siesta and apparently is not aware of what has happened) to have intercourse with her. Finding herself pregnant soon after, Christine spends the rest of the novel worrying about whether the child will be Sultan's or her husband's; on the last page of the book she is relieved to be shown a baby who looks completely European; it is never clear whether she, or the author, understands or cares that such a baby, despite its fair skin, might not be her husband's. Whatever the case— and it is part of the overriding ineptness of the book that we never know just what the case is—once again the subcontinent destroys the repressions and suppressions of a lifetime and even magically confers fertility on the barren.

It is not surprising that novelists with pronounced limitations resort to the stale concepts that have typified the Indian sexual myth in order to confer a dubious energy and excitement on their work. Rather more surprising is the survival of the myth in the work of so talented a writer as Ruth Jhabvala. Her work will be discussed in detail in the next chapter, but here it will be useful to consider this aspect of her fiction. Despite the frequent cynicism, weariness, despair, and the general numbness of the style in the later works, this fundamentally romantic (or, better, melodramatic) concept of Indian sex plays its role and helps to confirm my view that—much more than has been recognized—Jhabvala, far from being the "Indian" novelist she is generally held to be, in fact continues the traditions of the colonial British novelists of the half-century preceding Indian Independence.

Jhabvala employs two basic patterns several times to dramatize the myth. In the first, an English girl marries or has an affair with an Indian which quickly turns sour, leaving the girl isolated, desolate, and sometimes desperate. This is the structure of several stories, for example, "The Alien," "The Young Couple," "Passion," "A Young Man of Good Family," mostly from the earlier period. The girls are trapped by the irresistible sexual attractiveness of Indians whom they fail to understand. In "The Young Couple," Cathy marries Naraian only to discover that he is (despite his earlier typical bachelor's coffeehouse free life-style) an ordinary traditionalist, settling down into his family's old-fashioned way of life. Christine and Betsy in "Passion," Daphne in "A Spiritual Call," and Georgia in "A Young Man of Good Family" all offer variations on the unhappiness coming from a sexual surrender to an Indian without any fundamental understanding. These stories from *A Stronger Climate* are all part of the section called "The Seekers," all the seekers being apparently lured into traps in their search for sex and beauty. They do not seem particularly different from the characters in the book's other section, "The Sufferers," except that these tend to be older. In other stories there are variations on the pattern; women are sometimes the seducers. In "A Course of English Studies," it is an Indian college girl at a Midlands university who, in her affair with an English professor, comes close to destroying him, while she herself remains fundamentally childlike, even infantile, naïve, and untroubled except by homesickness. In "In Love With A Beautiful Girl," a naïve young Englishman is tempted, bewildered, and left high and dry by Ruchira, a wealthy young Delhi girl. In all these stories there tends to be a sameness to the young Indian tempters. In "A Course of English Studies," the girl "smiled at him, and indeed as she did so, she radiated such warmth, such a sun all of her own, that he, who had looked up briefly, had at once to look down again as if it were too strong for him."[9] For his part, the professor "was rather short . . . and thin, and exceptionally pale; his hair was pale too, and very straight and fine, of an indeterminate color which may have been blond shading into grey."[10] These are familiar types—the Prufrockian intellectual and the sexually lustrous semitropical personage—and they will haunt Jhabvala's fiction. In "An Indian

Citizen" the young Indians, in comparison with the Europeans, looked like "a higher kind of being, with their healthy, brown, glowing skins and their brilliant dark eyes and strong teeth and hair."[11] To the English girl in "Miss Sahib," her countrymen are incapable of *"real love."* "Even physically the English looked cold to her, with their damp white skins and pale blue eyes, and she longed again to be surrounded by those glowing coloured skins; and those eyes! the dark, large, liquid Indian eyes! and hair that sprang with such abundance from their heads."[12] All the Indians have "beautiful eyes"; since this is so predictable and so rarely qualified, it becomes a commonplace in Jhabvala's work. Ruchira, in "In Love with A Beautiful Girl," has "soft, dusky skin" and "a superb smell."[13] The Indian lovers are frequently shown in a scene where they are completely or partially naked. Naraian, for instance, in "The Young Couple," is "pale brown, spare, hard, and muscular, not tall but beautifully put together."[14] The fondness for describing these types—or really type, for there is only one—is found in similar scenes in some of the novels, for example, *A Backward Place* (Kishan Kumar) and *Travelers* (Gopi); and in all these instances the character scarcely exists beyond the single dimension of his very generalized physical description. In one later story, "A Star and Two Girls," the now expected good-looking, vain, and infantile Indian, in this case a star of the Bombay cinema, comes out the loser, as the two visiting English girls baffle and ultimately reject him. Indian women are also sometimes victims of the attractive, predatory, and hopelessly immature young man (Durga in "The Widow" and Chameli in "A Bad Woman"). Most of the European women in these stories are in general so passive and apathetic that they may, as in *Heat and Dust,* succumb to a mediocre and even unattractive Indian man.

Even in her first non-Indian novel, *In Search of Love and Beauty* (1983), Jhabvala appears unable to do without a return to the pattern of apathetic involvement. Marietta, already of a certain age, goes to India and falls automatically, as it were, into a series of sexual encounters too brief and trivial to be called affairs or relationships of any sustained kind. "They were eager Indian youths who were excited by being in an expensive hotel, and also by her. They examined the clothes she had unpacked and sprayed themselves with her scents. They slept with her and were ashamed if their lovemaking was too frenzied to be sustained. But she didn't mind—it wasn't for sex that she liked being with them, it was for themselves. They were charming and pure."[15] This seems merely sentimental and indulgent. Even the typically Jhabvalan turn of phrase ("excited by being in an expensive hotel, and also by her") is stale, trivializing the characters and serving to diminish the writer's involvement with them. The book's title, with its high Platonic resonance, is first used in connection with Marietta's homosexual son, Mark, whose sexual taste is first made explicit in India—inevitably, even in this novel set mainly in New York.

In the second pattern, itself only a variation on the first, young English visitors to India, with the focus primarily on women, succumb to the hypnotic or sometimes violent attentions of a swami. We see this in "A Spiritual Call," "How I Became a Holy Mother," and *Travelers*. In the title story of *An Experience of India* (1972), both patterns are combined. The European heroine, bored with her journalist husband, has a series of sexual encounters with Indians, although she "didn't like sleeping with all those people, but felt I had to."[16] In describing Indian love-making, she notes that middle-aged men "get as excited as a fifteen-year-old boy, and then of course they can't wait, they *jump* and before you know where you are, in a great rush it's all over. And when it's over, it's over, there's nothing left."[17] Two of her encounters are described in some detail: one with Ahmed, an eighteen-year-old musician who is infantile and narcissistic, and one with a swami who, though he doesn't look very spiritual, has hypnotic eyes. The swami, like her other lovers, wants to know how many men she has slept with and then calls her "Bitch!"—at which she laughs in relief. Despite her surface sophistication, she is, like so many other Western women in Jhabvala's fiction, utterly passive when confronted with Indian men, particularly one with pretensions to spirituality, whether she accepts this as authentic or not. In the end, the unnamed protagonist decides to stay on in India after her husband has returned to sanitary Geneva. She concludes, "Yet it's still like an adventure, and that's why besides being afraid I'm also excited and most of the time I don't know why my heart is beating fast, is it in fear or in excitement, wondering what will happen to me now that I'm going travelling again."[18] This particular pathological study may be considered a kind of prelude to the novel that followed, *Travelers* (1973, titled *A New Dominion* in Britain), where one of the central figures, Lee, follows a similar path.

The collection *How I Became a Holy Mother* (1976) represents a modification of the two patterns in Jhabvala's work. In two of the stories happy marriages between Englishwomen and Indians are described, though in each case there is a counterpoint of a more Jhabvalan nature. In the first, "Two More Under the Indian Sun," Margaret is disturbed and angered by the happiness of her younger friend Elizabeth with her Indian husband. Sadie, in "The Englishwoman," after many years of marriage to an Indian, her children all married to Indians, feels an irresistible urge to return to England, to experience again its climate and landscape—an anticipation of the author's own return to the West. Both these stories are skilfully told and in their departure from the old mythology seem to represent a maturing of the writer's talent, though this estimate must be measured against the decline we find in *In Search of Love and Beauty*, where, among other weaknesses, there is the falling back on the old sexual patterns pointed out above. In the title story of the collection, although the external pattern is familiar, there are interesting variations. At twenty-three, Katie, after "boyfriends, marriages (two), jobs (modelling), best friends that are suddenly your best enemies,"[19] goes off to do the ashrams of India one after the other, until she finds one she prefers because "the scenery was very picturesque"[20] and the atmosphere is better because the "Master" is "full of pep." In the ashram, through the promotional planning of the swami and a European lady of dubious background known as the Countess, Katie and her Indian lover are said to be "revealed" as embodiments of the Guru and the Mother principle and travel to the West ("it's just a job we do"[21]), remembering with some nostalgia the mountains they have had to leave. Like many of Jhabvala's stories, especially the later ones, this one is successful because the standard mythology is allowed to disintegrate and the characters to evolve more freely and imaginatively; the tone too is different, more subtle, ambivalent, funny with less bitterness. Still, it is interesting to observe how powerful the old mythic patterns remain, as Jhabvala, in so many stories and most of the novels, continues to fabricate a basic structure in which individuals are somehow employed to dramatize the powerful and often destructive fascination of race, sex, and spirituality—an apparently indissoluble and threatening Indian trinity that seems still to dominate virtually all Anglo-Indian fiction. While many of Jhabvala's stories debunk the myth to some extent, they subtly reinforce many of its elements: India *does* destroy, Indian men, no matter how fatuous and without character, remain irresistible to European women, while most of the Western men portrayed are dull, ineffectual, colorless, and often homosexual.

Some will defend the stories as being satires of the defective perceptions of both Europeans and Indians regarding one another. Jhabvala of course must know that not all Europeans in India and not all the limited variety of Indians they encounter are like her characters. But this defense also helps to define the limitations of her art, for throughout her work one can scarcely ever discover a different reality to contrast with the desolate human realm she has made her sphere. This may well be the reason why her short stories satisfy in a way her novels in general do not. For the full-length novel craves a broader, more varied, and, above all, more generously observed world.

It remained for Paul Scott to integrate the elements of the old tradition of India and sex into a new, significant structure in which they cease to be generalizations and stereotypes. Scott's work will be discussed in detail later; here I wish only to cite some of the elements of the Indian sexual myth as they are particularized in *The Raj Quartet*. The central incident that dominates all subsequent action in the four novels is the love affair of an English girl and an Indian and the raping of the girl by unknown hoodlums. The girl is plain, the Indian remarkably handsome. Scott here is deliberately evoking Miss Quested and Aziz, perhaps to emphasize the profound difference both in his conception of such a potential situation and in his attitude toward the relationship of India and England. Ronald Merrick, a policeman, very different from Forster's Ronald, is motivated to play his villainous part in the tragedy of Daphne and Hari Kumar to a large extent by the overwhelming attraction he feels toward the latter (while courting the former), as well as by the challenge to his conviction of absolute and explicit white racial superiority. His homosexuality is not fully revealed until far along in the *Quartet*, but in retrospect we understand how the conflict of his desires with his beliefs concerning race, class, and the responsibility of the British mission undermines his character and is the source of his physical as well as moral destruction.

What Scott has done is to make sexual excess, deviation, and aberration a near-inevitable correlative of the Imperial process; the greed and the moral and ethical blindness that inspire and sustain colonialism in the sphere of public action are accompanied by a parallel degeneration in the private sphere, where sexual problems, violence, and confusion reveal and symbolize the same moral failures. All of this is a far cry from the conventional use of the mythology that, especially in this century, has been used in fiction largely as an exotic source of titillation to produce commercial success or, in a superior writer like Ruth Jhabvala, as a kind of touchstone to reveal the defects of character (and common sense) in the Europeans seduced by India and the crass, characterless Indians they are apt to encounter.

4

Ruth Jhabvala

So I am back again alone in my room with the blinds down, and the air-conditioner on. Sometimes, when I think of my life, it seems to have contracted to this one point and to be concentrated in this one room, and it is always a very hot, very long afternoon when the airconditioner has failed. I cannot describe the oppression of such afternoons. It is a physical oppression—heat pressing down on me and pressing in the walls and the ceiling and congealing together with time which has stood still and will never move again. And it is not only those two—heat and time—that are laying their weight on me but behind them, or held within them, there is something more which I can only describe as the whole of India. This is hyperbole, but I need hyperbole to express my feelings about those countless afternoons spent over what now seems to me countless years in a country for which I was not born.

RUTH JHABVALA[1]

Of the recent novelists who have written about India, with the exception of Paul Scott, Ruth Prawer Jhabvala, because of the special nature of her case, seems to me the most interesting, whatever the limitations of her work. When I speak of her "case," I mean the question of how she is to be classified by the literary historian—as British or Indian—and the far more serious and complex question of the relationship between her work and her own conception of her identity.

Ruth Jhabvala was born in 1927 in Frankfurt, Germany of Polish Jewish parents. *Who's Who of Indian Writers* lists her native language as Yiddish. In 1939 her parents took her to England. She lived there until 1951, when she married a Parsi architect and went with him to Delhi, where she lived for the next twenty-five years and brought up three daughters. During this time she wrote all but the last one of her nine novels, as well as four volumes of short stories and various screenplays, including the prize-winning *Shakespeare Wallah*. In 1975 she left India and settled in New York,

Part of this chapter appeared in *Modern Fiction Studies* 30, no. 4 (Winter 1984): 669–81) with the title "Ruth Jhabvala in India."

which has become the principal setting, if not precisely the subject, of her most recent novel, *In Search of Love and Beauty*, and the screenplay *Roseland*. Most Indian and Western critics alike regard her as an Indian writer, one of the "Indo-Anglian" school, which includes such diverse novelists as Raja Rao, Mulk Raj Anand, Anita Desai, Salman Rushdie, and R. K. Narayan. I believe, however, that she should not be viewed as an Indian writer but that she actually belongs to the tradition of the Anglo-Indian writers discussed in earlier chapters, those novelists who for the most part regard India with the critical and often indignant eye of the superior (if lonely) outsider. Not to recognize Jhabvala's kinship with this tradition seriously compromises the possibility of a genuine comprehension of the significance of her work, its virtues, and its failings.

Let us first consider the basis for regarding Jhabvala as an authentic Indian voice: her marriage to an Indian and her long residence in India. If this evidence were sufficient in itself, then by the same standards Kamala Markandaya, married to an Englishman and living in London, must be judged British. If we consider the question from the viewpoint of her material, which is mostly Indian in setting with a fair mix of Indian and Western characters, Markandaya, for her part, could again just as fairly be called British. The question is further complicated by Jhabvala's recent abandonment of India for the United States. The solution to this puzzle of national identification is not idly speculative, for on it hangs the greater mystery of Jhabvala's sense of her own identity and its relation to the world she has created, a world populated by wanderers, refugees, Westerners who have lost all sense of a national identity.

Describing Indo-Anglian writers in general, Klaus Steinvorth writes: "The position of Indo-English novelists is on the periphery of their own society, they are partly even separated from it by emigration or expatriation, which does not mean they are sufficiently integrated in their new society. . . . Almost every one of them feels, or is considered, an outsider standing between India and the West, often led to believe that these two complex and abstract ideas can be reduced to a pair of simple opposites."[2] The curious thing about Jhabvala, of course, is that, unlike the other novelists Steinvorth is concerned with, she has been exiled not from but to India. Her position is therefore that of a kind of permanent refugee, a point whose significance I shall return to later. Steinvorth also maintains that Jhabvala's fiction is strongly molded by Hinduism, to an extent even greater than one finds in the work of a Hindu writer such as, say, Manohar Malgonkar.[3] The un-likelihood of this thesis should become clear in what follows.

The view that Jhabvala is an Indian writer is one held by critics but not by the novelist herself. In an interview with Ramlal Agarwal, when asked if she would like to be considered an Indian writer, she answered, "No, how could I be? I'm not, am I? There's no getting away from that fact. I write differently from Indian writers because my birth, background, ancestry, and traditions are different. If I must be considered anything, then let it be as one of those European writers who have written about India."[4] Elsewhere she has said:

The central fact of all my work, as I see it, is that I am a European living permanently in India. I have lived here for most of my adult life and have an Indian family. This makes me not quite an outsider either. I feel my position to be at a point in space where I have quite a good view of both sides but am myself left stranded in the middle. My work is an attempt to charter this unchartered territory for myself. . . . My books may appear to be objective but really I think they are the opposite; for I describe the Indian scene not for its own sake but for mine. . . . My work is only one individual European's attempt to compound the puzzling process of living in India.[5]

This straightforward and candid statement, made in 1972, offers useful clues for the interpretation of Jhabvala's fiction, but it has been largely ignored by critics and reviewers, who continue to consider her an Indian novelist.

From Jhabvala's point of view there is, of course, a considerable advantage in being thought of as Indian. It allows her to be ruthlessly critical of both traditional and "modern" India without incurring the odium attaching to a hostile and uninformed outsider. In writing of that India which she knows from her own experience, she has the additional advantage, as she suggests, of being both of it and out of it. To her observation of Indian city life she brings both a European irony that can come only with a certain detachment and an insider's knowledge of detail and nuance that few other non-Indians could hope to command. At moments (and I believe they are her best) she writes with a finely controlled irony and an unsentimental sympathy that is neither necessarily Indian nor European but very much her own individual manner—an accomplishment few genuine Indo-Anglian writers can claim, though there are notable exceptions, such as R. K. Narayan and Anita Desai.

India: The Early Phase—Indian Family Life

Jhabvala's first five novels may be said to constitute the first phase of her work. With the exception of *Esmond in India*, they are not particularly involved with Europeans but portray, rather, Indian family life and its constant preoccupation with finding suitable husbands for younger daughters. Although the tone darkens after the relatively sunny first novel, *Amrita*, the principal characters are viewed, in general, with some compassion and their eccentricities as, for the most part, endearing. The third novel, *Esmond in India*, the first to take up what may be called Jhabvala's international theme, is noticeably more bitter in tone. It seems as though a European presence automatically calls up tension, anxiety, and disappointment. The novel that followed, *The Householder*, is again a mostly Indian story, one in which Jhabvala achieves her most sympathetic insight into middle-class domestic life, with nuances both tender and melancholy; its only defect comes from the intrusion of minor European characters, caricatures who anticipate the hippies and other questers who flocked to India in the sixties and who were to become almost an obsessive preoccupation in Jhabvala's later work. *Get Ready for Battle*, her fifth novel, is also the last one in which she concentrates on an India uninvolved with the outside world.

In *Amrita* (1955, published in Britain with the title *To Whom She Will*) Jhabvala develops the basic pattern of new comedy in terms of contemporary upper-class Delhi life. Amrita, the heroine, thinks she is in love with a superficial young man, who is considered unacceptable by her mother and aunts because his family is cruder and less affluent. They in turn plot to marry her to the son of one Lady Ram Prashad, but this fails because the boy, while abroad, marries an American, and finally Amrita's mother settles on a former lodger, Krishna Sen Gupta, as the proper match for her daughter at about the same time that Amrita and Krishna realize that they are in love with each another.

Out of this slender plot Jhabvala creates a romantic comedy of considerable charm and even tenderness such as she was never to write again. There are some satirical elements, especially in the presentation of Jhabvala's bête noire, the wealthy society woman (in this case, Lady Ram Prashad) whose do-gooder activities are called into question by her egotism, snobbery, and lack of genuine kindness. Amrita herself emerges as a spirited girl, and, like Sen Gupta, she is given an individual (which means of course on some occasions unpredictable) character, so that the reader does not come to view them as examples of fixed Indian sociological types. Rather, despite the local color created by frequent references to Indian foods and types of clothing, for example, one more or less forgets that this is a story that could take place only in India. Some of the minor characters are crudely sketched; Mira Auntie exists only in terms of her gormandizing; Hari's relatives are all too flat and predictable examples of a traditional family of their caste and community; and so on. However, many of the other second-string characters are well individualized, with some complexity in the form of contradictory traits, for example, the grandfather, Tarla Auntie, and particularly Radha, Amrita's mother. Radha is something of a snob, resents her sisters' greater wealth, holds traditional views about marriage, but has herself married a Bengali (as her daughter ultimately will do), so that she has broken the confining circle of both caste and ethnic identity. Anticipating the situation of Lalaji in *The Nature of Passion* (where it is more explicitly developed), Radha also has a genuinely deep love for her daughter and is concerned that the girl be happy.

Unlike many of the later novels, *Amrita* contains much less explication of the specifically Indian context. In this respect the book is closer to what one has come to expect of a novel by an Indian writer (although even novelists like Khushwant Singh and Markandaya introduce material obviously intended to clarify for a non-Indian audience).[6] And again, as in Indo-Anglian fiction in general, in *Amrita* foreigners are of no importance. When they do intrude, as in the person of Jhabvala's favorite butt, the German specialist in Indian culture, the satire is facile and obvious.

"If we want to show to our foreign guests the real, the true, spirit of India," the Professor continued, "we must show them not the degenerate city life with its evil Western influences, but life as it is lived in the villages, unchanged for generations, unruffled by the comings and going of conquerors. Pure as water drawn from the clear sparkling well"—a phrase which he hoped to be able to fit in the evening's lecture—"the Indian village reflects the very soul of India, forever still and at peace, oblivious of Time, lost in its contemplation of the infinite." And then it was time for lunch. . . .

Professor Hoch was kept very busy. Besides eating, he had to talk Art
with Vazir Dayal, Amrita with Radha, Social Work with Lady Ram Prashad and Tarla, and admire Dr. Mukherji's simple ways. The last was the
most thankless task, for Dr. Mukherji did not even glance at him, although
he very ardently commended the beauty of cotton saris and boiled vegetables.[7]

But in general Jhabvala's inclination to satire of an especially
cutting sort is kept banked. One might say that in *Amrita* the author's attitude toward life is brighter, more relaxed, even a bit
more optimistic than it was soon to become. If there is a weakness
in this comedy as comedy, it derives from the fact that the happy
resolution of the characters' problems and the banishment of their
illusions comes about not through their exertions but rather as
the result of a fortunate play of circumstances unassisted by them.
Amrita herself, though she at first plots and struggles to achieve
happiness, as she at that moment conceives it to be, is ultimately
passive, surrendering to her fate. This passivity will come to per-
vade the ensuing novels, particularly the Western characters,
where it often seems to reach a degree that can only be called
pathological and removes them from the realm of comedy altogether.

The Nature of Passion (1956) marks a significant development in
Ruth Jhabvala's art. The romantic comedy of *Amrita*, in which the
chief characters evolve—or escape—out of stereotypes to become
satisfyingly individualized human beings, gives way to a more
acerbic and even cynical presentation of people so limited that
each comes close to being an illustration of a single humor. The
apparent objectivity with which they are portrayed is, in fact, a
device for diminishing and ridiculing them. Unlike those characters dominated by a single capacity or obsession whom we encounter in Jonson or Molière, say, these in *The Nature of Passion*
are so predictable and unimaginatively sketched that they fail to
interest.

The meager plot of *Amrita* is fulsome by comparison with this
novel's, which consists of a series of vignettes of the life of a rich
Panjabi family settled in Delhi after fleeing from Lahore at the
time of Partition (Jhabvala's first study of refugees, though, like
the German Jews of *In Search of Love and Beauty*, they appear to
have no link at all with their past, nor even any recollection of
it). The center of the novel is Lalaji, a millionaire, fat and corrupt,
whose only distinction is his affection for his daughter, whom

eventually he is willing to trade off to gain a lucrative contract. His oldest daughter and son are cast exactly in the family mold, while the youngest daughter and son are rebellious—both long to go to England—although in the end they will follow the path charted for them by their parents. As in *Amrita*, by a lucky coincidence a marriage is arranged for Nimmi with the young man she has been only half-consciously attracted to but comes to love. But in this novel the happy resolution is made possible only by the weakness and triviality of character exhibited by the principal actors and is unexpected after the negative tone of what precedes. In the subplot Lalaji's oldest son has written an indiscreet letter that has been put in a government file just as there is to be an investigation in a bribery and corruption case. By chance, the file has found its way onto the desk of Chandra, Lalaji's second son, a government officer. When Lalaji attempts to make Chandra give him the letter, Chandra's wife, Kanta, a self-righteous, pseudointellectual social climber, protests. But after a long argument with Chandra, she realizes that if the letter is not removed from the file, her husband's career may be compromised, along with Lalaji's generous contributions to her household, which make their summer vacations in the hills possible. She is then obliged to reverse her position and persuade Chandra that he must remove the letter.

Using a technique that she will employ frequently in later books, Jhabvala avoids presenting the moments that might have been genuinely dramatic and moving: Nimmi's discovery that, against her most passionate wishes, her family is planning to marry her; or her later discovery that her betrothed is the man who has already fascinated her; or the crucial moment when Kanta realizes that she is going to have to dispense with her scruples and rationalize what she knows is corrupt. A dangerous strategy, for the understatement may, as here, end up by undermining the interest of the narrative. So also the characterizations, where a host of mostly older women (mother, mother-in-law, widowed aunt, ayah, etc.) all recite set pieces that identify them as typical Indian household characters. They appear in a series of strung-together episodes so dull that they rather give the impression of creative writing assignments: a naïve girl on her first date, a dinner party for the host's boss, the gathering of the clan at the birth of a grandchild.

The style contributes further to the flatness of the novel. There is, first of all, the matter of the dialogue, which is innocent throughout of any contraction (as in most of the succeeding novels) and is rendered still more bizarre by the quaintness of the word order.

"A little sister you have got, a little sister like a pearl."[8]

"Take rest. We will cook for you, horseradish pancake we will cook for you."[9]

Eleven days old she is."[10]

The point of this word order is not clear to me. It does not match either Indian English or standard Hindi (or Panjabi), and it sounds rather more like English influenced by Yiddish or German; in any case, it is usually not clear which language, English, Hindi, or Panjabi, the characters are supposed to be speaking.

Like the dialogue, the narrative style is kept so flat that at times it seems fatigued, with repetitions and echoes increasing the monotony:

"It is a little hot," said one of the men sitting in the office. There were many people sitting in the office.[11]

The moment she came in they knew she had something special to impart, for her eyes gleamed with excitement and she wore a festive blouse of blue satin. They were a little apprehensive, whenever she came like this, she usually had something to their disadvantage to impart.[12]

The pervading dullness may, of course, be the meaning Jhabvala wishes to convey. If so, it shows us how early Jhabvala's unhappiness with India began, the unhappiness that would be revealed in 1972 in "Myself in India."

In writing about this novel Haydn Moore Williams cites Lalaji's clerk as an embodiment of the "highest Hindu religious spirit," which she was to develop more fully in subsequent novels.[13] I believe that this interpretation is mistaken on two counts. First of all, Jhabvala's sympathy with Hindu religious ideals is always ambiguous at best;[14] and second, the clerk, although he quotes scripture and is described as "pure, withdrawn, detached,"[15] is shown only as Lalaji sees him. All we know about him in fact is that he has a salary of seventy-five rupees a month and that in his only speech in the novel (apart from pious quotations) he sounds rather a bore. " 'It is written that a daughter is but a loan to her parents; when it is time for her to go to a husband's house, they must return this loan. This is written in the work of our great

Sanskrit poet Kalidasa.' '"[16] "Our great Sanskrit poet" betrays him as unreal, for even Lalaji doubtless does not need to be told who Kalidasa was. Or did Jhabvala feel that this intrusion was necessary for her Western audience? This, at least, would be one trait she shares with genuine Indo-Anglian writers, among whom Klaus Steinvorth mistakenly classifies her.[17]

It is interesting to compare *The Nature of Passion* with Hindi fiction that deals with the same stratum of Delhi society. Such novelists as Mohan Rakesh, Krishnā Sobti, and Agyeya are far more preoccupied with the particular than with the general, the individual drama rather than the exemplification of a clinical sociological pattern, with the result that their work seems, ironically, more securely located in the mainstream of Western realistic fiction (a genre that is itself a Western importation in India) than Jhabvala's.[18]

Jhabvala's first five novels stand apart from the four that follow by being concerned with middle-class domestic life in Delhi, a world in which Europeans are of little account except as facile caricatures observed briefly and from afar. This is true even of her third novel, *Esmond in India* (1958), for though Esmond appears to be a major figure in the story, he is in fact of little importance except as a kind of irritant that will stimulate and emphasize all that is typical of a modern middle-class Delhi family. It is clear from the beginning of the novel that Esmond and his Indian wife, Gulab, have nothing at all in common and interact only to make one another unhappy, a situation that will suffer no development or transformation in the course of the story. Gulab's mother tries to separate them, but the inevitable separation takes place only because a manservant has approached Gulab lewdly; Gulab, who has stayed with Esmond because she feels it is her *dharma*, now feels released because she has been defiled and Esmond has not been there to protect her. At the same time, ironically, Esmond, without her knowledge, has decided to leave her and return to England.

Most of the novel is taken up with Har Dayal and Madhuri making plans for the marriage of their daughter Shakuntala, while Ramnath, Gulab's uncle, and his wife, Lakshmi, plan a marriage for their son Narayan. Jhabvala initiates complexities that are not resolved or, for that matter, explored fully. Though the novel is more ambitious in scope than the two preceding it and, in its characterization of Indian parents, more engaging and subtle, it fails because, in the midst of its psychological realism, Jhabvala introduces an incident that she avoids confronting: Esmond's casual seduction of Shakuntala. It happens offstage, so to speak, and Shakuntala, incredibly (anticipating the passive and apathetic females who are to become a stock feature of Jhabvala's work) accepts the event without any more effect than a tendency to gush when alone with Esmond. As presented, it is simply not believable that a girl like Shakuntala, portrayed as intelligent, gilded with sophistication but utterly innocent in matters of sex, and rather fatuously romantic, could sleep with Esmond and then go about her business as though nothing had happened. Jhabvala seems unwilling to explore this crucial event all the while she expends her considerable analytical powers in revealing the inner workings of what is already obvious, by which I mean such elements as Madhuri's resentment of Uma, Gulab's mother, for allowing her daughter to marry Esmond instead of (as originally planned) her own son, and so on.

But the Indian characters are by and large treated sympathetically, as humans first, Indians second. A comedy comparable to *Amrita* seems in the offing until Esmond makes his delayed appearance, at which point it all goes sour—a foreshadowing of what will happen to Jhabvala's work when the international (or interracial) theme comes to obsess it.

In contrast to the later novels, in *Esmond in India* it is the Indians who tend to emerge as individuals. For Esmond the author does not conceal her distaste, and she diminishes him at once, perhaps unconsciously echoing Dickens on the Veneerings, obliging the reader to share her scorn.

> He sat alone at his smart little dining-table in his smart little corner and ate his cheese salad. Everything on the table was colourful and modern.[19]

> He decided to go and see Betty. He always, whenever he felt particularly oppressed by Gulab, went to see Betty. Her flat was so light, modern, and airy; she herself so light, modern, and airy.[20]

Esmond is the first of her major European caricatures, just as Sarla, in *Get Ready for Battle,* may be said to be the last of her real, believably human Indians. Vasant Shahane, in his book on Jhabvala, correctly observes that Esmond, in his inability to adjust to India, to accept it as it is, has a problem "similar to the problem of Jhabvala herself: 'Should one want to try and become something other than what one is?'[21] It is essentially a problem of identity. Can Esmond in relation to India allow himself to be crushed by the environment?''[22] If this is true, then one wonders if it is fair of Ruth Jhabvala to satirize her characters mercilessly for failings (or, better, problems) that may well be her own? (Her identity problem, in any case, is not trying to become something other than what she is but rather simply to discover *what* she is.) Also interesting to note is Jhabvala's dark view of interracial marriages and affairs: few throughout her oeuvre are happy, and when they appear to be, as in the case of Bal and Judy in *A Backward Place*, the Indian husband is exasperatingly childish and foolish, while his wife remains so placid as to appear defective in sense and pride. As the stories of *A Stronger Climate* (1968) confirm, it is always the Indian spouse or lover who disappoints, reverts either to a strongly molded and predictable caste (and class) type (Naraian in "The Young Couple," Har Gopal in "Passion") or to an equally predictable superficial, modish, and modern social type (Ruchira in "In Love with a Beautiful Girl," Manny in "Passion.")

After *Amrita*, Jhabvala's next book, *The Householder* (1960), is her most relaxed, least problematical novel. Its chief action is the development of Prem, a shy teacher in a mediocre little school, toward a sense of selfhood, a process in which the chief element is his gradual falling in love with his wife. This scheme allows Jhabvala to present a touching and ironic picture of the typical circumstances of so many arranged marriages in present-day India. The charm and novelty, for a Western reader, come of course from the very idea of a man coming so late to understand and sympathize with and ultimately love his wife, who at the point the story opens is already several months pregnant.

The minor characters (Prem's mother, the school principal, and the like) are mere devices, and the two European characters nothing more than cartoon wraiths, the caricatured Western seekers who will come unfortunately to play an ever larger role in Jhabvala's subsequent novels without gaining much if anything in substance or depth. Hans, a German proto-hippie, comes out with statements like " 'My theory is that where there is greatest unemployment among the educated classes there is also greatest spiritual development,' ''[23] and not much else, while Kitty, darning a stocking, will say, " 'The way you talk anybody'd think there wasn't such a thing as the Infinite,' '' and " 'We mustn't forget the Eternal Essence, must we?' ''[24] The swami, whom Prem visits twice, is more ambiguous, shadowy, unconvincing.[25]

Jhabvala uncharacteristically maintains a single point of view (Prem's) throughout the novel, so that the minor figures and caricatures do not make the story founder, as they are apt to do in the later novels devoted to East-West questions, works that sometimes appear to be mere salmagundis of minor personages with nothing to hold them together except for the satirical, even contemptuous point of view of the author. Prem, as Haydn Moore Williams points out,[26] remains sympathetic despite his shallowness and immaturity. One can feel for him in his botched attempts to get a raise in salary from his principal and a cut in the rent from his landlord; one can even suffer with him in the fine comic scene of the principal's tea party, where he watches, helpless on the men's side of the room, while his wife violates the rigid protocol and gorges on the sweets long after the other women have stopped. In the course of the story, we are made aware that youthful Prem's inexperience is gradually giving way to a genuine maturity. Although terribly inept, he is less passive than the major figures in many of the other novels, and his faults are not stamped upon him like irredeemable curses. As in *Amrita,* a sense of genuine fun is mingled with the condemnation of the selfish and self-serving, even in the case of the swami. And above all one feels that the writer still believes that Indians can be happy (without being shallow and monstrous hedonists), that she is celebrating simple virtues, domestic ones at that, possible in her created world, and not dismissing that world as hopeless.

The last of Jhabvala's novels centered on Indian domestic life is *Get Ready for Battle* (1962). The central character is Sarla, a woman committed to the service of the underprivileged. She has long ago left her husband, Gulzari Lal, and conducts her life according to her understanding of the Bhagavad Gita. The main action of the novel derives from her attempt to save a squatters' colony from eviction and her son from following in the money-grubbing, corrupt life of his father. Despite her energy and passion she fails in both these attempts; vested interests want the eviction in order to enhance the value of adjoining property, even though it means shifting the residents to a site many miles from their work (an all too common occurrence in Delhi and other big cities), while Sarla's son, turning down an invitation from an idealistic friend to open a school or go wandering, decides to go into business for himself. Around Sarla moves the world we have come to expect from Jhabvala: shallow society people aping Western life-styles, cynical and grasping businessmen, Gulzari Lal's tough and practical middle-aged mistress, self-aggrandizing do-gooders, and the like. Sarla is the most memorable of all Jhabvala's Indian characterizations, presented without the usual corrosive irony; if she fails, it is at least not because she is apathetic. She is also the single embodiment in a major character in all Jhabvala's fiction of a genuinely Hindu point of view, at least in terms of the Hinduism of the Gita. There is, in fact, nowhere else in Jhabvala's work an Indian character so positively conceived, so worthy of admiration and so universally and touchingly human.

With *Get Ready for Battle* the first phase of Jhabvala's fiction comes to an end. Except for *Amrita* all the novels strike a melancholy note, a note that will become more depressing and angrier in the works to follow. In all five novels the Europeans are objects of derision, and the idealists or simply the decent people are oppressed by India, drained, rendered ineffectual in the paralyzing, mechanical and virtually unchangeable structure of traditional values, caste, and near-universal selfishness, while the morally seedy flourish. The atmosphere of moral bankruptcy and inertia is confirmed by the dullness of Jhabvala's style, in which not a metaphor enlivens a single moment. This is not the methodically precise control we find in Tolstoy or Chekhov but rather the creation of a joyless world, in which fleeting pleasures are without exception trivial, corrupt, and as little pleasurable as possible. This is not the comedy it is usually dubbed by careless or ignorant critics but a harsh and puritanical view of life unsustained by faith or hope.

India: The Later Phase—East Versus West

A Backward Place (1965) is the novel that initiates Jhabvala's second phase, in which the international theme becomes all-important. As in all of Jhabvala's fiction, the focus here is on women; there are few memorable male characters in all her work. In this case the central figures are three European women who represent in varying degrees the East-West malaise exemplified in the typical situations that recur throughout her fiction: the troubled marriages and love affairs between Indians and Europeans, the romantic, vaguely questing Westerner, the adventuring and fight for survival of bored, trivial, and Indophobic drifters—all mirrored by their egomaniacal, mindless, and predatory Indian counterparts. In *A Backward Place* the Indian characters, with two minor exceptions, Shanti and Bhuaji (*sic*)[27] are characterized by shallowness and mediocrity, combined in individual cases with infantile selfishness, cupidity, stupidity, and extravagant vanity. They are, in short, caricatures, occasionally amusing and generally predictable. The Western characters demonstrate only slightly more individuality.

The action of the novel is of the simplest. Judy, married to Bal ("child"), who is unemployed and unemployable, works in the office of the Cultural Dais until, finally, she gives in to her husband's harebrained scheme of going to Bombay to look for work in films. Clarissa, an adumbration of the later hippies, is a painter, an expert sponger, and wildly in love with an elemental India of nature and villages, about which she knows nothing. She says that Romain Rolland's *Life of Vivekananda* inspired her to come to India, and she has "rejected all Western values." Etta, a Hungarian refugee, is a fading blond who survives by having affairs with Indian businessmen. Unlike Clarissa, she clings to everything Western. This limited material is sufficient for Jhabvala to present a cutting satire of the way foreigners—some foreigners—live in New Delhi. Her fiercest scorn is reserved for a German exchange economist at the university and his wife, a couple who are victims of the reverse Indian myth, a gushy, uninformed Indophilia sustained by the good life their government grant guarantees ("Even the furniture was provided by the government").

[The Hochstadts] saw in it a reflection of the spirit of India as a whole— of that new India, which strove to bring itself in line with the most highly developed technical achievements of the twentieth century and yet retain its own culture: its art, its religion, its philosophy (and where in India, as Dr. Hochstadt so aptly remarked to his wife, can one draw a dividing line between these three manifestations of the human spirit?) which had ever been, and would ever be, an inspiration to the world. . . . Another few months and Dr. Hochstadt's assignment would be at an end, and it would be time to return to the normal course of their duties. In a way they were not sorry: all good things must come to an end, and they were beginning to miss the cosy flat in St. John's Wood . . . and several other features of their normal settled lives.[28]

The Indian characters are just as cruelly satirized. Mrs. Kaul, the rich patroness of the ineffectual Cultural Dais (which presents a farcically inept performance of Ibsen's *Doll's House*), is a modern variation on Dickens' Veneerings:

Then some of her own friends came, and they were very much more acceptable. They were all well dressed, spoke good English and had been abroad; in short, they were cultured people.[29]

"Last year we were in Berlin where Mr. Kaul was head of the economic mission at the International Conference of Civil Servants. We were shown many interesting cultural events such as the State Opera and the Berliner theatre. From there we went to U.K. and saw *Rosenkavalier* at the Covent Garden Opera House. This too was a beautiful experience. In Moscow we saw the Bolshoi Ballet—oh my own dear Bolshoi Ballet!" she cried and clapped her hands and shut her eyes for joy.[30]

Mrs. Kaul is even more pungently satirized for her moral shoddiness: she would like to fire Judy so as to be able to oblige some influential friends by hiring their daughter.

He pointed out that it was hardly possible to slide one person out of a job for no better reason than that you wished to slide another person into it; but here she could not follow him, for as far as she was concerned it was entirely possible.[31]

Most of the other Indians in the novel are even less attractive: Guppy, the writer's usual grossly self-indulgent businessman; Kishan Kumar, a mindless, narcissistic film star; snobbish, Europe-mongering Mr. Jumperwala; the pompous Doctor, among others. Jaykar, the editor, feels some indignation at the idleness and silliness of the young Indians who crowd the coffeehouses, but he expresses it only in editorials composed in a desolatingly trite style. "Now is the time it behoves our Youth to leave their cushioned chairs, gird up their loins and stride out into those areas of our vast land where the trumpet of Progress has not yet sounded its first triumphant notes."[32] Sudhir, who has decent instincts, is, like so many of Jhabvala's characters, passive, ineffectual, and ultimately futile.

Judy, the most sympathetically drawn of all the characters, seems to promise the possibility of a sane middle path between Etta's Indophobia and Clarissa's gush. She is happy to work to support her husband and children, content in the society of her sister-in-law and husband's aunt, a conventional religious old Hindu woman. But Judy herself is without any strong motivation or discrimination and seems indeed to be almost simpleminded; her capitulation to her husband at the end of the novel, in a kind of irrational, euphoric surrender, is difficult to credit. It seems as though India has sapped her will and her native Cockney common sense, for it is all too clear that in Bombay her husband will fail in his assault on the bastions of filmdom and Judy will have to keep working to feed him and the children.

Apart from its exotic interest as a reflection of Indian experience, it is as a triumphant example of comedic art that Jhabvala's work has been most consistently praised. The comparison of her work to Chekhov's has been so frequent as to be a reviewer's cliché. To cite only one instance, V. S. Pritchett, reviewing another novel, finds her "an ironical observer of what Chekhov called the false emotions, the comedy (in the sternest sense) of self-delusion without drastic condemnation of the deluded."[33] But drastic condemnation is certainly present, even in this best of Jhabvala's satirical recreations of the lives of foreigners in India, as the examples quoted above suggest. The classical conception of comedy as a literary process in which illusions and confusions are dispelled, in which, above all, true identities at both symbolic and literal levels are reestablished and the protagonists given, as it were, a second chance (the point at which comedy decides not to be tragedy) so that their lives are clarified, sweetened and, in short, redeemed—none of these concepts, obviously, can be applied to *A Backward Place*. In Chekhovian tragicomedy, as Pritchett remarks, the author does not condemn or disdain his creations. Furthermore, in Chekhov the melancholy view of human experience is constantly counterpointed by currents of joy, of pleasure, of hope, no matter how often it is cruelly disappointed: at the end of *Three Sisters*, Olga can still say that "life isn't finished yet for us," and Anya and Trofimov are described as gay and excited when last heard of in *The Cherry Orchard*. In *A Backward Place* the outcome of each character's quests and conflicts (themselves deliberately trivialized) is merely sour and negative. As so often in Jhabvala's work, there is a persistent concentration on the perverse, the mediocre, and the disappointing that is actually not the correction of the exaggeratedly romantic but merely its opposite extreme, too unbalanced to be considered realistic; it is rather a facile cynicism of the kind an unhappy Indian experience can breed so effectively. Here we have something like the world of Evelyn Waugh's early novels transplanted to Delhi and gone stale.

As in the earlier novels, in *A Backward Place* the pessimism and emotional deadness are reinforced by the prose style. It is self-consciously flat. There are hardly ever any conjunctions except for *and* and *but;* consequently, there is scarcely any subordination of clauses, which in turn means a heavy restriction on the expression of any kind of sentiment, indignation, or approval. Superficially this may seem like Hemingway, but in Hemingway, at least in the earlier novels and stories, the coolness and evenness of style are used to communicate and enhance extraordinary events, intense emotional shocks, and a definite moral viewpoint. In *A Backward Place* the apparent indifference does not serve any such purpose. Instead of lending conviction to passionately felt experiences and hard-won stoicism in the face of tragic losses, the style merely confirms the obvious mediocrity of the novel's characters and situations. Almost any paragraph chosen at random illustrates this. "Bal had a brilliant idea. He woke up with it one morning and couldn't wait to tell Judy. Unfortunately she had already left for work—he was always the last to get up, for he got home late at night and liked to make up for it in the morning—so he had to lie there and think about it by himself. He lay for quite a long time, but in the end jumped out of bed for he had got so excited about his idea that he felt he had to share it with someone, even if it was only Bhuaji who wouldn't understand properly. But she had gone out too, and the children were at school, and the servant in the bazaar."[34] Even at a moment that is charged with some emotion, the writer downplays it to rob it deliberately of serious impact. " 'She has insulted me!' he suddenly shouted. With a vehement gesture he flung away his chicken leg (Mrs. Hochstadt, who hated to see litter, had to check an impulse to run after it and pick it up and put it in her special disposal box). He shouted again, 'I have been insulted!' "[35]

This is farce rather than comedy, and it is based not on insight but rather on facile generalizations and accurate observation only of the surface of things. Chekhovian comedy depends on a swift recognition of what is typical and expected, but its effectiveness derives from the way this is set off by what is neither typical nor expected; the apparently placid surface conceals and gradually reveals a depth and tension, a sympathetically conceived human personality, not a clinically sound diagnosis followed by a scornful dismissal. In Chekhov, laughter and tears are natural partners, and there is usually a sense of wonder at the extraordinary qualities of surprise and mystery embedded in the most ordinary experience. *A Backward Place* is a dry and occasionally humorous chronicling of the bleak totality of Indian experience, as the author conceives it; the Indian characters are vain, shallow, self-indulgent, deceitful; and India itself becomes not a searchlight but an instrument used to diminish and denigrate the characters.

As I mentioned before, Clarissa anticipates the arrival of the hippies on the Indian scene and the shift of Jhabvala's attention from the Indian family to the Western drifter as the center of her plots. The hippie is a kind of refugee, and the refugee has always fascinated Jhabvala, who in an interview in 1974 said of herself, "I was practically born a displaced person."[36] So the hippies offered to Jhabvala a whole rich new field to explore, a field in which she could also approach more closely than she ever had before the particular nature of her own situation in India. This is not to say that the various kinds of philosophical and emotional escape artists who now crowd into her fiction are simple projections of herself, but obviously they do relate to her in many ways, reflect, and even parody elements of her own Indian experience. "My books may appear to be objective but really I think they are the opposite." And in any case, with *Get Ready for Battle*, Jhabvala had exploited the Indian family to its limit; the atmosphere engendered by its traditional, almost mechanical mode of operation had become suffocating and offered less and less material that a maturing writer could relate to herself.

Travelers, the novel that follows *A Backward Place*, might well have been called *Refugees*. The two central Indian characters, Asha, a middle-aged rani, and Gopi, a young sponger, drift from one place to another as their affair progresses. Raymond, a young middle-class Englishman in love with Gopi, follows them around despite his disillusionment with Gopi's shallowness and rapacity. Lee, an American girl, one of several foreign spiritual questers, floats sometimes with them, sometimes away, drawing them after her; she sleeps with Gopi, or rather lets him sleep with her, remaining not very interested throughout, and certainly not emotionally involved with him. The other ashram dwellers and pilgrims from overseas are even more apathetic. They seem almost to mistake apathy for illumination; when one of them dies of the diseases that afflict them all, they can scarcely be said to react. At the end of the novel, a weary Raymond sets out for home, mother, and the family business. Lee, who has been seduced, almost raped by a swami, is apparently on her way back to his ashram. The swami, a particularly nasty Dickensian caricature, is a monster of ambition, greed, and lust. *Dickensian* is inaccurate: he appalls us but he does not make us laugh. Like all the major characters, he is always close to caricature.

The novel is divided into three parts, "Delhi," "The Holy City," and "Maupur." These titles curiously echo those of the three sections of Forster's *Passage to India*—"Mosque" (Delhi is noted for its numerous mosques), "Caves" (the setting for disillusionment with religion), and "Temple" (the temple is located in Mau). In the second and third parts of *Travelers*, Jhabvala makes one of her rare departures from Delhi as the setting for her longer fiction, moving the action first to an ashram in Varanasi and then to a raja's broken-down provincial palaces, settings that are the stock-in-trade of several of her screenplays. To emphasize the author's distance from the material, the novel is further subdivided into mostly very brief scenes, each with its title, for example, "Gopi Is Displeased with Raymond," "Lee and Gopi Eat Kebabs," "Asha Feels Old."

V. S. Pritchett writes, "A large number of these passages are perfect as short stories in which the light changes from the bizarre to the poetic, from the comic to the horrifying, from the thoughtful to the mischievous—all with an allusiveness, a susceptibility to mood, a tenderness of which Chekhov was the exemplar."[37] Again, I find it difficult to see much that is Chekhovian, or for that matter tender and poetic, anywhere in *Travelers*, where the style and technique appear calculated to dispel any suspicion of charity on the author's part by reducing events to something like the panels of a comic strip.

Pritchett finds the Western characters less successful than the Indian. "The Hindus are Mrs. Jhabvala's complete characterizations—above all, the ancient Princess Asha and the impossible young Gopi."[38] But Asha (who may be fading but in middle age is hardly "ancient") and Gopi, far from being complete characterizations, are hardly recognizable as Hindus. (Perhaps Pritchett means Indians.) As certain Indian types, perhaps—types made familiar by Hindi-language musical films of unashamed fantasy. The only characteristic that distinguishes Asha and Gopi (and the swami) from the Europeans in the story is their capacity to exercise their willpower, in their relentless and sometimes crafty grasping. The Westerners are once again apathetic, passive, unmotivated, will-less, and vague, and once again the style of the novel serves mainly to render them insignificant. What we have is a series of vignettes, in which nobody is more important than anybody else, nothing much has value, and nothing much matters: the depressed world of voluntary displaced persons who fail even as refugees.

If we return to the question of whether to consider Ruth Jhabvala an Indian novelist, it is relevant to point out that nowhere else in the work of either Indo-Anglian or vernacular novelists do we find such a gallery of consistently unsympathetic Indian portraits. This suggests to me how much of an outsider in India Jhabvala must have remained (and felt) during her quarter-century sojourn there. Speaking of her "dual nationality," Haydn Moore Williams says, "Since she has 'chosen' India, she can afford to be critical without offence . . . India is not a 'problem' to her, as it appears to be to so many earnest investigators, but a life."[39] This was written in 1972, the same year in which Jhabvala's "Myself in India," a title that ominously echoes *Esmond in India,* revealed just how much of a problem and what sort of a life India had been for her, though I believe that the writer's discontent was implicit already in much of the fiction written before this time.

In the fourteen pages of "Myself in India," Jhabvala describes with a raw intensity we do not expect from her her own private anguish over her Delhi life and the unsettling ambivalences, familiar to so many who have lived a long time in India, of being unable to live with the country or without it, a very special kind of *odi et amo,* or, as she candidly terms it, a disease. Even the most commonplace social pleasures are fraught with malaise. Of a Delhi hostess she writes:

In her one may see the best of East and West combined. She is interested in a great variety of topics and can hold her own in any discussion. She loves to exercise her emancipated mind, and whatever the subject of conversation—economics, or politics, or literature, or film—she has a well-formulated opinion on it and knows how to express herself. How lucky for me if I could have such a person for a friend! What enjoyable, lively times we two could have together!
    In fact, my teeth are set on edge if I have to listen to her for more than five minutes.[40]

Jhabvala presents her conclusion as a surprise, but she has given it away at the very outset of her description of the woman, laden as it is with the deadliest clichés ("best of East and West," "interested in a great variety of topics," etc.); it is nothing less than venomous, and we know at once that the person so described—

artificial, mechanical, without any individualizing characteristics, any personality of her own—must be an intolerable bore.

Very well, then, if one does not enjoy the limited and factitious society of the Civil Lines or the rich new colonies and if, on the other hand, one is not a "strong person who plunges in and does what he can, a doctor, or a social worker," as she puts it, then what is left? Extraordinarily, Jhabvala can summon up only a handful of isolated images to express her sense of all the rest of the subcontinent: a smiling leper, the carcass of a dog, a human sacrifice, Shiva on Mount Kailash sporting his necklace of skulls, outlaws with the hearts of wild beasts, the naïve and touching devotion to the cow—none of which, significantly, ever figure in her fiction. One cannot suppress a decided disappointment that this intelligent observer should feel compelled to evoke the shade of Katherine Mayo. Her Delhi life is haunted by the knowledge that she is "on the back of this great animal of poverty and backwardness. It is not possible to pretend otherwise. Even if one never rolls up the blinds and never turns off the airconditioner, something is bound to go wrong. People are not meant to shut themselves up in rooms and pretend there is nothing outside."[41]

So we are back in India as experienced by so many of the earlier British novelists who have tried to come to grips with it: Europeans are not meant to live there (some would say that nobody is, as N. C. Chaudhuri contends),[42] with the possible exception of egoless drifters like Lee; the spiritual claims of Indian thought are mere pretensions; the sexual craving that the country seems to accentuate and then to gratify so easily leads only to disappointing and destructive erotic adventures; and Europeans and Indians are forever doomed not to understand one another.

Heat and Dust is the last of Jhabvala's Indian novels to date and was published in 1975, the year she moved her residence from Delhi to the United States. In it there is an attenuation of the attitudes prevalent in the preceding books. At first glance it appears to be an apologia, almost a refutation, of the earlier novels. Although caricature and stereotyping have not disappeared completely, the major characters (all English, for the Nawab is barely sketched in) are more fully delineated; and for the first time, in the conclusion there is at least some ambiguity, a vague possibility of affirmation won from Indian experience. The unnamed narrator comes to India in part to unravel the story of Olivia, her grandfather's first wife, who had caused a scandal by becoming the mistress of a nawab and renouncing England forever—whether happily or not we are never permitted to know. In the process, the narrator herself becomes fascinated with India, is made pregnant by her Indian landlord, and, unlike Olivia, resolves to have her baby. We last see her awaiting its birth in the lower Himalayas and planning vaguely to go eventually to some mountain ashram.

A certain (and unwonted) element of allegory is discernible in this novel. The Nawab's palace is near a village called Khatm, "finished" in Urdu, and Olivia and the narrator reside in Satipur, the "city of the faithful wife," a rather obvious irony. Satipur is notable for its English cemetery, like Paul Scott's Pankot. This cemetery, with its graves of British soldiers, their wives, and children, overgrown with weeds, its tombstones and statues broken, is all that remains of the Raj in Satipur. The only English in evidence today, including the narrator, herself the descendant of an old British colonial family, are partially Indianized vagrants. Whereas Olivia aborts her half-Indian baby but remains faithful to its Indian father, the narrator, in a more enlightened age or perhaps merely a more cynical one, discards her Indian lover, but, after unsuccessfully trying to abort her child, decides to have it and is filled with rapture at the thought. Although Pritchett had found *Travelers* Forsterian rather than Chekhovian, that adjective is more applicable to *Heat and Dust.* The concern with "bridging" is treated more seriously than anywhere else in Jhabvala; the possibility of a positive value in at least some Hindu holy men and women is suggested; and even Forster's tendency to sententious and sometimes intrusive observations of a moral nature can be found.

Part of the mythology of the West accepted by many Indians is the belief that European women are sex-crazed, immodest, and eager to jump into bed with any Indian who invites them. This stems in part, obviously, from the differences in codes of manners and dress governing women of the two cultures, as well as from the Hollywood fantasies Indians see so often on their cinema screens. It is interesting that Ruth Jhabvala seems to accept this mythology as sociological fact. If we survey the complete cast of Western women in her stories and novels, excepting the caricatured memsahibs who appear occasionally, we see that most of them succumb to the extremely dubious blandishments of a wide assortment of Indian men (many of them described in repellent terms) without hesitation. In *Heat and Dust*, Olivia, married to a loving if fairly conventional military husband, seems hypnotized by the Nawab, who is also (as she knows) a bandit—it is all dissonantly romantic in the Jhabvalan world of disappointment and ineluctable mediocrity. The narrator, for her part, succumbs, without being terribly interested, both to her landlord and to Chid, an English hippie suffering from hepatitis whom she finds utterly sexless. "I don't know why I let him go ahead. I'm much bigger and stronger than he is and could easily keep him off. But it seems as if there really is something, some emanation, that does not come from him but from some powers outside himself. Because he himself is quite sexless."[43] The "powers outside himself" must be the effect of his austerities, his life as a *sadhu*, or holy man, although of course we can never know since the writer has retreated from the real question, as she always does: what in the personalities of her women makes them so passive, so willing, in these bizarre situations? It is significant that in the screenplay version of the novel the narrator (given a name to reinforce her doubtful reality) rejects the advances of Chid, who for his part has been turned into an American from Iowa; whether these changes were Jhabvala's own ideas (she wrote the screenplay) or were imposed by the producers in the interest of plausibility (the narrator's rejection of Chid) or the American market (Chid becomes Iowan) must remain conjecture for the moment.[44]

It is difficult to assess how much of a development in Jhabvala's sense of India *Heat and Dust* represents. As so often in her work, the author has remained elusive, difficult to pin down. Unlike Forster, say, who expresses his moral viewpoint in his fiction in his own person, Jhabvala never does. What Etta or Raymond or the unnamed narrator thinks may or may not coincide with her personal ideas. We must try to draw conclusions only through a process of inference by examining the consistency of story patterns, the fate of each of the characters, and the dominant elements of the narrative style. In all these respects, *Heat and Dust* has after all not advanced very far beyond the world of *A Backward Place*. The irony of the later book may be deliberately blunted, the value of Indian experience for Europeans less defined (and therefore at least potentially positive), the attitude toward India's victims (including the indispensable hippies) a trifle more sympathetic. But the fundamental modality is still flatness of presentation, with the major characters passively drifting without will. In both her sexual adventures (they cannot be called love affairs) the narrator remains inert. By the very nature of the novel's structure—present-day events recorded in the narrator's matter-of-fact diary and the distant past reconstructed from Olivia's letters, then retold by the same narrator—we are excluded from the opportunity to confront people and situations directly, with either intensity or certainty. The technique, characteristically, provides a skillful screening device that allows the writer to remain uncommitted to any position that might hint at the sentimental, the emotional, or the charitable. Just as in the later Hemingway the controlled concealment of feeling leads one to suspect that there is very little feeling to conceal, so here one is troubled by the deadpan mask and the predictable let-down.

In none of these novels does an Indian or European experience a moment of fulfillment or even pleasure. In "Myself in India," Jhabvala herself records no agreeable Indian experience apart from the enjoyment of *bhajan*, traditional devotional songs. In the same essay she writes:

> However, I must admit that I am no longer interested in India. What I am interested in now is myself in India—which sometimes, in moments of despondency, I tend to think of as my survival in India. I had better say straightaway that the reason I live in India is because my strongest human ties are here. If I hadn't married an Indian, I don't think I would ever have come here for I am not attracted—or used not to be attracted—to the things that usually bring people to India. I know I am the wrong type of person to live here. To stay and endure, one should have a mission and a cause, to be patient, cheerful, unselfish, strong. I am a central European with an English education and a deplorable tendency to constant self-analysis. I am irritable and have weak nerves.[45]

At the end of the essay she says that she gets bored after a time in Europe and finds it difficult to stand the European climate. "I have got used to intense heat and seem to need it."[46] Nevertheless, in 1981 she writes, "In 1975 I left India and am now living in and writing about America—but not for long enough to be able to make any kind of comment about either of these activities."[47] It is obviously too early to say whether without India's "intense heat" Jhabvala will develop in new directions or whether, after a respite, she will return to India as her subject with a new perspective and greater depth. Until the present her Indian fiction has constituted a clever and disarming set of variations on the long tradition of the Anglo-Indian novelists. Although her earlier novels, like those of any Indian writer, tended to deal with Indians

as people first and only secondarily as Indians, in her later ones
this is reversed as the East-West theme comes to obsess her. Her
characters become increasingly emblematic and less human, the
impoverishment and mediocrity of the Indian society she knows
is presented more and more bitterly, and in consequence the alleged comic nature of these books appears ever more dubious.
Their relation to her "constant self-analysis" can only be specu-
lated on in the light of her abandonment of India, but it seems
likely that she will come to be regarded less and less as an Indian
novelist, a correction in classification long overdue. The third
phase, the American, has only now begun, bringing with it, it is
safe to assume, ever greater contradictions and complexities.

Postscript: America

In Ruth Jhabvala's early novels the Indian family, coherent no
matter how big and extended, supplies the central material for
both plot and point of view. The middle novels, *Esmond in India*,
and *A Backward Place*, and the short stories of that time show Europeans cut loose from Europe and finding a home—usually a
disappointing and unlovable home—in the same kind of Indian
family. The later novels and stories portray Europeans adrift in
India; no Indian family can save them or give them even a temporary harbor. This evolution parallels Jhabvala's increasing pessimism and her general disaffection from India, and it reminds
one of the remark quoted earlier, "I was practically born a displaced person." By this I mean to suggest that the evolution of
the novels somehow confirms the refugee's longing for a stable
center, a traditional family not threatened with dissolution and
even physical annihilation, and the subsequent failure of this
longing to be fulfilled. For the writer one displacement has followed upon another: in the case of her parents, from Poland first,
and in the case of Jhabvala herself, from Germany, England, and
now from India. The world darkens, the writer becomes more
pessimistic and less and less productive, with seven years between
Heat and Dust and the novel that followed it, *In Search of Love and
Beauty* (1982), while the search for a milieu, a home to be integrated
into, a home that would stabilize and confirm an identity, goes
on.

In Search of Love and Beauty, by means of flashbacks, covers some
five decades in the lives of a handful of refugees from Hitler's

Germany who have settled in New York. The curious thing about all of them is that even those who grew up in Germany seem to have no relationship to their earlier lives, either to their culture or to their family histories. They also are emotionally numb, capable, it would seem, of no feelings beyond lust and jealousy, which are described with clinical coldness. There is no point of view that emerges but mere nihilism reflected through deadened sensibilities. The Indian sections, which were briefly described earlier, seem irrelevant, a bit of irresistible *Heimweh,* perhaps. The critics who have compared this novel to those of Proust must have read him a long time ago, if ever. Unlike Proust, Jhabvala here offers no meticulous development of character in relation to background, heredity, will, talent, or individual and unpredictable traits. In Proust, everything, and particularly the evolving of the work of art from mere autobiography, is inextricably bound to a moral point of view. Proust's estheticism accepts that not only moral awareness but moral commitment, courage, or *virtus,* if you will, is necessary to give value to the work of art. For Proust, the moral equals the passionate exploration and fearless criticism of human actions and human relationships, not the clever cartoon representation of human silliness, shallowness, and despair, where even refugees from Hitler's Germany appear as nobodies from nowhere.

Where in her Indian fiction Jhabvala's eye for the typical action and ear for the characteristic utterance of her milieu are usually dependable, both eye and ear fail in *In Search of Love and Beauty.* In the American dialogue perhaps Jhabvala's ear betrays her through its tendency to parody. "I got her the cutest little outfit you ever saw—cerise, with a darling row of buttons here and its own little blue blouse."[48] It sounds perfect but in fact it is wrong: the woman who says, "cutest little outfit" is unlikely to say, "darling row of buttons." The woman, a minor character, is in any case only another British comic American. Another American says, "It was quite a favorite sweater,"[49] an even greater gaffe. Other Americans in the novel, that is, Americans unrelated to the refugees and their progeny, range from midwestern homey types to sexually ambivalent (or merely indifferent) young people, borderline hippies. One suspects here the uprooted person's desire, shown in part by becoming something of an expert on it, to belong to a particular milieu. At the same time, the stuff of the novel, despite its exotic new setting, adds nothing to what Jhabvala had said before. One of her refugees even becomes a guru, girls flock to him (even when he is impotent—a problem the swamis, at least, never seem to suffer) and he continues to exert his mysterious, charismatic spell, mysterious only because, as with the other seductive gurus, there is never any accounting for it except the indifference, boredom and passivity of his victims. The America of *In Search of Love and Beauty* is still in fact Ruth Jhabvala's India, its German Jewish refugee families hard to distinguish from the Panjabi refugee families of the early novels, its disappointments, boredom, and isolation the same as one has suffered in Delhi and Bombay.

5
The Early Novels of Paul Scott

I began with poetry, went on to plays and graduated to novels, the most exacting form of literary composition there is.

PAUL SCOTT[1]

He heard the doors banging and the bell and the mournful call of the boy selling tea, and over it all the fierce music from the bazaar.

   Now it was going. Oh, hold it, his heart cried, oh, enter it: dig deeply with the hands into it and raise out of it all the love and pity and compassion the music sings of. But now it is going. The light in the sky is going. The singing is fading. And the train is moving into the plain where night holds and the deep silence is broken only by the muffled drumming of the wheels and the distant cries of jackals.

PAUL SCOTT[2]

One turns with relief from the world of Ruth Jhabvala, devoid equally of joy and of tragedy, to Scott's splendid series of Indian novels, where the real is not equivalent to the trivial and the possibility, at least, exists for "a glow, grandezza, the wild hope." Let me say at the outset of my discussion of Scott's Indian novels that they are far and away the best fiction dealing with Anglo-Indian relations not only since Independence but since the very beginning of such fiction. "Best" comports two specific areas of excellence: first, the depth and breadth of understanding of the British who lived and worked in India; and second, still more important, the sheer novelistic power and technical resourcefulness grounded in an observation of manners both objective and compassionate—the qualities one often thinks of as specifically Tolstoyan. Of all the novelists dealing with Scott's subject matter before him, only one, E. J. Thompson, surpassed him in knowledge of the subcontinent and its problems, and though Thompson is an unjustly neglected and underrated writer, he is not a match for Scott in his portrayal of human character and situations.

In his "Indian" novels Scott draws upon all the important elements of the tradition to refashion them and enhance and transform their significance: the visitor caught up in a whirlwind beyond his control (Daphne, MacKendrick) or encountering new philosophies or magic (Tom Brent); India as a destructive sexual force (Merrick); India as a heightened theater for British virtues and vices (*The Raj Quartet*); and India as fallaciously romantic, the embodiment of the delusion of Empire. In the *Quartet*, Scott boldly parallels Forster's *Passage to India*, taking as his central incident the alleged attack by an Indian on a European woman, and treats this incident and its consequences in far more exhaustive detail but also with greater depth and inventiveness than the earlier novelist. Characteristically, in Forster there was no attack, there was nothing; in Scott the Indian is not a would-be rapist but a lover.

All eight novels preceding the *Quartet* and *Staying On* have some connection with India. Two of them, *Johnnie Sahib* (1952) and *The Mark of the Warrior* (1958), both stories of military experience and the central significance of a man's career in his life, are set in India but have little to do with it or its specific problems, although it is worth noting that in *Johnnie Sahib*, Scott's first book, Eurasians appear briefly and are regarded with sympathy. In *A Male Child* (1956) the protagonist, Ian Canning, suffers from a mysterious disease contracted in India; the country does not otherwise figure in this work. A character in *The Bender* (1963) is Eurasian, "from Islington-pore," as she says; shallow in conception, she is a weakness in this brilliant and undervalued work. Tom Brent, the narrator of *The Chinese Love Pavilion* (1960), comes of a family with a long tradition of service in India and says, "India was of my bone,"[3] but both a year in Bombay and four more on an experimental farm in the Panjab bring him only disillusionment; most of the book is set in Malaya following the end of World War II and is preoccupied with his love for the mysterious Teena Chang and his quest for the even more enigmatic "God-hunter," Brian Saxby. Although the beginning of the book, in Bombay, is richly observed, with minor Eurasian characters talking of "our home in Shropshire," India quickly ceases to be important in the development of the story, which, for all its ingenuity, never seems able to integrate its many disparate elements. This was a problem Scott was to handle with greater skill and far more success in the two important novels that preceded the *Quartet*, *The Birds of Paradise* and *The Corrida at San Feliu*.

The Alien Sky

The Alien Sky (1958) is Scott's first attempt to write a novel set
entirely in India and concerned very largely with the problems
of the British there at the time the Raj was coming to an end. It
has generally been viewed as the weakest among Scott's thirteen
novels and of interest mostly because of certain anticipations of
the later work. It is flawed, but it also has clear virtues in its own
right that make it worth consideration.

Set mainly in Marapore,[4] it describes the tumult in the city in
June 1947, two months before the end of the Raj. The novel is
diffuse, with several strands of plot that are not always satisfac-
torily related and resolved—the problem that Scott was to solve
so brilliantly by the more leisurely and exhaustively detailed approach of the *Quartet.* There is first of all Joe MacKendrick, an
American, who has come for obscure reasons to find his dead
brother's mistress, Dorothy Gower. Dorothy's husband edits a
small paper and runs an experimental farm; he is strongly pro-
Indian, and his tragedy is that, with coming Independence, his
Indian friends and colleagues, egged on by various extremists,
reject him as too moderate and, ultimately, too alien. Gower at
times seems to speak for Scott. " 'In not disputing India's intention
to rule herself we're avoiding the danger of taking action. We
recognize we're in too great proximity to forces we don't begin
to understand. I think if we're to blame for anything in the years
we've ruled it's our failure to understand these forces even at the
moment of departure. All we understand is that individual kindness isn't enough. But perhaps our strength lies in the fact that
we don't understand what *is* enough. Perhaps we don't want to
understand.' "[5] When he speaks of going back to England, his
wife categorically refuses to return with him; he assumes that it
is because she is having an affair with Steele, his assistant, but
in fact it is because she is part Indian and fears that her carefully
guarded secret would be exposed if she "returned" to the England
she has actually never seen. Cynthia Mapleton, a widow in fi-
nancial straits, is planning to leave for Kenya; she is a cynical and
malicious woman and a shameless sponger. She has a particular
contempt for Eurasians and, in a painful dinner party scene,
needles and humiliates a Eurasian girl named Judith Anderson,
a former schoolmate of Dorothy's. Judith gives Dorothy's secret

away to MacKendrick, who persuades Dorothy to abandon her husband and leave Marapore with him. Radical students burn down Gower's experimental farm, Steele shoots a servant who appears to be attacking him (and who quite incidentally has blackmailed Dorothy—an echo, perhaps, of Forster's Antony), and is himself assassinated on the day of the judicial inquiry by a student named Vidyasagar (not to be confused with the Vidyasagar of *The Jewel in the Crown*).[6] Gower, who has been promised a new post in a princely state, learns that the job has fallen through and attempts suicide, after which Dorothy returns to him and MacKendrick leaves Marapore.

The anticipations of the *Quartet* are obvious: the general climate and constant threat of violence of 1947, the plight of the person of indeterminate culture, the predilection for judicial inquiry as a device to move the plot (the district magistrate's informal interrogation of Steele is one of the most successful scenes in the novel) and, above all, the emotional and spiritual crisis of the British as the Raj begins to crumble. Harriet Haig, an elderly retired schoolteacher, a bit crazy, sometimes out of emotional control, is a slight preliminary sketch for the memorable Barbie Batchelor, while Cynthia's homelessness and her anxiety about where she can stay foreshadow Barbie's trials in *The Towers of Silence*; Cynthia also provides an early study for the snobbery and meanness of spirit that characterize the Pankot women in the *Quartet*.

The material of the story is too various, too rich to be contained and developed adequately in this two-hundred-page novel. One wonders first of all why Scott chose an American for his central observer (insofar as there can be said to be one), as this introduces the complexity of a three-way cultural divergence. In Joyce Cary's *American Visitor* (1933), one of the few novels with a comparable triple international theme,[7] the interplay of American, Englishman, and Nigerian is wonderfully controlled and directed toward an ironic embodiment of the book's vision. But in *The Alien Sky*, MacKendrick, a grim, humorless and unappealing man, serves only, it would seem, to allow various British characters to explain to him their views on India and the crisis of the moment. MacKendrick as an American can also be the vehicle for a view of the departing British too harsh to be expected from one of their own countrymen as he sums up the situation in Marapore in June 1947. "They were stubborn, these Britishers on the point of departure, stubborn like the aged and the dying. About them was the smell of decay, the smell of the sickroom. They were clearing out of India and leaving the smell behind them. If you sniffed, now, it smarted in your nostrils. Decay. Death. An end to ambition. A burial of pride."[8] His own personal drama seems to be a quest for some kind of liberation from the haunting presence of his brother, who had treated him with extreme sadism; perhaps finding another of his brother's victims who has survived—Dorothy—or winning her for himself could bring him this liberation, but Scott's intention remains vague: even MacKendrick himself does not appear to understand what he is doing.

The question of people of mixed English and Indian race, which obviously interested Scott so much in the very early phase of his career and returns again as a very minor theme in *The Corrida at San Feliu* and *Staying On*, provides the main tension of the novel.[9] First of all, there is Dorothy's frantic attempt to keep her secret. In one of the book's chief ironies, Dorothy pays her blackmailer because she assumes that he has found out she is Eurasian, when the secret he thought he had discovered, that she was MacKendrick's mistress, was in fact a mistake. There is the pathos of Judith Anderson, who aspires only to marrying her lover, a coarse and brutish British major. And of course there is the reaction of MacKendrick, the observer who stands outside the problem. He is watching when Gower and Jimmy, the maharaja, meet Judith Anderson. "Gower's eyes had the same look as Jimmy's. MacKendrick caught its meaning. Try as one would to ignore it, instinct said: This girl is a freak. Half-European, half-Asian, the only unity she has is a sexual one. Because of the colour of her skin one's mind immediately recalls an act of union."[10] This, of course, reveals more about the state of MacKendrick's own psyche than anything else. His own prejudice in the matter is made no clearer than this, but he does seem to feel some pity for Judith Anderson, and he is not repelled when he learns Dorothy's secret; but when he is about to make love to her, "he was appalled by her indifference to what had happened to Tom [Gower]. He was repelled by the physical hunger he had released in her,"[11] and their lovemaking is a failure. Dorothy Gower herself is, all in all, unappealing: dry, cold, deceitful. At only one moment does she speak in a way that commands some sympathy, when she tries to describe her own "Indianness." " 'There's something else, too, something to do with roots, feeling they're here, in India, wanting them, or pretending they're there. Sometimes I think I have no roots at all. Then there are times when I look at India and know it's inside me as it was in my mother, and her mother, and her mother's mother. Failing a different sort of love, there's always that sort to be looked for and found.' '"[12] Only, as she confesses, she has not found it, and at the end, defeated, she can only return to her husband and an uncertain future either in England or a new India where neither she nor Gower will be at home.

The problem of the Eurasian ceased to engage Scott deeply after *The Alien Sky*. I believe this is mainly because the question presented itself to him as a diversion from a far more engrossing problem, in his view: the conflict of cultures. A genetic mixture is a much too facile embodiment of this conflict, which in any case for the Eurasian need not be a conflict at all. I feel that Patrick Swinden is mistaken when he refers to Hari Kumar as the "principal 'half-caste' character in the *Quartet*."[13] I shall return to Hari later, but at this point let me indicate that his tragedy lies precisely in the fact that he is *not* a mixture of anything but actually *entirely* English in culture and outlook: wounded, Philoctetes remains Philoctetes. Hari Kumar is wholly free of any kind of "half-caste identity," as Swinden terms it, and this makes his predicament all the more intense and poignant. In contrast, his half-Indian, half-English daughter, Parvati, will grow up happily as Indian and nothing else. For Scott the question of racial composition is a mere technicality, meaningless except when it is made the basis for prejudice and cruelty—a far cry from the Kipling of "His Chance in Life." Dorothy Gower *is* English, whatever bizarre equation expresses her precise racial make-up. Her tragedy is one that begins in her own mentality, her underlying contempt for herself, which ultimately embraces all those close to her. But she is not challenging enough to fascinate Scott for long, and he leaves her more or less in midstream, and with her India as a major theme, to be taken up again only when he had acquired the technical mastery needed to produce the *Quartet*.

Perhaps the most striking passage in the whole book is the final paragraph, quoted as the epigraph to this chapter. But its passionate lyricism is strangely out of keeping with the rest of the novel, particularly with MacKendrick, whose feelings it is apparently intended to represent. Only vaguely "American," with no precise geographical origin or attachment in the United States, still unformed, MacKendrick is not sufficiently defined, like Dorothy not deep enough, to fill the role of observer at these moments of great personal and general cataclysm. This role will be filled successfully in the *Quartet* by the unknown researcher of the opening volume and by Guy Perron of the final one.

The Corrida at San Feliu

Leaving *The Birds of Paradise* (1962) aside for the moment, out of its chronological order, I want to speak briefly of *The Corrida at San Feliu* (1964). Although one story, one episode, and part of the novel-in-progress it contains are all located in India, that country provides little more than setting for incidents in the life (and fictional creations) of Edward Thornhill, the protagonist of this complex construction of interchangeable names and identities. In the novel it would seem that Scott was working out for himself some of the esthetic problems he had to solve before beginning the *Quartet.*

Scott uses the bullfights at San Feliu, attended by Thornhill (who, like himself, has a horror of blood sports), as the medium for considering these esthetic questions. Quite incidentally, Scott's treatment of the corrida shows up the crudeness and fatuity of Hemingway's celebrated writings on tauromachy—what F. R. Leavis would no doubt have dismissed as "mere hobbledehoydom," if he had been minded to notice them. Scott presents the bullfights from three points of view: first (and riskiest), the bull's; then the torero's; and finally Thornhill's own.

Thornhill, after sympathetically and imaginatively recreating the psychological state (or what one might term the existential reality) of both bull and bullfighter as it must seem to each, attempts to understand and justify the corrida's claim to being a form of art. But whereas in all other forms of art a stasis is reached, the corrida concludes with the total stasis of death. "Any piece of sculpture would be monstrous if it moved, and the end of Hedda Gabler unbearable if the actress actually shot herself. I mean monstrous and unbearable in the terms of art, not in terms of life because we are, God knows, inured to death by violence, so long as the show is free and we come upon it accidentally and not by design. But here in the corrida is an art that defies the principle of simulation and so is unique."[14] But the corrida fails as art, as tragedy, even as comedy: it is mere melodrama and harlequinade and cannot satisfy Thornhill when he asks himself why he has come and why he has sat through the horror. He concludes that in the last analysis he does not care about any of them, bull, horse, torero, and the rest.

In the crowded plaza de toros, I sit alone, with a full belly and an empty heart: a two-legged animal with opposed thumbs and a tragic inheritance of speech; waiting for the personal revelation of what he really means when he says, as he has said so often, so glibly, for nearly sixty years: I love, I care, let justice be done, teach us to forgive; hoping that once, today, through the medium of this art that is unique because it defies the law of life arrested by artifice, there will be a glimpse of the reality behind the illusion that man can care for someone other than himself.
But there has not been any such glimpse.[15]

Thornhill's failure to care is the source of the failure of his art. He has sought a love that is not possessive, not destructive, not incomplete, a love that is not merely "an extension of unrelated fear," as a character in *The Bender* calls it.[16] But while he seeks, he is compelled to spy on his wife with his binoculars as she swims each day with an unknown young man and to suffer agonies of jealousy. He cannot go beyond the existentialist notion, as Iris Murdoch might have it, of the absolute nature of the individual, a nature that automatically excludes all other realities, although he suffers more than others of this sort because he is convinced that the notion is wrong and must be fought against. Conrad's theory of the necessity, for creating fiction, of that "conviction of our fellow-men's existence" is what is lacking in both Thornhill's art and his life. The failure of his art, and his suicide, are entirely consistent with (indeed, almost inevitable as a consequence of) his failure to love.

The Birds of Paradise

One of the special distinctions of *The Birds of Paradise* is that in so short a novel Scott has sounded so many diverse themes and integrated them successfully into a meaningful and harmonious whole. All these themes had appeared in his earlier fiction and would reach their triumphant final development in *The Raj Quartet.* They may be described, in no particular order, as follows: the relationship of the private lives of individuals to history; the relativity of what we know as "truth"; the epistemological question—

the difficulty of arriving at truth; the isolation of individuals; the relation of a man's life to his vocation or career; the lost childhood and the quest for paradise; the distinction (and frequent conflict) between the "consumers," those who cultivate and batten on illusion, and the questers, those who suffer from the inability to sustain their illusions; and the real and symbolic significance of man's relationship with the nonhuman natural world.

The focal event of the entire *Raj Quartet* is the so-called Bibighar incident and its aftermath, the catastrophic result, in large part, of an educational experiment in which an Indian child is turned all too successfully into a public school Englishman in a world unable to accept him on any terms at all that he is capable of meeting. For the rest of his life Hari Kumar will regard the happiness of his sixteen years in England as his own paradise lost. Now, *The Birds of Paradise* is, in effect, the inversion of Hari Kumar's situation: an English child born and raised in India who, without becoming in any superficial way Indian,[17] has imbibed some subversive strain in his early experiences that can never be reversed by his subsequent education (starting at the age of ten and a half) and adult life in England. A particular kind of sensitivity and a near-mystical bond with the natural world that are not part of the conventional British mentality but are commonplace in India seem to have become ineradicable elements in his psyche.

On Manoba, an island in the Malay archipelago where he is spending a sabbatical year away from his London office, William Conway recollects the various stages of his life. The overall sequence of the flashbacks is chronological, though from his vantage point, surveying the totality of his life as far as it has been lived, Conway is free in his reflections to interrupt and reverse this order, flash back or anticipate within a flashback according to the natural association of his thoughts. He has spent the first ten years of his life in Indian princely states, mostly in Tradura, where his father is assistant to the resident. This may be called a romantic period in which reality and illusion intermingle in ways never to be completely disentangled. Conway's mother has been dead since he was four; her place is taken variously by a governess and his Aunt Sarah. Though his father appears cold toward him and cannot communicate (or even seem to want to), Conway respects him as one of those who are above even the princes, a man who is fulfilling the British imperial mission. As Mrs. Canterbury, his governess, puts it, " 'Men like your father have put down all the old

feudal injustices,' 'Men like your father have given them standards,' "[18] and more of the like. Like Grayson-Hume, his tutor
later on, she instils in him the idea that he is the heir of this father
and his mission: " 'it will be your job to go on helping these people
to live better lives.' "[19] So it is no surprise that the boy's favorite
subject to study is the British in India. He is also gifted with a
lively imagination, shaped not only by the illusory history he
studies but by authors like Henty and Wren. He even has an
imaginary dog named Digby after one of the latter's Geste brothers. It is this imagination that will constantly open up vistas of
understanding, unexpected sympathies, and temptations to further and ever deeper inquiry, which marks him off from most of
his kind in India in the twenties and provides both the cause and,
perhaps, the compensation for his future suffering. Significant in
this Indian childhood is his annual reception, on his birthday, by
the old Maharajah, who, though he is only a symbolic power
(compared to the elder Conway), nevertheless bestows on the boy
some of the paternal affection and consideration Conway's real
father cannot. The visit to the Maharajah each year is the stuff of
which romance is born: he is sent for in a royal carriage, saluted,
and received in the grand durbar hall. Tradura, which seems so
perfectly to fulfill an English boy's romantic conception of India,
he recognizes as illusory;[20] and thirty years later, when he returns
to the subcontinent, he avoids going back to see it. "Tradura
wouldn't be dead either, but I didn't want to see its flower; to
find, for instance, that the iron gateway from the agency bungalow
looked too narrow for a horse-drawn carriage to pass through
with dignity."[21]

Young Conway's friendship with Krishi, the *rajkumar* of a nearby
princely state, and his dawning love for Dora Salford, an English
girl of his own age, complete the formation of his sensibilities and
the principles that will dominate his adult life. Through Krishi he
finds the stuffed birds of paradise in their immense cage on the
little island near the Jundapur palace. The birds, identified variously with the British on their way out of India, then with the
native princes themselves, their finery and style beautifully preserved, but lifeless, come eventually to fulfill a greater symbolic
role, which I shall discuss below. Through Dora, William Conway
experiences not only the beginning of a complex love for another
human being that, as it turns out, is never to be surpassed, but
also, as a spontaneous complement of this love, the recognition

of his place in creation, the limitations of his claims, and, as it were, the illumination that the world is greater than himself. He has gone with Dora to sit in a *machān*, a hunter's raised platform in the jungle, to wait for a fierce prowling tiger everyone is trying to track down. He is prepared to shoot it with Krishi's gun until the tiger actually appears.

I saw him emerge from the shadow into the morning sunlight and stand arrested, staring at something that aroused his curiosity in such a way that mine was aroused too, and almost unconsciously I turned my head and so saw not what the tiger saw, or fancied he saw, but Dora's profile: the small speckling of sweat on her upper lip, the partly opened mouth and lowered jaw, her perfect stillness, the isolated pulsing movement of a vein in her neck; her appearance of being bewitched and totally unafraid.

At once the waves of her enchantment made themselves manifest in a faint vibration, a sawing of the air all about the *machan;* a compound of our breathing and the tiger's breathing. The tiger stood quite in the open now, but I made no move to bring the gun to bear on him. He made a perfect target. The phrase "perfect target" was in my mind but there was something wrong with it and presently, when quite unexpectedly he lost interest in whatever it was he had been looking at or listening to and moved to a patch of dappled sun and shade, lay down and began to lick his paws, I knew it was the word target that was wrong. There was no target in that place, just myself and Dora, the surrounding forest and the tiger washing himself.

And then it was not a question of being awestruck by the tiger's burning bigness or of seeing in it a kind of savage nobility. Big it was, and in the sunlight seemed to burn so that later Blake's poem came to me with an authority it would not otherwise have done. It was savage and, I suppose, noble in its way. It was a question of being awestruck by something quite other than these things: by the realization that it had a right to be where it was, as much right as I and Dora; not *more* right, but as much right.[22]

I have quoted this passage at such length because it seems to me to be of central importance for understanding not only *The Birds of Paradise* but the *Quartet* as well. It describes what we may term a natural religious experience, as opposed to an existential perception of one's place in the world, and it exemplifies the way in which Scott is in the great tradition described by Iris Murdoch in "The Sublime and the Beautiful Revisited," the tradition of the novelist who is tolerant, objective (rather than solipsistic), whose fiction is something more than the working out (therapeutic or otherwise) of a private neurosis. Describing the fiction of the writers she places in this tradition—Sir Walter Scott, Jane Austen, George Eliot, Tolstoy—she says: "There is in these novels a plurality of real persons more or less naturalistically presented in a large social scene, and representing mutually independent centers of significance which are those of real individuals. What we have here may be called a display of tolerance. A great novelist is essentially tolerant, that is, displays a real apprehenion of persons other than the author as having a right to exist and to have a separate mode of being which is important and interesting to themselves."[23] This description applies most particularly to the *Quartet*, which so admirably fulfills all its particulars, but it is very specifically the sensibility and aware imagination of William Conway, sitting with Dora in the *machān* observing the tiger, that makes the novels of this tradition possible.

The succeeding sections of *The Birds of Paradise* tell of Conway's life between Tradura and Manoba: his experiences in the war, including three and a half years spent in a Japanese prisoner-of-war camp in Malaya, where he has acted as assistant to a doctor named Cranston; and after the war his unhappy marriage to Anne, his failure to engage the affection of his son, and subsequently his divorce; and finally his return to India, his visit with Cranston and to Jundapur, where Krishi is now Maharajah and Dora once more a houseguest in the hot weather before the rains. Then, in Manoba itself, his quest both for the living birds of paradise and for Daintree, the doctor whom Cranston had so praised, are disappointed: the birds are not found, and Daintree, the last (or most recent) of the succession of fathers Conway has found, beginning with his own and leading through the old Maharajah, Grayson-Hume, his Uncle Walter, and Cranston, is almost completely isolated from human communication because of his alcoholism.

Each of the four sections of the book derives its title from a particular experience or, better, vision—Scott's way of providing a thread through his labyrinth. The first, "The Wheeling Horsemen," alludes to a kind of mirage in which Conway at ten charges on his pony against an imagined group of horsemen to "save Dora." Did it happen, did he daydream it? He is never to be sure, but what is certain is that the dream fulfills the aspirations of an imaginative child, who, in a way more profound than he then understands, has fallen in love, a child nurtured on Henty and Wren with a conception of heroism and romance that also reflects his sense of India and the British mission, a conception that is touching but, as he will discover, all too appropriate to his age. Even at this early stage Conway has intimations, revelations even, of the harshness and cruelty of the splendid world he inhabits.

According to Dora, when she and I talked about the procession recently, I was concerned about "that old woman in rags." Dora still had a clear picture of her; the way she knelt by the roadside holding out her palm. I remember no old woman in rags, but I remember the feeling of the splendour suddenly gone. I think what happened was that both Dora and I saw the old woman, even discussed her, but that afterwards I retained a general impression while she retained the particular one. What I have never forgotten is how the procession suddenly looked unreal and tawdry. The way I would describe it now is to say that in the midst of the magnificence I saw the face of damnation.[24]

In "On the Banks of the Water," Conway conjures up the bitter disappointment when, standing by a stream called "the Water," his father told him he was not to pursue an Indian career but would go into business in London with his Uncle Walter. He reflects on how his father has in a sense hoodwinked him into thinking that he cared for him and that a career in India had value. The boy now sees "the guardians of the trust" as "whoring imperialists," and he is now quite sure that his father never cared for him at all. And he concludes that, all the same, "Life's not half bad . . . no thanks to Father."[25]

"The View from the Terrace" describes the horrors of the prison camp; Conway's sympathy for those Indians who have joined the Indian National Army (to fight the British under Japanese direction), an important theme in the *Quartet;* and the importance of Cranston to Conway in his quest for an ideal. "The illusion of my life had been that a man should love his job, be dedicated to it, born to it. When I met Cranston I saw that he was the only man I had ever met who did and was."[26] Conway returns to India to recuperate; he spends days sitting on the terrace observing the landscape with its major and minor mysteries. His "view" refers chiefly to his new (though far from complete) understanding of his father and the British role in India. In a game of chess with the older Conway, he concludes that the British will desert the princes who, for their part, had always stood by the Raj with devotion and loyalty and who still believe that they will be rewarded.

Wavell would see to it. So would men like my father.

But Wavell wouldn't be able to see to it. Neither would men like Father. They were pawns dressed up as knights. Logic demanded that one day we should say to a land we had loved and hated, bled and bled for, felt in our cold northern bones as a source of warmth and in our God-rotten souls as a burden too hot to handle: Yes we will go, we will go on such and such a day. Logic demanded that we add: And on that day we are finished, the princes are on their own, it is up to them to whom, if anyone, they pay tribute.[27]

Later, in England, "reading the accounts of this new decline and fall, I was lost sometimes in admiration of the way we English could twist an essential retreat until it looked like a voluntary advance, could seem to shrug our shoulders in paternal amusement at the antics the jackals got up to and tap our feet in the background as if we had been waiting for thirty years and not three months for them to decide what to do about their freedom."[28]

It is a part of the folklore pertaining to the birds of paradise that they never land on earth and fly always against the wind to save themselves from being entangled in their long, trailing plumage. "Against the Wind," the final section of the novel, recapitulates and focuses with greatest intensity on the polarities that preoccupy William Conway. That the birds always fly against the wind is of course only a folk belief, but all the same it is their beauty that brings about their destruction. "The bird of paradise, it had been thought, was too beautiful a creature to inhabit the natural world,"[29] Conway writes, and if we change the word *inhabit* to *survive*, we come close to the significance of the birds in the scheme of the book. Only the "consumers" can remain blind to the fragility of their own illusions. It is a potent element in the underlying pessimism of this novel that even the best and strongest cannot sustain their ideals. Cranston, when Conway visits him in Bihar, has given up his mission to go out and look for the sick who cannot come to him—sold out, as it were, to a richly endowed foundation and "become reconciled to his own role of consumer, ready to consign the Muzzafirabad laboratories—outwardly perfect but inwardly no doubt already short of essentials—to the heap of brand new rubbish that seems to surround us always."[30] Daintree, who had devoted his career to the difficult treatment of yaws, is in a sense put out of business after the war by the discovery of penicillin and has now been farmed out to Manoba, where, in his alcoholism, it is felt he cannot do too much harm. The birds themselves are probably extinct on the island, and when the natives tell Conway to listen, for they may still be heard if not seen, he assumes they are imitating the birds' song for his benefit. Of the two Manobas that Conway discerns, the one is fouled with trash and garbage, and the other is "a dark, forgotten island whose warriors challenge your approach, make magic out of tins and mysteries out of birds."[31] The second is a dream to set against the first, which is also the world of his wife, a world of *maya*, a "world that had never existed and never could exist," which the consumers use

as one of the few remaining means by which they could forget that if they suddenly closed their eyes and listened the only real sounds in the world would be those of chewing and swallowing and champing and regurgitation, the gasp of dying animals, the crash of tree trunks, the snap of stalks, the whirr of machinery turning things into other things, the ring of hammers, the screech of chisels, the crunch of bone on bone and of mind on mind.

Not that Anne would hear any of that, for she is a great consumer, wholly committed to it. I am hard on her, I know, but she is content with what she thinks she is, and is therefore nothing in my opinion. For her nothing has any meaning until she has got her teeth into it. Whatever she touches she ravages with her ignorance of its previous existence, her greed for it while she wants it, her destructive dismissal of it when she has finished with it. For her the world was born on the day that she was born and will die when she dies.[32]

Set against this is what Conway has felt for Dora on the *machān* and feels again when, thirty years later, he stands with her in the cage beneath the now rotting stuffed birds of paradise. "She stood in profile, as in the *machān* on the day of the tiger. The tangential lines at the corners of her eyes, with the yellowing patches on her neck, the husky, ragged, memsahib voice became, briefly, focuses for my tenderness, and acquired beauty as did all the traces left upon her by her years, for her years were my life, and I had loved her as a child."[33]

Dora and Krishi make a gift of a Paraguayan parrot named Melba to Conway as he sets out for Manoba. He calls her his "mock bird of paradise" and builds for her an immense outside cage that re-creates the island cage of the *paradisaeidae*. He and Melba, as he puts it, "are acting out the part of lovers," and they "are committed to each other."[34] For him alone Melba sings the wild songs of her Paraguayan highlands, becomes jealous, sulks, tries to please. The mainstay of her vocabulary is his name and "Wurrah Yadoor-a!" ("Where are you, Dora?" with an unmistakable echo of Tradura), so that in her speech and music Melba, whose name is another echo (Manoba, which Conway tells us is pronounced Man'ba) sums up all that is most important to Conway. "I feel that it is my youth she has been singing and not her own and at times like this I go up to her cage and we stare at each other and try to break down the terrible barrier that exists between man and beast."[35]

The truth is relative, Conway decides, and the past largely one's own creation. He, Dora, and Krishi have mostly quite different memories of the past, and only certain moments, like the experience on the *machān*, seem to possess an absolute reality. The barrier between man and man is as terrible as the barrier between man and beast. When Conway learns of the death of Mrs. Canterbury, he realizes how very little he actually has known about her, and her life remains "mostly shrouded in mystery."[36]

After his unsatisfactory reunion with Cranston, he can only say, "There is no end to the misunderstandings that can exist between man and man."[37] More important, he learns that his father, whom he had come to think of as one of those who let the princes down, had actually made an attempt, in public, to dissuade the Maharajah of Tradura from giving in to the new Indian government. The attempt is not appreciated but, like Gower's pro-Indian stand in *The Alien Sky*, earns him the hostility of those he has intended to help. This new dimension to the elder Conway leads his son at the conclusion of the book to "bitterly regret that not once in my life did I sit with him and let him feel that I understood how vulnerable is the illusion that a man has of his own importance, not of his importance to others, but of his importance to himself, and how to speak of what drives him to sustain the illusion, of the means he finds to drive himself, of the dark that falls on him, when the illusion is gone, is virtually impossible."[38]

In *The Birds of Paradise*, Scott has mastered a metaphorically rich style superior to anything in his earlier fiction. Symbols shift and expand their meanings constantly. An example is the birds of paradise themselves, which finally come to stand for more than British or princes and embody the ideals that are found to be "too beautiful to inhabit the natural world"; the fanciful folklore about the birds is made real by the rapacity of those who destroy them. Artificially preserved after their slaughter, they will eventually rot, their beauty real only in the memory or the imagination. The touching relationship of Conway and Melba of Paraguay (with its echoes of paradise), herself named after a great singer, a diva, or divine one, adds a new dimension to the paradisiacal ideals, giving Conway his only opportunity to express, or better, exercise, a selfless love in his commitment to the bird, which, despite all the difficulties, he will not abandon. Scott's triumph in *The Birds of Paradise* is that, as in the *Quartet*, he is able to give life, dramatic impact, a universally meaningful human dimension to this story, which is served by (rather than succumbing to) its technique, its metaphorical or symbolic apparatus, and its philosophical intentions. Where, perhaps in despair, Jhabvala, with her stance of objectivity camouflaging an essentially solipsistic view of the world, reduces everything to the trivial and contemptible and (occasionally) the pathetic, Scott is genuinely objective and views his creation with the greatest seriousness, one might even say respect. Even in Conway's harsh judgment of his wife, there is not meanness but a passionate need to define her without sentimentality, and his view of himself is no less ruthlessly critical. Wide and deep as Conway's character is, however, it is not vast enough to encompass the conception Scott was forming of the historical climax of Indo-British relations, a conception out of which the *Quartet* would evolve, a scheme or structure in which a great variety of voices will be heard speaking for themselves in a context of objectively observed incident and detail that simulates the condition of history and, transcending that, the complexity and richness of life.

6

The Raj Quartet

It is merely an illusion that some of us stand on one bank and some on the opposite. So long as we stand like that we are not living at all, but dreaming. So jump, jump in, and let the shock wake us up. Even if we drown, at least for a moment or two before we die we shall be awake and alive.

PAUL SCOTT[1]

Mildred's enemy was history.

PAUL SCOTT[2]

Earlier studies of *The Raj Quartet*[3] have found it useful to begin the exploration of this immense work from the point of view of history: the sequence of historical events that provides Scott with the external structure of the four novels and his development of a theory of history, his characters as victims of history, his success (or failure) in bringing into focus a comprehensive and clarifying vision of the significance of the end of the Raj. The limitations of such an approach seem to me to be obvious, and its choice only an admission of the magnitude of the task of presenting a comprehensive and coherent study of the work. For my part, I believe it may be possible to understand Scott's fundamental intentions more readily by viewing the history that provides the background and structure for his fictional happenings as secondary; history, indeed, may, just as readily as the reverse, be viewed as the victim of people and human character. The *Quartet* embraces what may be called a double intention: the presentation, on the one hand, of individual, private dramas, and on the other, of a historical perspective more general and universal than recent Anglo-Indian conflicts, which for their part provide an instrumentality for Scott's purpose, much as the Napoleonic wars serve Tolstoy for the portrayal of a specific society operating within a framework of universal laws. Scott had in mind, I am convinced, the dramatization of certain elemental human impulses or instincts that, in conflict with one another, lead inevitably to tragedy at both the personal and the broadly historical levels. In *The Corrida at San Feliu*, Edward

Thornhill's imprisonment in envy and contempt, two key words in the *Quartet*, make it impossible for him to achieve a loving relationship with anyone, and failures of this sort are dramatized in *The Raj Quartet* on a colossal scale. Possessive love and sexual starvation or envy play significant roles in most of the human relationships and catastrophes that make up the *Quartet*. In this, Scott is closer to Proust than to the Tolstoy of *War and Peace*— which is not to deny that Scott and Proust are both historical novelists par excellence.

The relationship of Britain and India, as Scott portrays it, is allegorized as a sexual embrace. Scott introduces the theme at the private, personal level on the first page of the first novel. "This is the story of a rape, of the events that led up to it and followed it and of the place in which it happened. There are the action, the people, and the place; all of which are interrelated but in their totality incommunicable in isolation from the moral continuum of human affairs."[4] Scott proceeds immediately to consider the wider implications of this event, invoking, as he will so often through the work, a kind of vague historical chorus: "people have said," "people say," and so on. "The affair that began on the evening of August 9th, 1942, in Mayapore, ended with the spectacle of two nations in violent opposition, not for the first time nor as yet for the last because they were then still locked in an imperial embrace of such long standing and subtlety it was no longer possible for them to know whether they hated or loved one another, or what it was that held them together and seemed to have confused the image of their separate destinies."[5] Accordingly, the very first image of these four novels so rich in imagery is of "a girl running," and the final one, in the last line of the last novel, of "the girl running with the deer" from the pursuing bowman. The first girl running is of course Daphne Manners, but the second, a mere image in a poem written a century or so before, suggests a universal and constantly recurring tragedy to be experienced long after the Imperial embrace has been dissolved and forgotten.

The existence of another kind of love is also asserted to provide a kind of countervailing symmetry for the whole *Quartet:* in the beginning of the first novel, Mr. Chaudhuri dying to protect Miss Crane; and at the end of the last, Ahmed Kasim offering himself up to the mob of Hindu fanatics to appease them and probably assure the survival of the English in the train compartment with him. Patrick Swinden writes: "The *Quartet* ends, in human terms, where it began: with a dead Indian on the road, being tended by representatives of the English ruling class who are powerless to help him. . . . It is an imbalance which gives some indication of the solemnity and often depressive quality of Scott's vision of life."[6] Swinden apparently sees only futility in the sacrificial deaths of Chaudhuri and Ahmed, and futility precludes tragedy. But Mr. Chaudhuri and Ahmed Kasim are both heroic in their resolve and devotion; their deaths may be viewed as acts of love. Scott's placing them, like monumental pillars, at the beginning and end of his epic story must surely be intended to represent more than futility, and though (or precisely because) they reinforce the intention of presenting a tragic vision, they cannot be intended to depress. That Scott's vision of life is solemn and dark is unquestionable, but redemptive elements constantly assert themselves, usually in the form of some kind of human loving that is selfless and giving and able to contradict (or correct) the mistaken version of events that passes as history. The redemptive figures in the novels (Sarah, Perron, Barbie Batchelor) from an instinctive devotion to truth constantly strive to reconstruct the events of the recent past in defiance of the generally accepted myths that have grown up about them and obscured them.

In *The Raj Quartet,* Paul Scott explores a complex of illusions and their consequences both for those who sooner or later see through them and for those who do not. There are some minor characters, like Major Jimmy Clark, who do not seem to care; we are not permitted to know if he was always cynical or became that way as a result of any specifically Indian experience. Where other writers discussed earlier, such as William Buchan, see the declining days of the Raj mostly in terms of what the change brings to the life-styles of the Anglo-Indians, Scott is interested in the more profound spiritual dislocation that the end of the old regime will produce in a wide variety of human beings, not only British but Indian as well.

Each of the four novels is dominated by a single figure—Daphne Manners, Sarah Layton, Barbie Batchelor, and Guy Perron respectively—but all the major characters, with one exception, are allowed at one point or other to have their say, give their personal and private point of view on what has happened, not only through dialogue but by means of interior monologue, journals, letters, confidential reports, and the like. The exception is Ronald Merrick, whose ideas and feelings are known only through dialogue and actions; this is significant because he is the only important character to play a major role in all four novels. Also, in the first novel we are not precisely introduced to but rather made aware of a researcher, a kind of historical investigator, who is seeking to establish the correct version of the Bibighar affair; this figure, never identified, disappears after *The Jewel in the Crown*. It is tempting to think that perhaps he is the historian Guy Perron or his student, young David Turner, whom Guy and Sarah commend to Lucy in *Staying On*, but this must remain no more than speculation.

In the short introductory paragraphs quoted above, Scott states his main subject, the "story of a rape," presumably Daphne Manners', but by extension India's. He then begins *The Jewel in the Crown* (1966) with what appears to be a diversion from the main narrative, the chronicle of the life and death of Edwina Crane, a mission school teacher noted for her pro-Indian sympathies. In her study hang two pictures: a portrait of Gandhi and an allegorical painting, "The Jewel in Her Crown," which represents, in its crowded scene, a native prince offering a gem to Queen Victoria while Disraeli flourishes the map of India and all the subcontinent joyfully looks on—princes, merchants, and "remarkably clean and tidy beggars." Miss Crane, a spinster who has spent thirty-five of her fifty-seven years in India, is aware of the delusions that the painting embodies. At the same time, she recognizes the difficulty, impossibility even, of communicating with her Indian friends, including Mr. Chaudhuri, the teacher at the school in Dibrapur, some 70 miles distant from Mayapore.[7] Miss Crane returns from Dibrapur with Mr. Chaudhuri on 9 August, the day after Gandhi's arrest and the outbreak of anti-British violence in many parts of India. On the way her car is attacked, whether by radical nationalists or by mere hoodlums is not made clear; Mr. Chaudhuri is murdered as he tries to protect Miss Crane. Later, Miss Crane puts on a sari and burns herself to death in an act of suttee.

The attack on Miss Crane occurs the same day as the Bibighar affair and, like it, will haunt the rest of the *Quartet*, gathering significance as subsequent events unfold and different characters become aware of it and ponder its wider meaning. It is important to note that Miss Crane, who has never experienced a complete love (or for that matter, a loving) relationship and who has been troubled for so long by the difficulty of understanding, respecting, and loving Indians, achieves a kind of communication and even fulfillment as she drives Mr. Chaudhuri along the Mayapore road toward what will prove his death. After his murder, "she sat down in the mud at the side of the road, close to him, reached out and took his hand. 'It's taken me a long time,' she said, meaning not only Mr. Chaudhuri, 'I'm sorry it was too late.' "[8]

The scene of the central incident of the *Quartet*—or, better, incidents, since Daphne Manners' consummation of her love for Hari Kumar is symbolically quite as important as her subsequent rape—is called the Bibighar, the house of women, or wife's house. Scott has chosen the name deliberately and audaciously, for it is charged with ominous resonance for the British: the house in Kanpur where the British women and children were massacred in July 1857 was known as the Bibighar. According to the popular legends that pass for history in Mayapore (as indeed, Scott implies throughout his work, they do everywhere else), the Bibighar was built by a prince for a singer he loved, a girl who always eluded him, so that his passion was never consummated. After their deaths the prince's son lets the Bibighar decay and builds for himself another house for his courtesans; this prince is later deposed by the British because of his corruption, and the house is remodeled by a Scottish merchant named MacGregor. MacGregor burns down the Bibighar, perhaps because he had been rejected by an Indian girl he wished to maintain there, although there are many different versions of the story. In the Mutiny, MacGregor is killed by mutinous sepoys and his wife murdered on the veranda of her house, to be known forever as MacGregor House, with her baby in her arms. "A Muslim servant called Akbar Hossain died defending her."[9] (The preciseness with which Scott names this servant emphasises the theme of loyalty and selfless love, in the face of what some would call absolute futility, that will be sounded and varied so often throughout the *Quartet*.) The MacGregor House, Lili Chatterjee says, is the place of the white, and the ruins of the Bibighar the place of the black, and thus Scott defines the point where Daphne Manners begins her journey and her destination. Janet MacGregor's ghost haunts the MacGregor House to warn Europeans living there that it is not a good place for them. Daphne has come to stay there on a long visit with her aunt's old friend, Lady Chatterjee. For Daphne the house is good, as it marks the beginning of her discovery of a greater, expanded world, even though that discovery proves full of dangers.

While being courted by the District Superintendant of Police in

Mayapore, Ronald Merrick, whom she finds vaguely and unaccountably distasteful, Daphne meets and falls in love with Hari Kumar, a young Indian who has lived and been educated in England between the ages of two and seventeen and who, by his accent alone, would pass for an upper-class Englishman; even his name has been Anglicized to Harry Coomer and he has never actually known himself as Hari Kumar. On the evening Daphne and Hari Kumar consummate their love in the Bibighar Gardens, six hoodlums attack them and rape Daphne. Afterward Daphne exacts a promise from Hari Kumar that he will deny that he was at the Bibighar, a promise that he keeps despite Merrick's efforts, later on, to make him confess it. His silence becomes a key element in affirming not only his courage and passionate attachment to Daphne but also his "English-ness"; those English who assume he is lying simply cannot understand this silence. "Connie said, 'I expect it's frightfully silly of me, but you know if Hari Kumar had been an Englishman I could have understood his silence better, although even then it would have had to be a silence imposed on him by a woman.' "[10] Hari Kumar is, of course, an Englishman in all but color, and the silence was imposed on him by a woman, not to protect herself but, as Daphne has rapidly figured, to protect him. As will happen often in the *Quartet*, a minor personage, in this case Connie, will hypothesize a version of the incident closer to the truth than the official one, but as usual the version will not be credited, in this case even by its creator.

Hari Kumar and five students are arrested, and Merrick, whose confused feelings concerning Hari are clarified only later, plants Daphne's bicycle at Hari's house to incriminate him. Daphne resolutely denies that she knew any of her attackers, claiming they were dirty country people and one of them was circumcised, so must have been a Muslim, and consequently none of those arrested could have had anything to do with the attack. She is not believed but the case is dropped, in part because of her refusal to cooperate and her threat to suggest in an inquiry that the men could have been British with blackened faces. But the six young men arrested are not released but held on political grounds, since the attacks on Miss Crane and Daphne both occur at the beginning of widespread anti-British agitation that was brought about by Gandhi's refusal to cooperate with Britain in its war against the Axis and by his arrest. Later it is learned that Daphne is pregnant; to everyone's surprise she determines to have the baby and, with her aunt, goes to Kashmir, where she gives birth to a girl, Parvati, and dies.

In the course of the novel, the reader is given accounts of the Bibighar affair through the reminiscences of Lady Chatterjee and Sister Ludmila, a mysterious European woman who cares for the sick and homeless; Daphne's letters and diary; the deposition of Vidyasagar, a journalist arrested soon after Hari Kumar; the memoirs of a General Reid; the comments of Robin White, the Deputy Commissioner; and the interior monologue of Hari Kumar. All of these are attempts at establishing a coherent "history" of the affair, which must remain incomplete for the reader until the revelations in *The Day of the Scorpion,* when the action moves away from Mayapore (the "city of illusion"), which, ironically, has been the theater for the unfolding of history on both the personal and the international level. As for the characters in the four novels, most will never know the truth about Bibighar but must remain content with official versions; only those who are capable of love— Sister Ludmila, Sarah, Barbie, Guy Perron—will intuit the real story.

The Day of the Scorpion begins with the introduction of the Kasim family, aristocratic Muslims whose ancestors have included a great Urdu poet, Gaffur. Mohammed Ali Kasim, an important Congress leader and kinsman of the Nawab of Mirat, has been arrested following the violence of 8 August. His elder son[11] is with the British-Indian army in Burma; the younger, Ahmed, is acting as social secretary to the Nawab of Mirat. Mohammed Ali in prison reflects on what is happening in India and the difficulties of his own position as a Muslim freedom fighter in a predominantly Hindu world. The anomalies of the Kasim family in some ways dimly parallel the situation of some of the British in India: like them, the Kasims, no matter how Indian they become, remain even now on the fringe of that Hindu world, rarely loved and trusted despite the fact that their entry into India preceded that of the English by several centuries; like them, they have achieved neither mastery nor integration.

We next meet the Layton family, the father a prisoner of war in Germany, the mother an all-too-typical snobbish and bitchy memsahib, given to drink and infidelity, while the two daughters, Sarah and Susan, represent polarities of British awareness. Susan, the younger and prettier, is shallow, unstable, selfish, and utterly unconcerned about the morality of the Raj or its future; Sarah, like Daphne Manners, is constantly troubled by these matters and her responsibilities to both her family and India.[12] Other parallels between Daphne and Sarah are shown: Sarah too is courted by Merrick and finds herself drawn, more in friendship than romantically, to an Indian, Ahmed Kasim; she becomes fascinated by the Bibighar affair and tantalized by the inconclusiveness of both official and unofficial versions. The Laytons have come to the princely state of Mirat for Susan's wedding to a Captain Teddie Bingham, with Merrick stepping in to replace the best man, who is ill. The wedding is marred by ominous incidents: a stone is thrown at the car carrying the groom and Merrick to the ceremony; the Nawab, host to the wedding party, is denied entrance to the reception at the Gymkhana Club by overzealous British military police eager to keep natives off the premises; and on the railway station platform a woman, Hari Kumar's aunt, throws herself at Merrick's feet in a highly embarrassing scene. The Nawab's chief minister, a Russian exile named Bronowsky, is the second in the story (after Sister Ludmila) to suspect Merricks' homosexual inclination. A homosexual himself, but living the most austere of lives, Bronowsky for the rest of the *Quartet* will be a dedicated inquirer into Merrick's career and the Bibighar case.

The second half of *The Day of the Scorpion* begins with a long section that brings us back to Hari Kumar. Lady Manners, Daphne's aunt, has arranged to listen, unobserved, to an interrogation of Hari by a Captain Rowan and an Indian lawyer. The very long cross-examination (almost a hundred pages, and a favorite technique of Scott) at last reveals what has happened to Hari Kumar after his arrest, though he still resolutely refuses to say anything about his presence in the Bibighar Gardens and his relationship with Daphne, even when told of her death. He describes objectively and in detail his treatment at Merrick's hands: how he has been stripped, bound to a trestle, and sexually abused by Merrick, who nevertheless failed to get him to admit to involvement of any kind with Daphne. This extraordinary treatment by Merrick has been subtly prepared for and justified by the comments earlier of Sister Ludmila, who has observed the way Merrick watched Hari, and of Count Bronowsky. Lady Manners is convinced of Hari Kumar's innocence, as is Captain Rowan, an old boy from Chillingborough, the same public school Hari had gone to, and he will be released from prison, though, as Lady Manners asks pessimistically, "To what?"—a question answered only in the final volume. The importance of Rowan, who will return in the final volume as a friend of Guy Perron and provider of much information on Hari Kumar and Bibighar, at this point is to play devil's advocate, coming only slowly to a conviction of the young Indian's innocence.

By this point in the novel, Sarah Layton has already emerged as its most significant character. Before her sister's wedding, while with her family in Kashmir, she alone has visited, secretly, the houseboat where Lady Manners is living with her infant grand-niece, Parvati. The other Laytons had considered it somehow embarrassing and infra dig even to acknowledge the existence of the people on the other houseboat. It is Lady Manners who suggests a bound volume of Gaffur's poetry as a suitable guest gift for the Laytons to present to the Nawab of Mirat at the time of the wedding. Sarah's visit to Lady Manners thus becomes an act of great emblematic importance that not only links together many divergent strands of the story (Daphne and Hari Kumar, the Laytons, Ahmed, and the Mirat court) but also establishes Sarah's independence, moral awareness, and growing involvement in the Bibighar affair.

After Teddie Bingham is killed in action in Burma, and Merrick, who has tried to save him, is hospitalized in Calcutta, badly burned and mutilated, Sarah is sent to visit him. While in Calcutta she is seduced by a coarse and brutally hedonistic man named Clark. On her return to her family in Pankot (a hill station and military depot), while changing trains at Ranpur, she meets Count Bronowsky and is introduced to Captain Rowan. All of them are linked by their interest in and opinions about Merrick, and Sarah hopes for an opportunity to quiz Rowan privately concerning him and Hari Kumar, but, as happens often in these novels, at the point where someone is close to gaining important knowledge of the Bibighar affair, a casual intervention (in this case, Count Bronowsky's insistence on seeing Sarah to her train) frustrates further revelation.

At the end of the novel, Susan, who has given birth to Teddie's son, suffers what is apparently a postpartum psychosis and attempts to kill the baby by setting him in a circle of fire, just as she has heard a scorpion was destroyed by a servant when she was a child.

We also become acquainted with Barbie Batchelor, a retired schoolteacher obsessed with what she comes to understand as the heroic example of Edwina Crane. Barbie has been living with Sarah's Aunt Mabel[13] in the hill station called Pankot at Rose Cottage, a house that, like the Bibighar and MacGregor House, has great symbolic importance in the volumes that follow. Mabel, strongly pro-Indian, had refused to contribute to the General Dyer fund after the Jallianwallah Bagh massacre in 1919 and instead donated a sum for the relief of the families of the victims. She is so haunted by Jallianwallah that a quarter-century later she murmurs the name frequently in her sleep, a name that Barbie hears as "Gillian Waller" and takes for a person of some importance in Mabel's life; and the name remains an unsolved mystery. Mabel and Barbie both take their place with Edwina Crane, Sarah, and Lady Manners, in contrast to the complacent memsahibs of Mayapore and Pankot, among those troubled by the role of the British in India and their personal responsibility in that involvement. Barbie's presence at Rose Cottage is an affront and aggravation to Mrs. Layton, who wants the cottage for herself. When Mabel dies, Barbie is moved out with indecent haste to find temporary sanctuary with Reverend Peplow and his wife. The revealing of Mabel's death at this point in the narrative is typical of Scott's technique, for most of the following novel will flash back to a detailed description of the relationship between Barbie and Mabel.

Near the end of *The Day of the Scorpion,* we also learn that Mohammed Ali Kasim's elder son, who has been captured by the Japanese, is collaborating with them as an officer in the Indian National Army, formed specifically to fight the British. This represents a tragic and dishonoring development for Mohammed Ali, who is himself renowned for his absolute integrity and idealistic devotion in all circumstances to the rules of the game.

The Towers of Silence (1971), the third novel of the *Quartet,* is like the adagio movement of a cyclic symphony that develops themes in new and unexpected ways, a long, reflective, unwinding narrative that presents again and in far greater detail events previously related. It begins in 1939 with Barbie Batchelor's retirement and her coming, in answer to an advertisement, to live at Rose Cottage with Mabel Layton; continues on through 1943, with the deaths of Mabel and Teddie Bingham, and a climactic confrontation between Barbie and Merrick; and concludes with Barbie's death in a Ranpur hospital in August 1945.

Barbie, who is held to be mad at the end of her life and has long intervals of what would be clinically considered derangement,

is also a quester after truth and at times seems to have the intuitions of a seeress, a gift not at all out of keeping with her fragile
sanity. She is fascinated by the Edwina Crane and Daphne Manners affairs; it is in fact her acquaintance with Edwina that leads
her on to the Bibighar mystery, the two events being so closely
associated. She guesses with an extraordinary leap of the imagination that Sarah has visited Lady Manners and the infant Parvati,
a happening known to no one in all Pankot outside Sarah's immediate family. She feels drawn to both Daphne and Hari Kumar
and suspects that the official version of events is incorrect. In a
nightmarish scene, defying (as is her wont) the civil and social
taboos of the hill station, she forces her way into the morgue where
Mabel, eyes still open, is being embalmed. She stumbles onto the
loveless and mechanical lovemaking of Mildred Layton, Sarah's
mother, and Kevin Coley, a Pankot officer, which leads Mildred
to attack her with violent abuse. The station gossip hints that Barbie has an unnatural affection for Sarah and Susan; the truth is
of course that she does love them, and Mabel even more—here
Scott is implying a Proustian distinction between profane and sacred love. Barbie's importance as a spiritual force, capable of the
highest devotion and the deepest discernment, is triumphantly
revealed in her meeting with Ronald Merrick. She has just returned to Rose Cottage after Mabel's death to collect her enormous
trunk when she finds Merrick there—a presence that makes "the
air difficult to breathe."[14] He is accompanied by a "noxious emanation that lay like an almost visible miasma around the plants,"
so that she experiences nausea. Then, in a long, polite conversation, they discuss the Laytons, Edwina Crane, and the Bibighar
affair. Merrick betrays his jealousy and uneasiness to Barbie's
preternaturally sharp perception, and later she is to think that
"God had shone his light on her at last by casting first the shadow
of the prince of darkness across her feet."[15] As she rides down
the hillside in a tonga with the too-large trunk beside her, the
horse slips, the tonga overturns. Though she recovers from the
accident, she never quite regains her wits after the meeting with
Merrick.

To Barbie, Scott gives one of his most eloquent images for his
own feelings about the Raj. "But tonight she found herself slowed
down, struck by the significance of her surroundings, the reality
of this ordinariness, this shabbiness, this evidence of detritus behind the screens of imperial power and magnificence. The feeling

she had was not of glory departing or departed but of its original and continuing irrelevance to the business of being in India."[16] Like Edwina Crane, Barbie has a copy of the picture "The Jewel in Her Crown," and as was the case with Edwina, along with her loss of respect for the Raj, her faith in the Church of England God is eroded. The final link between the two spinster teachers is established when at her death Barbie is described in this way: "They found her thus, eternally alert, in sudden sunshine, her shadow burnt into the wall behind her as if by some distant but terrible fire."[17] The day is 6 August, and the fire of course is not only the reflected memory of Edwina Crane's suttee but also Hiroshima.

In *The Towers of Silence* we are given the barroom version of the Bibighar mystery by one Captain Mackay, a version that ironically is the closest to the truth of any of the many speculations by Scott's fringe characters (the "people, "they," "one") who invent history. Mackay—whose interpretation is almost "the real Mackay"—is not taken seriously, and of course his inebriated audience will never know how close to the truth he came.

In this novel also, Sarah makes an unhappy journey to Calcutta to have an abortion. This points up the barrenness of her affair with Clark and is a reminder of Daphne's insistence on bearing her half-Indian child. Throughout *The Towers of Silence* the view of the British continues to darken, especially as demonstrated by the detailed account of social life in Pankot, its hollowness, and the growing dreariness of its rituals. When Lady Manners comes to Pankot, she stays on the Indian side of town and, to emphasize her rejection of Anglo-India, pointedly ignores the English community; her presence in the hill station, indeed, is known only from her signature in the governor's visitors' book, though both Sarah and Barbie, symbolically privileged beings, observe her from afar on different occasions.

The Towers of Silence is the shortest of the four novels in the *Quartet* and, through the concentration on Barbie and the Laytons, the most sustained and dense as well as the most morally and spiritually explicit. The succeeding novel, *A Division of the Spoils* (1975) is the longest and in some ways the most diffuse.

In this final novel, Guy Perron, a sergeant in field intelligence and, like Hari Kumar and Nigel Rowan, an old Chillingburian, is the closest we come to a conventional hero in the *Quartet*. He is resourceful, independent, ruthlessly honest, gifted with abundant humor and imagination, and, like the other morally aware char-

acters throughout the four novels, he becomes profoundly interested in the Bibighar affair; he also finds himself the most directly
in conflict (after Hari Kumar) with Ronald Merrick. It is Merrick's
misfortune that, with his inferior education and inferior accent,
he is constantly confronted by brilliant and attractive Chillingborough graduates, and one may feel that Scott has rather stacked
the cards against him. Perron, unfortunately, falls into his clutches.
As he puts it, " 'Merrick looks around, his eye lights on someone,
and he says, Right, I want *him*. Why else do you think I'm here?
I'm a chosen one. I expect Coomer was.' "[18] But Merrick cannot
hold onto Perron, who eludes him eventually and gets himself
ordered to a new posting, though not before he has had a brief
love affair with Sarah Layton, which will lead (we learn only after
the end of the *Quartet*, in *Staying On*) to their marriage.

More incidents in the life of Merrick are revealed, including the
way he is harassed by bicycles abandoned on his doorstep to remind him that the Hari Kumar matter is not forgotten; his cruel
entrapment of an inoffensive and timid nascent homosexual
named Pinky; and his role in driving an Indian noncommissioned
officer, formerly under Colonel Layton's command, to suicide.
Merrick nonetheless is able to get on well with Susan and Teddie
Bingham's little son, and eventually he marries Susan. A year
after his marriage, in 1947, he is brutally murdered; across the
mirror in his room his assassins have written "Bibighar" with a
make-up stick. The circumstances of his death are hushed up—
it is reported that he has died as a result of injuries sustained in
a riding accident—and so, like so much in the *Quartet*, pass into
history in a completely untrue version.

Count Bronowsky delivers what must be the last word on Merrick in a conversation with Perron; he suggests that Merrick deliberately put himself in the way of what was to happen to him.

"What I mean by a revelation is revelation of the connexion between the
homosexuality, the sado-masochism, the sense of social inferiority and
the grinding defensive belief in his racial superiority. I believe—although
you may not—that Aziz was the first young man he had actually ever
made love to, and that this gave him a moment of profound peace, but
in the next the kind he knew he couldn't bear, knew he couldn't bear
because to admit this peace meant discarding every belief he had. I think
he realized that, when he woke up after his first night with the boy. And
I think that when the boy turned up the following night he just found
himself punished and humiliated. And I believe that when Merrick beat

him with his fist he was inviting retaliation. I believe he knew why Aziz had arrived. I am sure that finally, Mr. Perron, he sought the occasion of his own death and that he grew impatient for it."[19]

All of this is perfectly consonant with Perron's assessment: "He's the man who comes too late and invents himself to make up for it."[20] As Perron sees it, Merrick's inverted snobbery leads him to take the Raj seriously. " 'Can't the fool see that nobody of the class he aspires to belong to has ever cared a damn about the empire and that all that God-the-Father-God-the-*raj* was a lot of insular middle- and lower-class shit?' "[21]

The situation of the princes, which interested Scott so much in *The Birds of Paradise,* is developed in great detail as we see Count Bronowsky trying to solve the dilemma of Mirat, hoping to save the state by incorporating it peacefully into the Indian union without violence and without losing the modernizing advantages he has introduced. Mirat, like Hyderabad-Deccan and Junagarh, though ruled by a Muslim, is predominantly Hindu, which renders its situation still more precarious. Bronowsky hopes to solidify his plans by having the Nawab's daughter marry Ahmed Kasim, a plan that will be frustrated by historical accident.

In the course of the narrative, Guy Perron learns from Rowan and his own researching most of the truth about Bibighar. In 1947, just on the eve of Independence and some of the bloodiest Partition riots, he returns to India to participate in the ending of the Raj and the final catastrophe in the story. He is riding in a train with Sarah, Susan and her little boy, Ahmed Kasim, and others when Hindus attack it to slaughter all the Muslims they can find. When they demand that Ahmed give himself up, he complies, thus sparing the compartment a violent assault, steps out of the train, and is hacked to death.

A Division of the Spoils concludes with Perron's unsuccessful attempt to track down his old schoolfellow Hari Kumar. In a Ranpur newspaper he has read an article by him, signed Philoctetes, that states with the greatest poignancy the tragic situation of one individual caught in the loveless operations that attend the demise of the Raj. " 'I walk home, thinking of another place, of seemingly long endless summers and the shade of different kinds of trees; and then of winters when the branches of the trees were bare, so bare that, recalling them now, it seems inconceivable to me that I looked at them and did not think of the summer just gone, and the spring soon to come, as illusions; as dreams, never fulfilled, never to be fulfilled.' "[22] Ironically, the article is a commentary on the opening of a new government college in Ranpur, described earlier in the same newspaper in stilted prose, with quotations from the even more painfully stilted and hollow speeches of the presiding dignitaries. Hari Kumar's article, along with the poem of Gaffur that brings the whole *Quartet* to a close, is an elegiacal epilogue in a completely personal vein to the mammoth historical spectacle that provides the background for the *Raj Quartet*, and another way for Scott to assert the overriding interest for him of the private lives of individuals seen against that background rather than the reverse, the predominant concern with history that some have seen merely illustrated by scattered private lives.

So skeletal a summary of the four complex novels cannot convey their richness and brilliance but is unhappily indispensable for further consideration of their significance, a consideration that must begin with a more detailed discussion of the central characters.

As so often in Scott, one finds in the conception of Daphne Manners a Forsterian parallel, almost as though, consciously or not, the writer were responding to a challenge to outdo the book that is so widely accepted as the finest novelistic study of Anglo-India. Like Adela Quested, Daphne is not a conventionally beautiful woman; her awkwardness and nearsightedness are also emphasized. She too has come out to India—not accompanying but to stay with a much older woman. Like Adela, Daphne will find her standing in the British community and her whole life threatened by her involvement in a scandal of alleged violation. At this point the differences from Forster's character proliferate. Daphne has felt a spontaneous sympathy for Indians early in her visit, from the moment she observes the crude disapproval of some Englishwomen reacting to the presence of Lady Chatterjee in their railway compartment. Most important, contrary to the case in Forster, the rape and the love and the ability to know "the real India" are not imaginary, neither mysteries nor muddles, but realities. Just as Scott, unlike Forster, ties his fictional events to historical actuality, so also Scott's drama of personal relations is revealed through a succession of actions too fleshly, too bloody, and sometimes too sordid for Forster's pen.[23]

To Daphne, Scott attributes an awareness of the unreality of racial feeling that must have been close to his own. I say unreality rather than injustice because, as Daphne first becomes conscious of it, she is not indignant but merely objective, trying to view the problem sensibly. So (with some irony) part of the resonance of Bibighar is that it serves as an instrument for Daphne's enlightenment.

When I first saw the Bibighar I thought: How Indian! . . . But when you say something like that, in circumstances like that, I think you're responding to the attraction of a place which you see as alien on the surface but underneath as proof of something general and universal. I wish I could get hold of the right words to say just what I mean. The Taj Mahal is "typically Indian," isn't it? Picture-book Moghul stuff. But what makes you give out to it emotionally is the feeling of a man's worship of his wife, which is neither Indian nor un-Indian, but a general human emotion, expressed in this case in an "Indian" way. This is what I got from Bibighar.[24]

By falling in love with Hari Kumar, even before they are separated forever by the events at the Bibighar, Daphne has attained a remarkable clarity as the world around her expands. Her dislike of the Raj becomes all the greater as she realizes that it depends so much on pretense. "Seeing Hari in my imagination looking over the shoulder of every pink male face and seeing in every pink male face the strain of pretending that the world was this small. Hateful. Ingrown. About to explode like powder compressed ready for firing."[25] Daphne goes on to theorize about the sexual implications of the Raj—one of Scott's fundamental concerns—after all the moral force "has gone sour," because "the whole bloody affair of *us* in India . . . was based on violation. . . . What happens when you unsex a nation, treat it like a nation of eunuchs? Because that's what we've done, isn't it?"[26] She continues prophetically, "God knows what happens. What will happen." Just as Edwina Crane has traced all the trouble to "this little matter of the colour of the skin, which gets in the way of our seeing through each other's failings and seeing into each other's hearts,"[27] so Daphne wonders about the "old primitive savage instinct to attack and destroy what we didn't understand because it looked different and was different always got the upper hand. And God knows how many centuries you have to go back to trace to its source their apparent fear of skins paler than their own."[28] She finds dishonesty on both sides, the Indians engaged in a vulgar scramble for power "and an equally vulgar smug hanging on on ours."[29]

But Daphne, in the words of Sister Ludmila, jumps from the bank into the stream, goes to a Hindu temple out of curiosity (she seems more at ease in it than Hari) and finally, though it costs her her life, bears an Indian child in a final redemptive act of love. (A comparison of Scott's treatment of this subject with Jhabvala's unnamed narrator and her decision to bear an Indian child in *Heat and Dust* provides a touchstone for revealing Scott's seriousness and depth in comparison with Jhabvala's vague and sketchy presentation and the neutrality with which she views it; or, rather, her failure to accord and define any significance in it.)

It is characteristic of Scott's novelistic technique that some characters tend to merge with others, borrowing, as it were, their identities and in some cases their destinies as well. I have already shown that, through the image of fire at her death, Barbie Batchelor may be said to have become Edwina Crane, though it would be more accurate to say that Edwina becomes Barbie, since her ideals, her disillusionment, and her capacity for love continue and in a way are fulfilled in Barbie. In the most striking example of this interchange of identities Perron, who has been so much preoccupied with the story of Daphne and Hari Kumar, after making love to Sarah Layton for the first time in a place known as the Moghul Room (echoes of Bibighar), is haunted by the echo of a statement from Hari Kumar's testimony ("We haven't seen each other since the night we visited the temple")[30] and observes, "While buttoning the cuffs a trick of light made my hands seem brown."[31] Immediately after this, there follows a passage in which Perron experiences, as though he were Hari, the attack by the rapists on Hari, whom they force to watch as they rape Daphne, and afterward Hari's conversation with Daphne. Indeed, except for a reference to the Moghul Room, we might simply assume that the passage was an interpolation from another place and time, a straightforward flashback, instead of a near-preternatural transference of experience, a haunting, or kind of possession.

The most elaborately developed interchange of identities is that of Daphne and Sarah. There are clear differences between them, and they are obviously not meant to be interchangeable, but their awareness, their common sense, their fairness of spirit, and even their physical resemblance are meant to make Sarah continue where Daphne left off, just as Barbie will extend the role and sensibilities of Edwina Crane. Because of these similarities between the two young women, it is not surprising that Sarah will become fascinated by the Bibighar mystery and the fate of Daphne and Hari Kumar, nor is it surprising that she alone of her family feels no repugnance toward the child of that unhappy couple and will make the visit, a symbolic pilgrimage of loving recognition, from the Layton houseboat to that of Lady Manners. So also we are allowed to follow in much greater detail than in Daphne's case Sarah's liberation from the smug and blind traditions of her family and the general racial intolerance of her class.

What might be termed Sarah's salvation is narrated against the background of her family's general decline. Her mother, Mildred Layton, and her sister, Susan, represent two stages in the collapse of the Raj. Mildred has a strong sense of holding up the tradition, keeping up appearances, and a fierce intolerance of anyone who does not, all the while she herself indulges in desperate drinking and the loveless love affair with Kevin Coley. As Mabel Layton sees it, the memsahibs care only about "representing." " 'Even when we're alone we're on show, aren't we, representing something? They come to make sure I'm still here and that we're all representing it together.' "[32] And while the future of the memsahibs becomes more and more doubtful, the women of Pankot "were in the habit of dropping in to make sure Mabel was still there and representing what had to be represented."[33] Mildred's blindness to the reality of her situation is best symbolized (a frequent device throughout Scott's work) by her relation to a place. After Mabel's death, when she is free to move back to Rose Cottage, Mildred Layton decides to restore it and discard its name so that it will be known, with delicious irony, as number 12 Club Road. "In restoring it to a likeness of its former self, Sarah knew her mother had intended to create a setting that would speak for itself and also for her and her family's claim on history through long connexion. . . . And she had succeeded, but at a cost. By cutting away inessentials, the accumulations of years, she had robbed the place of a quality that belonged to that accumulation, the quality of survival and the idea behind it—that survival meant change."[34] But as Scott has told us much earlier, Mildred's enemy was history, and we now see why. She goes on to commit the sacrilege of turning Mabel's rose garden, a universal symbol of love and innocence, into a tennis court, a symbol of discord and battle.

In a typical passage that demonstrates the crudeness and cruelty of the memsahibs' character, we find them complaining about the terms of Mabel's will, which has left a small annuity to Barbie.

"On top of which the estate has to fork out to buy an annuity for the woman and if she dies soon after it's bought it's hundreds of thousands of rupees wasted."

"Perhaps she won't live long enough for it to be bought at all," Nicky said. "Clarissa Peplow told me Captain Travers doesn't expect her to pull through."

"But she's been in hospital well over a week, nearly two, and she hasn't popped off yet. . . . Sarah says she only seems semi-conscious but reckons she's a tough old bird and will get over it. But whether she does or doesn't Mildred says the idea of an annuity could only have come from *her* because it's a typical lower-middle-class idea of upper-class security and respectability."[35]

Considering the situation of Mildred and her ilk, Perron writes in his notebook that for at least a half-century India has "played no part whatsoever in the lives of Englishmen in general," while "those who came out (those for whom England had to play a real part) became detached both from English life and from the English idea of life. Getting rid of India will cause us at home no qualm of conscience because it will be like getting rid of what is no longer reflected in our mirror of ourselves." But it will be sadder for "people like the Laytons," who "may now see nothing at all when looking in their mirror. Not even themselves? Not even a mirror?"[36]

Susan is more complex than her mother: she has, so to speak, less character and is made to suffer more. Comparing herself to Sarah, she says, "You're not like me. Whatever you do and wherever you go you'll always be yourself."[37] Her role as a member of a traditional Anglo-Indian military family is at the heart of her psychological problems. When Sarah tells her that it's nonsense to feel that she is merely a drawing that anyone can rub out, Susan tries to explain it.

"I felt it even when we were children in Ranpur and here, up in Pankot. I think it must have been something to do with the way Mummy and Daddy, everyone, were always talking about *home,* when we go home, when you go home. I knew 'home' was where people lived and I had this idea that in spirit I must be already there and that this explained why in Ranpur and Pankot I was just a drawing people could rub out. But when we got home it wasn't any better. It was worse. I wanted to tell someone but there was only you I could talk to and when I looked at you I felt you'd never understand because you didn't look and never looked like someone people could rub out."[38]

This sense of being without an identity, a self, makes inevitable her incapacity to love either of her husbands or her child. It is one of the ironies in the *Quartet* that she should marry Merrick, a man who despises her class for weakening the Raj and who, in any event, is unable to love her.

Mabel Layton, since the time she refused to contribute to the Dyer fund in 1919, has been considered hostile to the society of officers and memsahibs who represent the Raj in Pankot. Toward the end of her life, when she is unsociable at Susan's wedding party and leaves it without a word, people try to explain it away. But a point comes when this is impossible. "The truth could no longer be avoided. It had been a criticism of the foundations of the edifice, of the sense of duty which kept alive the senses of pride and loyalty and honour. It drew attention to a situation it was painful to acknowledge: that the god had left the temple, no one knew when, or how, or why. What one was left with were the rites which had once propitiated, once been obligatory, but were now meaningless because the god was no longer there to receive them."[39] It is this "critical" quality in Mabel that establishes her kinship with both Sarah and Barbie and helps to command Barbie's intense devotion. She has told Barbie of her wish to be buried in Ranpur beside her second husband (Sarah and Susan's grandfather). But Mildred and most of the others in Pankot consider this absurd, partly because to take Mabel's body down to Ranpur in the hot weather would be extremely inconvenient; so they conclude that Barbie has made it up or is hallucinating. Barbie tries heroically to accomplish her friend's wish, to no avail, and is insulted and abused for her pains. Her determination to carry out a wish she considers sacred is one of the strongest assertions of her belief in a spiritual reality that has nothing to do with the world of common sense. As with the Bundrens in Faulkner's *As I Lay Dying*, the intensity of her conviction defies reason, and after her near-fatal accident in the tonga, apparently in full possession of her senses, she announces, " 'I'm afraid there's been some trouble at the junction. Perhaps someone would kindly deal with it. I have seen the Devil. Have you a spade?' "[40] The "Devil" of course is Merrick and the spade for digging up Mabel Layton, but only Sarah, Barbie's friend, with compassionate intuition, understands this.

The accident, accompanied for Barbie by a great light, a giant explosion, anticipates her death on the day of Hiroshima but also looks back to Edwina. She is wearing, "like a bridal veil," the symbolic lace, with its fluttering, imprisoned embroidered butterflies, which Mabel had given her. The veil and the exploding lights remind one of Edwina's "suttee," the sacrificial self-immolation of the *sati,* the true wife. In this the two spinsters who "had never known the wilder secrets of life nor held the key to its deepest sensual pleasures,"[41] as Scott says of Barbie, are united in a different kind of loving. Both through their sacrifices have become seeresses of a sort. Their labors had embodied the highest ideals of the British mission, but neither can fulfill those ideals because, as both come to realize, it is nurtured on the usual colonialist self-delusion and upheld by unrelenting racial prejudice. That their love and compassion (and Barbie even feels compassion for Merrick at the end of their nerve-racking conversation) cannot prevail dooms the world inevitably to Partition riots, world wars, and Hiroshima. Among the unhappy wives of Pankot, Barbie is a kind of Cassandra, given the power to intuit and express what no one wants to hear and no one will believe.

And so it will be (Barbie thought) so it will be in regard to our experience here. And when we are gone let them colour the sky how they will. We shall not care. It has never truly been our desire or intention to colour it permanently but only to make it as cloudless for ourselves as we can. So that my life here has indeed been wasted because I have lived it as a transferred appendage, as a parlour maid, the first in line for morning prayers while the mistress of the house hastily covers herself with her wrap and kneels like myself in piety for a purpose. But we have no purpose that God would recognize as such, dress it up as we may by hastily closing our wrap to hide our nakedness and convey a distinction as Mildred did and still attempts. She has a kind of nobility. It does not seem to me to matter very much whether she appears half-dressed in front of Kevin Coley. But I think it matters to God and to the world that she rode with him into the valley and offered matriarchal wisdom to women older and as wise or wiser than she. For that was an arrogance, the kind which Mabel always set her face against, because Mabel knew she brought no consolation even to a rose let alone to a life. She brought none to me in the final count, but what distinguished her was her preknowledge that this was anyway impossible. So she probably forgives me about the grave and closes her eyes. It was not everyone who saw that they were open.[42]

Even more succinctly, when she faces Kevin Coley, she mocks "him not only for himself but for the whole condition. . . . The word was 'dead.' Dead. Dead. It didn't matter now who said it; the edifice had crumbled and the façade fooled nobody. One could

only pray for a wind to blow it all away or for an earthquake such
as Captain Coley's wife had died in. Barbie saw how perhaps
with one finger she might topple him, because there was nothing
to keep him standing except his own inertia."[43]

With Edwina, Mabel, and Barbie, those apostles of sacred love
in a violent and profane world, one must also rank Sister Ludmila.
This mysterious personage, perhaps French, perhaps German,
perhaps Hungarian, but probably Russian, has established a
sanctuary in Mayapore where she cares for the sick and homeless.
She acknowledges no religion and is frowned on by the established
churches. Later in life she becomes blind, fulfilling one of the traditions of the seeress. Significantly, it is to her that Scott gives
the first first-hand account about the relationship of Daphne and
Hari Kumar: she is the only one at the time to appreciate their
moral courage and moral intelligence. And she is the first to gain
an accurate insight into Ronald Merrick. There is nothing in the
least mysterious about her apparently uncanny knowledge: she
is both intuitive and a particularly keen observer. At a time when
Merrick's presumably still latent homosexuality is divined by no
one, Sister Ludmila notes that Merrick watches Hari Kumar "the
way later I saw Kumar watched on other occasions."[44] These other
occasions are when she observes European women watching him.
She grasps at once Merrick's anger that an Indian like Kumar is
far better-looking than himself (and even "in the western way"),
but, more than this, it is Hari Kumar's perfect upper-class English
accent that enrages Merrick. "For in Merrick's voice there was a
different tone, a tone regulated by care and ambition rather than
by upbringing."[45] She very quickly establishes the link in Merrick
between sexual desire (and sexual envy) and racial feeling. In her
words:

For he had long ago chosen Hari Kumar, chosen him as a victim, having
stood and watched him washing at the pump, and afterwards taken him
away for questioning, to observe more closely the darkness that attracted
the darkness in himself. A different darkness, but still a darkness. On
Kumar's part a darkness of the soul. On Merrick's a darkness of the mind
and heart and flesh. And again, but in an unnatural context, the attraction
of white to black, the attraction of an opposite, of someone this time who
had perhaps never even leapt into the depths of his own private compulsion, let alone into those of life or of the world at large, but had stood
high and dry on the sterile banks, thicketed around with his own secrecy
and also with the prejudice he had learned because he was one of the
white men in control of a black man's country.[46]

The "sterile banks" remind us of her advice to "jump in," quoted in the epigraph to this chapter, the course of action taken by both Daphne and Hari, the necessary action because, as Sister Ludmila says, there is no bridge between the place of the white and the place of the black, no bridge over the mile-wide river separating them where flow "the dark currents of human conflict, even after Bibighar was destroyed, a current whose direction might be traced by following the route taken by the girl running in darkness from one to the other."[47]

This leads me to a further consideration of Ronald Merrick. I have suggested earlier that Scott seems to have stacked the cards against him. He is certainly treated very harshly by fate, but it is to Scott's credit that we never question that it could be otherwise, given Merrick's personality and profession. As always fascinated by the relation between a man's work and his total significance, Scott discovers in the various personalities engaged in running the Raj a remarkably rich and varied field for his study. He *seems* at times to admire unabashedly the work the British have done.

> To leave the narrow streets and crowded chowks behind and enter the area once distinguished by the title Civil Lines, an area of broad avenues and spacious bungalows in walled compounds which culminates in the palladian grandeur of Government House, the Secretariat and the Legislative Assembly; to continue, still in an easterly direction, past the maidan, the government college, the hospital and film studios and enter the cantonment, which someone once described as Aldershot with trees planted to provide shade instead of cut down to make room, is to pass from one period of history to another and to feel that the people from the small and distant island of Britain who built and settled here were attempting to express in the architectural terms that struck them as suitable their sense of freedom at having space around them at last, a land with length and breadth to it that promised ideal conditions for concrete and abstract proof of their extraordinary talent for running things and making them work. And yet here too there is an atmosphere of circumscription, of unexpected limits having been reached and recognized, and quietly, sensibly settled for. Too late to reduce the scale and crowd everything together, each road and building has an air of being turned inwards on itself to withstand a siege.[48]

As one reads this passage, the subtle ironies become only gradually apparent, initiated by "Aldershot with trees," for of course it is not Aldershot, and India is not anybody else's country. Inevitably, a basic and essential guilt must attend all that Britain has done in India and all those who have made it possible, an anomalous situation that is, finally, perfectly defined by the wonderful image of the defeat of British aspirations and delusions of benef-icence: "to withstand a siege."

At one point Daphne defines the British judicial system in India as a "blundering judicial robot. We can't stop it working. It works for us even when we least want it to. We created it to prove how fair, how civilized we are. But it is a white robot and it can't dis-tinguish between love and rape. It only exists to punish crime."[49] Ronald Merrick is the perfectly appropriate instrument for this system in the *Quartet;* he is not a robot but rather a man who finds his own destiny perfectly realized by working for the robot, which allows him ample room to explore and exploit his own sa-distic proclivities. The only possible axes for a relationship are contempt and envy (mingled with fear), he tells Hari Kumar, and excoriates the present-day representatives of the Raj for pretending they do not feel contempt for the Indians. "The permutations of English corruption in India were endless—affection for servants, for peasants, for soldiers, pretence at understanding the Indian intellectual or at sympathizing with nationalist aspirations, but all this affection and understanding was a corruption of what he called the calm purity of their contempt."[50] Hari Kumar is able to admire the clarity with which Merrick expresses himself and, still more, Merrick's willingness to gamble to the limit in the "game," as he considers it, with the real possibility of getting himself into serious trouble.

Scott has skillfully delayed the long and painful interrogation of Hari Kumar by Captain Rowan, in which so much is revealed about Merrick, until well along in the second volume of the *Quar-tet,* following the events, in which Merrick plays his somewhat enigmatic role, in Mirat at the time of Susan's wedding to Teddie Bingham. In this way we are allowed to see him—despite Sister Ludmila's shrewd analysis, much of which is not completely clear until the interrogation—in several different lights: he is coura-geous, he can be kind to people (Daphne finds), he can appear lonely and vulnerable to Sarah, he can be the victim of the mean-spirited snobbery of a class he has reason not to love (Sarah's Aunt Fenny says of him, "I don't suppose Captain Merrick's family would bear close inspection. But he's quite the little gentleman, isn't he, and terribly efficient over detail. That's a sign of humble origin, too"[51]). The gradual revelation of his sadism is all the more chilling, particularly when one realizes, with Hari Kumar, that he is absolutely convinced of the rightness of what he is doing.

Scott clearly intends the Bibighar affair to symbolize two things, the obvious problems of the British-Indian relationship, and at a more universal level, the difficulty, human failings being as complex and apparently incorrigible as they are, of making love prevail or even survive in the world. With respect to the first of these, one notes how frequently Scott will suggest the way Bibighar stands for more than the disastrous events in the gardens on the night of 8 August. After hearing the interrogation of Hari Kumar relating to that night, Lady Manners feels that she has been "vouchsafed a vision of the future they were all headed for. At its heart was the rumbling sound of martial music. It was a vision because the likeness of it would happen."[52] Even the horror of the Partition massacres is related to it by Scott's favorite recurring image of a girl running: in *A Division of the Spoils*, boldly anticipating the massacres and Ahmed's fate early in the novel, he describes the situation, referring to Ahmed only as "the victim." "The victim chose neither the time nor the place of his death but in going to it as he did he must have seen that he contributed something of his own to its manner; and this was probably his compensation; so that when the body falls it will seem to do so without protest and without asking for any explanation of the thing that has happened to it, as if all that has gone before is explanation enough, so that it will not fall to the ground so much as out of a history which began with a girl stumbling on steps at the end of a long journey through the dark."[53] In the Bibighar affair both English and Indian are inevitably victims. In this case Ronald Merrick seems to represent not only British justice gone awry but the failure of the whole myth of Imperial benefaction. In him we see a microcosm of the Raj unmasked as hypocritically rapacious, guilty of brutal injustice and rape.[54] As so often in the *Quartet*, human error is associated with sexual error, that is, sexuality that is devoid of love and full instead of a lust for possession; a sexuality, also, that is most often not understood by those it drives. When Barbie calls Merrick the prince of darkness, she is not raving: Merrick is the personification of all the profane power in the world, a terrifying totalitarian intellect gifted with the mechanically perfect logic of hate and the capacity to destroy but not to create. He is also faintly comic, "high and dry on the sterile banks," in his inability, which amounts almost to stupidity, to comprehend the nature (or even the reality) of love and compassion, and ultimately pathetic as he stands so far outside the human circle of those who, to quote Daphne Manners, "trust because of the affection. You trust after you have learned to love."[55] Here one thinks too of Guy Perron's comment on "the comic dilemma of the *raj*—the dilemma of men who hoped to inspire trust but couldn't even trust themselves."[56] But though he is monstrous, Merrick is not unreal, and he and others like him exercise a disproportionately influential role in history—which seems to be an obsessive concern of many of the characters in the *Quartet*, whatever history may be.

As commonly understood, history is incapable of making sense (or, better, discovering the significance) of the Bibighar affair. This brings us to the question of what Bibighar means on the larger scale of human experience not confined or measured by the particular history of the last days of British India. For Scott, history, at times, seems be no more than the record of the cyclical repetition of human error. Pondering the paradoxes inherent in the conflict of Hari Kumar and Merrick, Perron reflects, "And yet how logical that meeting was, between Kumar—one of Macaulay's 'brown-skinned Englishmen'—and Merrick, English-born and English-bred, but a man whose country's social and economic structure had denied him advantages and privileges which Kumar had initially enjoyed; a man, moreover, who lacked entirely that liberal instinct which is so dear to historians that they lay it out like a guideline through the unmapped forests of prejudice and self-interest as though this line, and not the forest, is our history."[57] So history, unable to explain Bibighar—unlike an art such as fiction—will itself become a metaphor in Scott's strategy for coming to grips with that larger scale of human experience reflected by the private lives he has invented.

When Colonel Layton returns home to his family after years of imprisonment in Germany, we witness the happening through Sarah's eyes. But Sarah tends to see it in general rather than particular terms: the characters are described as husband, wife, grandson, and so on. It is all a "scene." "Beside her mother and sister she felt travel-stained, dowdy in her uniform, excluded from the scene: from what she recognized *as* a scene—for all its appearance of evolving naturally from a sequence of haphazard events."[58] Perhaps history then is no more than a succession of haphazard events leading to scenes that lead to more haphazard events. Any further organization may be no more than the imposition of the historian or the fiction writer, with their need for shape and order. But earlier, when learning of Teddie Bingham's death in Burma, Sarah has recognized a difference: scenes repeat themselves cyclically. "The situation was familiar. It had all happened before—people on a veranda and herself returning to join them. How many cycles had they lived through then, how many times had the news of Teddie's death been broken? How many times had Susan been taken indoors—almost dragged, stiffly resistant—in her mother's arms, while Mrs. Fosdick and Mrs. Paynton stood like silent supervisors of an ancient ritual concerning women's grief?"[59]

Sister Ludmila had earlier expressed a different concept of cyclical history when, in *The Jewel in the Crown*, she talks about the dancing Shiva and the cycle of creation, preservation, and destruction,[60] what she terms "a wholeness." While she talks to the unknown researcher about the story of Daphne Manners, she says that from his voice she can tell that "the word Bibighar is not an end in itself or descriptive of a case that can be opened as at such and such an hour and closed on such and such a day."

Permit me, too, a further observation? That given the material evidence there is also in you an understanding that a specific historical event has no definite beginning, no satisfactory end? It is as if time were telescoped? Is that the right word? As if time were telescoped and space dovetailed? As if Bibighar almost had not happened yet, and yet has happened, so that at once past, present and future are contained in your cupped palm. The route you came, the gateway you entered, the buildings you saw here in the Sanctuary—they are to me in spite of the new fourth building, the same route I took, the same building I returned to when I brought the limp body of young Mr. Coomer back to the Sanctuary.[61]

Sister Ludmila is talking about an Indian concept in which reality is outside time (like the reality of art, described as *extratemporelle*, in Proust's *Le Temps retrouvé*), since time itself, though it may be an "ineluctable modality" for the conception of events, is part of the *māyā*, the world, which we are obliged to take for at least qualifiedly real, and hence another illusion. But as Swinden points out, Sister Ludmila's idea of time also serves as the basis for Scott's technique, which depends heavily on the violation of linear time in favor of constructing a narrative that shoots ahead or curves back at will through past, present, and future.[62] This in itself is not unusual: the novelist stands at a point above his material, as on the apex of a cone, which lies before him complete, so that he may introduce any part of that material at any time he wishes without consideration of chronology. One thinks of *Nostromo* or *Eyeless in Gaza* or, in miniature, the "Wandering Rocks" episode in *Ulysses*. What is most interesting in Scott's treatment is that the narration always comes back to one particular moment, the events in the Bibighar Gardens and their immediate aftermath.

In *The Towers of Silence*, Barbie Batchelor begins reading Emerson, a volume of whose essays she has taken from the library for Mabel by mistake. " 'If the whole of history is one man,' she read, 'it is all to be explained from individual experience. There is a relation between the hours of our life and the centuries of time.' "[63] Through Emerson the philosophical life "impinged on her own like the shadow of a hunched bird of prey patiently observing below it the ritual of survival. It should have been an angel."[64] (In a way typical of him, Scott also anticipates in this passage Barbie's death in the hospital near the Parsi Tower of Silence, where the vultures consume the proffered corpses.) Pondering these lines of Emerson, Barbie comes to feel that "in her own experience lay an explanation not only of history but of the lives of other living people, therefore an explanation of the things that had happened to Edwina and to Miss Manners of whom she had only the vaguest picture."[65] So the consideration of history inspires this unlikely philosopher-historian to intuitions of the truth about Edwina Crane and Daphne Manners as well as the delusions that have determined her own career in India, intuitions about the events in the *Quartet* as profound as Scott allows any of his characters to have.

When Emerson writes, "Man is explicable by nothing less than all his history," the line that first captures Barbie's imagination,[66] he is talking about something impossible to acquire, except in fiction, where whatever history is given is all there is. Barbie later comes to reject Emerson. "She thought: Emerson was wrong, we're not explained by our history at all, in fact it's our history that gets in the way of a lucid explanation of us."[67] But as she imagines her history and other people's blowing away like leaves, "it occurred to her that among the leaves were her religious principles and beliefs." Turning then from abstract historical considerations, Barbie begins her series of "imaginary silences," spells during which she does not know if she has talked aloud or not, or even exactly what she has been thinking, but which lead to surprising new insights about Sarah, Merrick, and the mysterious figure of "the unknown Indian: dead in one aspect, alive in another,"[68] a figure who represents to her what her whole life in India has been about.

In *A Division of the Spoils*, Guy Perron, who is to become a professor of history, is already, at this point in his life, profoundly concerned with understanding the historical process (or processes). We have seen earlier how his understanding of Merrick is cast in a historical perspective. Merrick, he says, is "the unrecorded man, one of the kind of men we really are."[69] Like Barbie, Perron is interested in Emerson and, like her, tends to reject his theories. He quotes him and, coming back as usual to Merrick, refutes him. " 'Society is a wave. The wave moves onward, but the water of which it is composed does not. The same particle does not rise from the valley to the ridge. Its unity is phenomenal. The persons who make up a nation today next year die, and their experience with them.' Emerson failed to see that there were exceptions. People like you and me."[70] He goes on to explain that when the wave moves forward, people like himself and Rowan, to whom he is talking, move with it, while people like Merrick, with their limited outlook on class and institutions, fail to move, and "get drowned."[71] Furthermore, history seems to be made up of a series of unrecorded and unperceived responsibilities (or one could say irresponsibilities). For example, he is unable to make his Aunt Charlotte (who has never come to India) understand that she, like himself, is responsible for the one-quarter million deaths in the Panjab and other places in India. When he asks her who is responsible she replies, " 'But that is obvious. The people who attacked and killed each other.' "[72] But for Perron the ignorance and indifference of the English at home has been of overwhelming importance in British-Indian affairs. This is yet another step in his growing conviction that history is irrelevant to individuals, their aspirations, and usually their destinies. He had earlier been disturbed by the sight of Colonel Layton's bush-shirt hanging on the back of a chair. The bush-shirt, which no longer fits the colonel after his long imprisonment, is too big for the chair and cannot be made to look "perky." The way it hangs, Perron thinks, "ostensibly in possession of chair, room, suggested a claim to occupation, but . . . a claim made in awareness of the insecurity of any tenure. . . . The bush-shirt began to depress him; it was threatening to undermine his confidence in much the same way that the whole experience of being in India had so often seemed on the point of undermining it. Staring at the bush-shirt, on a perch it clung to which did not properly support it, he was struck by its mute indication of the grand irrelevance of history to the things that people wanted for themselves."[73]

The dark view of human history that seems to emerge from Perron's musings is never precisely codified as he considers various events and personages and interpretations. But it seems, ultimately, not to be so far removed from the lines, quoted earlier, with which Farrell concludes *The Siege of Krishnapur*,[74] and one is led to remember Conrad's pessimistic judgment. "The ethical view of the universe involves us at last in so many cruel and absurd contradictions, where the last vestige of faith, hope, charity, and even of reason itself, seem ready to perish, that I have come to suspect that the aim of creation is not ethical at all."[75]

As I have mentioned earlier, the history of Mayapore's past, like its present, is made up of rumor, gossip, unverifiable legends, myth. No one will ever be able to establish for certain which version, if any, of the past of the MacGregor House and the Bibighar is true. Similarly, the Bibighar affair will pass into history incomplete, inaccurate, tangled; even some of the participants will never be certain of everything that happened. The circumstances of Merrick's death are deliberately revised, and so recorded; Mabel Layton's wish for burial in Ranpur is not credited and her severe judgment of her step-daughter-in-law and the memsahibs discreetly forgotten. Even when someone stumbles close to the truth (Mackay's version of Bibighar), no one will believe him. "They," "one," "people" tend to accept wrong versions and perpetuate them—one thinks of Proust's *A la recherche du temps perdu*, where the Duchesse de Guermantes is regarded as an intellect, Vinteuil as a provincial organist of no account, and Charlus as a womanizer.

The kind of history that most profoundly engages Paul Scott's concern and forms the central theme of the *Quartet* is the spiritual record of individuals for whom "history," as we usually think of it—the fate of nations and the end of empires, the sweeping movements and transformations of societies and their institutions—is secondary to their spiritual pilgrimages. Scott titles one section of *A Division of the Spoils* "Journeys into Uneasy Distances"—the evolution of different kinds of loving; or the failure of love to evolve at all; or the way an individual defines his place in the world, whether he sees the world beginning and ending with himself or considers his own existence as merely a fragment, or manifestation, of some greater realm of being. The capacity for these journeys, these discoveries and evolutions, will be affected by the history of nations and societies, but history is not their source—the contrary, rather, is true. This is why Scott will devote so much of the *Quartet*, including virtually all of *The Towers of Silence*, to such considerations; nothing else will justify the pivotal significance he attaches to Barbie Batchelor, who, regarded from the wise world's point of view, is only a half-crazy elderly spinster schoolteacher. And this is why in *Staying On* (1977) he will return to a consideration of other "insignificant" personages for whom history is, after all, no more than a noise in the street, as irrelevant as Colonel Layton's bush-shirt draped and drooping over the back of a chair.

In Proust, time is redeemed through art and the mystical experience of *"mémoire involontaire."* Is there no redemption, even symbolically, in the *Quartet?* Scott carefully excludes the conventional "happy ending," the marriage of Guy Perron and Sarah Layton, saving its revelation for *Staying On,* where it is conveyed to the reader in a casual reference. The Partition massacres that climax in the final pages provide an overwhelmingly depressing instance of futility and unreason. And by this time we have forgotten Parvati, as Scott perhaps meant us to. But Parvati is a surprisingly vital, or durable image of innocence restored, a promising musical artist at the end of *The Jewel in the Crown,* the new flower of the ravaged garden. And since time is circular in the *Quartet,* it need not matter what page she appears on: her reality is assured. Again, a Proustian comparison may be useful. Toward the end of *A la recherche du temps perdu,* the narrator is moved by his meeting with "mademoiselle de Saint-Loup," the daughter of his old friends Gilberte Swann and Robert de Saint-Loup. The marriage of Gilberte and Saint-Loup represents the union of several conflicting elements—aristocrat and bourgeois, homosexual and heterosexual, Christian and Jew—just as the marriage of Gilberte's own parents suggests another blending of the worlds of banker and demimondaine, while Swann himself is a hybrid, a connoisseur of art sprung from mercantile origins. When the narrator meets Mlle de Saint-Loup, he finds that "time, colorless and unseizable had, so that I might so to speak see it and touch it, been materialized in her, shaped her like a masterpiece."[76] She presents a remarkable parallel to the heroines of Shakespeare's late romances, those innocent (and inviolable) girls whose purity and beauty redeem and, as it were, justify the sins of their parents; and, as Shakespeare makes clear, their very existence depends on their parents' fall from innocence. Scott does not go this far in introducing Parvati, the daughter of Daphne Manners and Hari Kumar, although her name has a resonance that subtly suggests "Perdita." Parvati will grow up as an Indian and an artist, a singer in the classical Hindustani (North Indian) tradition with every chance for a happy life before her. After the conclusion of *The Jewel in the Crown,* Scott does not refer to her again except as the crying infant on the houseboat in Kashmir. At the end of *The Jewel in the Crown,* we see her for the last time as a person, on her way to her music lesson. "One day, perhaps, Parvati will also sing in those western capitals, and then become a *guru* herself, instructing a new generation of girls in the formal complexities of the songs her English mother once described as the only music in the world she knew that sounded conscious of breaking silence and going back into it when it was finished."[77] Scott follows this by quoting, in translation, a poignant folksong in an eastern Hindi dialect. "Oh, my father's servants, bring my palanquin. I am going to the land of my husband. All my companions are scattered. They have gone to different homes."[78] Just as Mlle de Saint-Loup is a fusion of diverse elements, so Parvati reconciles in herself Britain and India, the old colonial family and the provincial orthodox Hindu, and, presumably, will one day bring to England her performances of a traditional Indian art, successfully bridging "the dark currents of a human conflict." And this, I think, is as much consolation as Scott is willing to allow us: it is perhaps all that is possible and it may suffice.

I have shown how Scott takes all the stock material of the Anglo-Indian novel—India and sex, the transposed racial identity, the value of the British mission (the white man's burden), India's power to confer illumination as well as to destroy—and transforms it into highly original fiction. In one area alone it may be said that his success is more limited: the creation of interesting Indian characters. When you survey the entire *Quartet,* you will observe that there are, after all, very few Indians around. Hari Kumar is only genetically and nominally an Indian; in every other respect he is a public school Englishman who does not even realize he is Indian, or what it means to be Indian, until he returns to the country he left when he was two years old. He is an interesting, complex conception, but his responses, his attitudes, his feelings, his way of thinking all stem from the environment in which he was educated. There are, to be sure, the members of the Kasim family, but one does not, I feel, even have to compare them with the immensely more richly conceived English characters to realize that they are noble bores, one and all, weak moments in an otherwise masterful succession of portraits. The Kasims are supremely "historical" figures, necessary to fill out the political background of the end of the Raj. Only Ahmed may be said to have some soul. In presenting them, Scott abandons his usually dependable irony and humor, and his imagination becomes somehow merely conventional. His most successful realization of an Indian is probably Lady Chatterjee, who, with her strongly English speech (the colloquialisms slightly exaggerated, Mayfair of the twenties phantasmally present in every sentence) is an affectionate characterization of certain educated Indian women of her generation, the wives of aristocrats, generals, and social reformers whom Scott came to know well during his visits to India. But again, it is an Anglicized personality that makes Lady Chatterjee emerge convincingly in Scott's characterization. In dealing with a more typical Indian, Scott has a fine ironic moment, the passage describing Hari Kumar's father's first impressions of England. "In England he had often been cold, miserable and shy, and not infrequently dismayed by the dirt, squalor and poverty, the sight of barefoot children, ragged beggars, drunken women, and evidence of cruelty to animals and humans: sins which in India only Indians were supposed to be capable of committing or guilty of allowing."[79] An Indian shocked by beggars and squalor in England—splendid material indeed for an ironist, and one wishes Scott had devoted a full-scale work to developing the theme. In his portraits of Indians he is probably closest to the mark in *Staying On,* where, in the Bhoolaboys, he shows, both more profoundly and more cuttingly even than Ruth Jhabvala, yet without caricature, the crassness, mediocrity of spirit, and desperate materialism of the new commercial class that has attained importance in India after the end of the Raj.

In *Staying On* (1977), his last novel, Scott offers a post-Raj look at the Smalleys, minor characters in the *Quartet.* In the section entitled "An Evening at the Club" in *The Jewel in the Crown,* he had already given a sometimes satirical glance at the English in India after 1947, their snobberies and the way they represent "new sahibs and memsahibs." But these were newcomers to India, unlike the Smalleys; here the treatment becomes sometimes comic, sometimes elegiac, sometimes tragic. *Staying On* is a brilliant novel, one of Scott's most beautifully sustained performances, a genuinely Chekhovian tragicomedy. In this work India as a "problem" ceases to matter; the more elemental problem of love uncommunicated and mostly incommunicable provides the central theme.

Staying On ties up many of the plot strands left hanging in the *Quartet*. We learn of Sarah's marriage to Guy Perron, Susan's third marriage, the death of Colonel Layton, and so on. We also find many ironic echoes of the Raj and its significance. "There really wasn't a single aspect of the nice civilized things in India which didn't reflect something of British influence. Colonel Menektara had impeccable English manners, as did his wife who was in many ways as big a bitch as Mildred Layton had been, but this comforted Lucy since it indicated continuity of civilized behaviour, and as the wife of a retired colonel herself she was in a position to give delicately as good as she delicately got which meant that she and Coocoo Menektara understood one another perfectly."[80]

Mrs. Menektara is one of the Indian characters who represent the new, successful middle-class entrepreneurs, viewed by Lucy Smalley as "wheelers and dealers who with their chicanery, their corrupt practices, their black money, their utter indifference to the state of the nation, their use of political power for personal gain were ruining the country or if not ruining it making it safe chiefly for themselves: a hierarchy within a hierarchy, with the Mrs. Bhoolabhoys at its base and at its peak people like the Desais, who had been nothing, were now as rich as Croesus and marrying their daughter into the family of a minister who himself had become rich by putting a price on his department's favours."[81] Descending from the theoretical to the concrete, Lucy reflects on Mrs. Desai, "who's always going to and fro between Delhi, Zurich, London, Paris and New York and comes back loaded with stuff from the duty free shops and other stuff that if she doesn't smuggle in must cost her a fortune at the customs."[82]

But Mrs. Desai is nothing compared to the formidable Mrs. Bhoolabhoy, who weighs 220 pounds and moves like a galleon. Mrs. Bhoolabhoy owns Smith's Hotel and its annex, known as the Lodge, where the Smalleys live. Motivated by a demonic greed, she has decided to join forces with the owners of the new glass-and-concrete Hotel Shiraz. She forces her husband to write a letter to the Smalleys announcing their eviction and thus provokes Tusker Smalley's fatal heart attack. The theme of eviction and the desperate concern over where to live reminds us of Barbie Batchelor's predicament and even evokes, faintly and at a mundane level, the origin of the Bibighar and the MacGregor House. Mrs. Bhoolabhoy is painted with broad Dickensian strokes: she is monstrous, but she makes us laugh the more we are shown both her absurdity and her viciousness. Even the malice of Scott's portrayal does not depress but is rather a source of pleasure; in keeping with the characteristic technique of the great novelistic tradition to which Scott belongs, Mrs. Bhoolabhoy, already immense, is not diminished but magnified for our wonder and enjoyment.

Typical also of that tradition is Scott's way of giving each of the characters, even the minor ones, an opportunity to speak for himself, or to act in some significant way before us for our objective and honest consideration, thereby teaching us, as the best novelists do, that to himself the most minor personage is the center of his own universe, our equal no matter how lowly he may appear.

The Bhoolabhoys and the other minor characters, who would have provided the entire stuff of a satirical novel, are in fact mere background against which to dramatize the retirement and old age of the Smalleys. In the *Quartet,* Lucy Smalley, condemned by her past as a stenographer to be at the bottom of the memsahibs' pecking order, is nevertheless the most astute woman among them, the only one who understands, at least in part, that the reason Sarah does not fit in is because she does not take them, their mission, the Raj, seriously. In *Staying On,* like so many of Scott's major characters, she appears as a woman tormented by concern over the ultimate significance of her life, and particularly her relationship to her husband, and the way his career and their retirement in India have both enhanced and darkened their chance to be happy. Starved for an assurance of some meaning in her life and the reality of Tusker's love, she lives at times in a world of socially acceptable fantasy, the movies. She holds imaginary conversations with characters, personified by her dog, from films like *The African Queen,* and she recounts in her mind past events in the history of Pankot, with a new view of the Laytons, Barbie, and others from the *Quartet*, to young Mr. Turner, whose visit she is expecting but whom she has never met.

In her interior monologues, her reminiscences, her letters (both real and imagined), and even her long addresses to Tusker full of reproaches and conjured memories, Lucy Smalley is an artist. In one form or another she will not stop talking. The unstoppable flow of her speech and thoughts is eloquent and potent in conveying the intensity of her feelings, and represents a triumph of art over circumstance—the only victory she can have in her tragic situation. Her remembrances of her early life in England sometimes lyrical, sometimes painful in their honesty, are marked by remarkable vividness; her interpretations of the past are acute and imaginative, an ideal history. Her art is not highly metaphorical, though she often wrings a simile out of sun and clouds, light and shadow. " 'We are people in shadow, Ibrahim,' she said, then stopped her slow pacing and glanced up at the glass and concrete structure that had helped put them there. 'And the dew does not so much nourish us as aggravate our rheumatism and our tempers.' "[83] Her style is devastatingly plain, even conventional, but bent to a ruthless confrontation with the truth, though ironically it most often finds expression in her fantasy conversations, as when she imagines telling young Mr. Turner, when he shows up, about Sarah.

> "Sometimes she seemed to be laughing at us, and it suddenly occurs to me that this may have been why she got on well with Tusker when she worked for him at Area headquarters because if you listen to Tusker now you begin to suspect that he was laughing too because really he hasn't a good word to say nowadays about anything connected with the past and this sometimes makes me feel, Mr. Turner, that my whole life has been a lie, mere play-acting, and I am not at all sure, Mr. Turner, if when you turn up and turn out to be self-reliant and young and buoyant and English and light-hearted and enthusiastic about your researches but look as if you will go home laughing at us like a drain that I shall be able to stand you, even though I yearn for you because simply by being here in this house you will be the catalyst I need to bring me back into my own white skin which day by day, week by week, month by month, year after year, I have felt to be increasingly incapable of containing me, let alone of acting as defensive armour."[84]

At the end she is destitute except for her art. With her husband's death she is left impoverished in an alien land, patronized now by servants and Eurasians. After a last imaginary conversation with Mr. Turner, she takes her brandy into the bathroom and sits on her "throne," as she terms it, next to one that was Tusker's. It is a daring strategy for Scott to end his novel with its most poignant moment set in so incongruous (some might think indecorous) a place; but the setting in no way detracts from but rather enhances the touching quality of Lucy's monologue. "Waiting on other people's verandahs for tongas, then, too, you took my arm, and in that way we waited. Arm in arm. Arm in arm. Throne by throne. What now, Tusker? Urn by urn?"[85] The combination of pathos (the words) and bathos (the setting) functions beautifully to reassert the tragic and comic elements of the novel, which are so inextricably woven together. Lucy, alone, manages to voice the melancholy longing of a generation of unimportant British colonials, committed hopelessly to India, when she says at the conclusion: "But now, until the end, I shall be alone, whatever I am doing, here as I feared, amid the alien corn, waking, sleeping, alone for ever and ever and I cannot bear it but mustn't cry and must must get over it but don't for the moment see how, so with my eyes shut, Tusker, I hold out my hand, and beg you, Tusker, beg, beg you to take it and take me with you. How can you not, Tusker? Oh, Tusker, Tusker, Tusker, how can you make me stay here by myself while you yourself go home?"[86]

In his treatment of the final days of the Raj, Scott has—incidentally, so to speak—presented a striking justification of the novel genre (in an era when it is said to be dying) as opposed to what is generally called history. His fiction, nourished by a remarkable objectivity and honesty and served by a highly original and refined novelistic skill, explores universal human potentialities and destinies for which history can provide only a deplorably inadequate record. Like the worlds portrayed in the best novels of the great European tradition, his is a world for us to wonder at, and this alone sets him apart from his contemporaries who have been challenged to make India their theme. His quality as a novelist appears to be in direct proportion to the quality of his personal relationship with India, a relationship he has summed up when he describes himself as one of those "in the West who have followed India's varying fortunes with affection and exasperation, admiration and nostalgia, and who maintain an overriding belief in her ability to plough the furrows we never plowed, and plough them straight, in the way (at our best) we imagined them."[87]

7

Kamala Markandaya and the Novel of Reconciliation

"He has never really recovered. . . . Some people have not been able to . . . it affects everyone, when a country is occupied. Both sides, I mean, overlords as much as inhabitants, it seems to twist them out of shape, out of any recognizable human shape. They ask, or at least their compatriots do, how could I do these things? How could such things happen? And nobody knows the answer."
                                        KAMALA MARKANDAYA[1]

"People aren't different, in the things that matter."
                                        KAMALA MARKANDAYA[2]

Like Ruth Jhabvala, Kamala Markandaya has become increasingly preoccupied in her fiction with the British involvement in India, both before and after Independence, but unlike Jhabvala she has mellowed rather than soured with time. Six of her ten novels to date treat of the relations of Indians and English, both in India and in Britain. Markandaya, married to an Englishman, has made her home in England for most of her adult life—a sort of mirror image of Jhabvala's experience. Her foreign residence distinguishes her from most other Indo-Anglian novelists, and the subtlety and elegance of her style marks her off from all but one or two of them (Anita Desai is the other most notable exception). Whereas Paul Scott triumphantly refashions the traditional themes of the Anglo-Indian novel into a unique masterpiece, Markandaya, in her most recent novels, ignores that material to dramatize the relations of Briton and Indian in an altogether new light.

Markandaya is best known for her first novel, *Nectar in a Sieve* (1954), a story of hard times and famine in South India. The novel has little to do with the international theme that will, as with Jhabvala, come to dominate her later work. The somewhat idealized portrait of Kennington, the English doctor, gives little promise of the subtly conceived English characters in *The Golden Honeycomb* and *Shalimar,* although Markandaya's fascination with construction projects and their effect upon traditional life-styles is already evident in the description of, first, a tannery, and later, a hospital.

Her second novel, *Some Inner Fury* (1956), is concerned with the love affair of a young Indian woman and an Englishman. Although the novel is set mainly in the troubled years of Indian agitation for independence (probably 1942 and 1943) the personal relations of Indians and Westerners described in it are curiously devoid of interracial or intercultural tension. The only moment when Markandaya alludes to any such problem is toward the end of the novel when the Indian heroine, the narrator, has to testify in defense of her foster brother, who is accused (presumably falsely) of murdering her brother; at this point she wonders whether her word will be believed against an Englishman's. Before any judicial decision is made, a mob bursts into the courtroom and spirits the foster brother away, so the point is left hanging. *Some Inner Fury* is a bad romantic novel, tending to vagueness and fine writing in its failed account of troubled personal relations; the vagueness extends even to the resolution of the story: the lovers are separated by the crisis, and—one judges by the opening of the novel, which sets up the flashback—they will not be reunited, though this is not certain and in any case there is no reason why they should not be. The book must be considered a false start for Markandaya, who for her next book, *A Silence of Desire* (1960), turned with great success to an entirely Indian subject and theme.

Markandaya reverted to the study of Indo-British relations in *Possession* (1963), the story of an Indian village artist named Valmiki who is taken up by an Englishwoman, Lady Caroline. She takes him to England, where he becomes a celebrity and also degenerates morally, but finally he returns to his village and a spiritual life: a fable of British possession of India, or, more precisely, of spirit (Valmiki) temporarily seduced by matter (Lady Caroline, who, as half-American, is even worse than English[3]). The story is weakened through being recounted by Anasuya, a young Indian woman, who remains remote and shadowy. Valmiki himself is seen as an abstraction: there are no concrete details about him except that he has gray eyes and, later, he is said to attain a normal weight after indulging in a Western diet. The crux of the tale is expressed in a conversation between Lady Caroline and Anasuya.

"I shall never really understand you," I said, and she nodded at once, looking at me with faint amusement.

"No. It's the classic ailment, isn't it?"

"What is?"

"That England and India never did understand one another."[4]

This point of view will be rejected in Markandaya's later novels as the theme of reconciliation gains ascendance.

Caroline, who "came of a breed that never admitted defeat,"[5] is grossly materialistic, hypocritical, unshakably sure of herself, arrogant, capable of deceit, a perfect embodiment of Anasuya's description of the British early in the book: "Wherever the British go, as the whole of the East knows, they live on the fat of the land, though the British themselves have no inkling of it. Simply by taking it for granted they have the hypnotized natives piling it onto their plates."[6]

Set in opposition to Lady Caroline is the mysterious Swami, mysterious because he has no ashram anywhere, nor even an address. The two are compared. Caroline, "who made casualness a religion, applying its supple standards and ingratiating gloss to all aspects of living; and the Swami, whose principles of morality were both inflexible and majestic, requiring a scrutiny not only of ends but of means, and rejecting as indefensible a plea of lack of knowledge."[7] He is not convincing because we are never told what his inflexible principles of morality are. But his followers are types we have come to know through Jhabvala's fiction, though here they are treated with less acerbity. They are described as they gather around the Swami in a Madras hotel.

European, American, a few Parisians, fewer Hindus: all of course affluent, for it cost money to breathe this rarefied air, and all with a less-evident common factor of subtle deformity—the pinched, down-drawn mouths of permanent discontent, the outthrust bosom and shoulders of an unrelenting aggressiveness, the painted, shadowed, wary eyes of people exhausted by their evolutionary move from being women happy to surrender, to women doomed to conquer, like those distant sea creatures that took their first steps onto land to collapse gasping on the beach.

The key being there the picture became clear, the presence of the Swami explicit. They craved tranquillity, he embodied it, the two had come together. The intervening process of encounter and suasion, like the postures and mock battles of mating byplay, was no more than intriguing trivia. The irreconcilable was the Swami himself, returning to a world he had renounced, and particularly to this morbid section of it; it was a conundrum only he could resolve.[8]

In Jumbo, a dispossessed maharaja, we have another Jhabvala type, close to caricature although sympathetically portrayed.

The abstractness of the characterizations emphasizes the novel's curious allegorical quality and the fatal tendency toward the universal unsupported by the particular. *Possession* is not a satisfying novel and is chiefly interesting for the contrast both in themes and technique with the fiction that was to follow.

The Coffer Dams (1969) is the first in the series of novels in which Markandaya presents a thoroughly mature consideration of Indo-British problems and points to the possibility of hard-won, unsentimental reconciliation of the two peoples. Like the later *Shalimar*, it is the story of a cooperative construction effort, in this case the building of a dam somewhere in South India several years after Independence. The purpose of the dam is to bring "progress" to the village districts, but, as it turns out, in order to do this the village itself has to be utterly destroyed, just as previously another village was evacuated and razed to provide a site for the builders' camp. Before the dam can be built, the river must be diverted by a series of coffer dams. In the course of the construction, both English and Indians die in accidents; the British want to leave two nearly irretrievable bodies of Indians in the river, but the local workmen threaten to strike until they have been reclaimed, and Bashiam, the engineer who is one of the protagonists of the novel, dies recovering them. The novel concludes with the death of the old village headman, signaling the end of an old order.

The divisions among groups and individuals in *The Coffer Dams* are many and complex. Some of the older English are still psychologically in the days of the Raj and complain about "the white man's burden." Rawlings and his wife, Millie, who have lived in Kenya, despise all "natives." "It was only in these extended limbs of Britain (as India still incredibly was, though not in name) that some of the old blood still flowed, injected with pickling fluid by memsahibs like Millie."[9] For their part, the Indian technicians, headed by Krishnan, still resent the British and nurture deep-rooted prejudice against them. "Strength: one spoke only from strength. The West understood no other language. The sensibilities that handicapped other races, the finer modulations of thought and behavior, all had been ground away, leaving only a superb act of public relations to fill the void with the belief that such qualities abounded. Well, thought Krishnan, there was no game under the sun that two could not learn to play. He brooded, his dark unlined face like a carved god's, while his subtle Brahmanical mind delicately picked up and dissected the Western techniques of seduction, persuasion and coercion."[10] Krishnan and his group also have contempt for Bashiam because he comes from the very tribal people who have lived around the dam site for generations. Only some of the younger people from both races— Helen Clinton, wife of the chief builder; Bashiam; Lefevre, the soil mechanics specialist—are unburdened by the Imperial past and without prejudice.

The direction of many of the ensuing conflicts is predictable, but these are treated with a delicacy and subtlety that are the hallmark of Markandaya's technique. Helen, with her deep sympathy for the tribal people, is driven further and further from her husband. " 'It's this blasted country,' he said, laying it where it belonged, all at one door, hoping she would join him so that all that was wrong between them could come right."[11] The increasing tension between Helen and Clinton is conveyed frequently by Cartesian exchanges that make one think of Scott's legal interrogations. With her "cool probing," Helen argues against having a party.

"A party today is rather the limit."
"Why?"
"With the laborers on short rations."
"Are they?"
"They've had their pay stopped," she said, and saw him stiffen. But why? He must know that she would know. "They live hand to mouth. Poor devils." . . .
He said sharply, "Coolies don't eat canapés, do they? You're close enough to them, you ought to know."
Helen looked up: "They eat," was all she said. Baldly. Neutrally.
"Do you mean," he said, and took a grip on himself and spoke carefully in case he was wrong, in case the neutrality was real, not a shell that housed live accusation, "are you trying to tell me they are facing starvation because they've been fined?"
"Oh, no," she answered at once, "no one will starve in a week. They have less to eat, that's all."
"And whom are you blaming for that," he asked heavily, "them? Or us?"[12]

But of course the "blasted country" is only a catalyst, not a cause, and their division grows. Helen has a brief affair with Bashiam, who has come to symbolize for her the link with a tribal past more important than the modern technology that obsesses her husband.

In sharp contrast to Helen is Millie Rawlings, who, starved for

sexual fulfillment and nourished only by her hatred for the country
and its people, suffers a mental collapse.

There are some fine psychological studies based on characters'
racial attitudes. Mackendrick, Clinton's partner, though of an older
generation, is sympathetic to his thin-skinned and sometimes un-
cooperative Indian colleagues. "In a way he understood . . . the
pulsing jealousy and pride that a poor nation could feel and trans-
mit to its nationals: the pride of an ancient civilization limping
behind in the modern race, called backward everywhere except
to its face and underdeveloped in diplomatic confrontation—a
euphemism of sheltering intent but dubious minting and no less
humiliation."[13]

There is Das, the Clintons' servant, who cannot understand
Helen's sympathy for the tribals and her lack of the expected
memsahib attitudes; in his eyes she lacks dignity, and his devotion
and approval are given entirely to her husband.

In Bashiam, Markandaya has portrayed the man between past
and present, one who, despite his technical training, still has a
profound respect for the powers of nature. It is this respect that
leads Clinton and others to think of him as either cowardly or
incredibly superstitious. Ironically, it is through the negligence of
the British technicians that he is killed while maneuvering the
giant crane to retrieve the bodies from the river; the crane, an
Avery-Kent, in a further irony, is addressed by Bashiam as Devi,
"Goddess." His recovery of the bodies at the cost of his own life
is an act of sacrifice for his people, as he understands it. "I must
do it, since they are my people, whom I cannot shed, although
I have tried. My people who are the impediment as they have
long been said and are now proving themselves to be, which it
is for me to remove."[14]

At the end, all the labors of both British and Indians are threatened by an early and violent monsoon, an elemental force that
might be expected to unite all factions; but when the rains come
to an end just in time to spare the coffer dams, the old occlusions
(a favorite word of Markandaya) that divide them are still in force,
and the villagers, their headman dead, are left in bewilderment.
Nevertheless, the possibility of reconciliation is now clearly confirmed in the various interracial friendships bred by the long and
painful experience of building the coffer dams, particularly in Helen's intuitive bond with the old village headman and her love
for Bashiam. But before Markandaya could affirm that paradisiacal

state in which all the old wounds were healed and hearts were open to spontaneous love, she had to test the possibility further in the experience of an Indian Everyman who has lived through the worst days before Independence in India and the difficult times in London during and after World War II.

The Nowhere Man (1972) is set in England. Its hero, Srinivas, has lived in England since he was about twenty. The major events of his life are described: his buying a house in South London, the death of Vasantha, his wife, his discovery that he has leprosy, his many years in the company of a Mrs. Pickering, who comes to live with him, his death as the result of a fire set by a fanatical racist hoodlum (who is trapped and killed in the fire). The heart of the book is a flashback to his earlier life in South India, the disappointed hopes for independence after the end of World War I, the humiliations he and his family undergo and, after his marriage, his decision to leave India with Vasantha. The bitterness of tone that characterizes these years is concentrated in the comments of Vasudev, Vasantha's brother, provoked by the massacre at Jallianwallah Bagh. " 'Over three hundred lives,' he said. 'A hundred Indians for each Briton. That is their scale, the scale by which they value themselves and against which we are measured. That is what we are up against: not their greed, or their anger, nor land hunger, nor the need to trade, but their arrogance, the mentality that produces such policies and acts.' "[15]

The central event of this period is the search of Srinivas's house by a British officer, who is introduced thus: "Yet already the climate had worked on him, seeding the blood with imperial implants, potent drugs that bore him to spheres from which he looked down, cold distant eye above the common run: an attitude which annihilated any basis of parity between the two human sides, substituting split levels of vassal and overlord."[16] The Englishman, "contained within an aura, a glittering envelope of subtle intimidation, and invested in the robes of authority which were colored khaki," suspects correctly that Vasudev, who has become a terrorist, is hidden somewhere in the house.

Smart alec, thought the Englishman, to whom the struggle under that alien skin was not apparent, and he remembered dimly what someone had told him, and resolved on no account to tangle in dialects. Wily Brahmin, he said to himself, won't look you in the eye and say yea or nay, oh, no; and his hands began to itch with a desire to knock down this smallish, brownish man trembling in front of him, though he too held himself intact, for he could not allow these people to observe him out of control.[17]

As it turns out, it is the Indians who remain cool, the Englishman who loses control.

[Srinivas] saw the change in color, pink gone to splotchy red, and the knife edge crease of the shorts ruined, risen to an apex above the bulging jockstrap. The Englishman also said nothing. He must be slipping, he thought, to be dumbstruck like this. His stick, which had rapped, was also swaggering, uncertain of its function. Suddenly he saw new scope for this exhausted tool in his hand, and bending slightly inserted it under the frill of Vasantha's skirt. What it did to him, this physical act, astonished and alarmed him. He would have withdrawn if he could, but now control had slipped away entirely. The supple cane flicked upward, and the flounces gathered soberly around Vasantha's ankles flew up over her head and left her naked, ready for bed as she had been, of her own though, which was an entirely different kind.[18]

After this violence, the "pink officer" regains control of himself and leaves the house. The grotesque conclusion to this disturbing episode comes when a large chest explodes from the pressure of the gases manufactured (in Markandaya's phrase) in Vasudev's corpse: he had taken refuge there, without the knowledge of the others in the household and suffocated.

The years in England are tranquil at first. Then with World War II, one son joins the army and marries an English girl. The marriage inevitably produces a rift in understanding with his parents. The other son becomes a conscientious objector and is killed by a bomb while driving an ambulance. His death is described in a style that Markanadaya had begun to develop with ever greater skill in *The Coffer Dams*, a style in which an ironic distance is maintained only to emphasize the tragic waste and the writer's compassionate view. "Seshu, speeding to hospital with the human wreckage from one explosion cramming the ambulance bays, was blown to smithereens by another together with his vehicle and half a terrace of shabby back to back houses on which a flying bomb had impersonally and wastefully landed."[19]

The growth of racial hostility after the war is chronicled in part through the conversations of the lower-class women of the neighborhood, memsahibs *sans le savoir*. Their shoddy minds have quickly been infected by the new feeling that followed the large-scale immigration of Indians and others from the former colonies in the fifties; it is the son of one of these women who is responsible for Srinivas's martyrdom. The suspicion of his leprosy has made him a special target, rendering him in a way the embodiment of all that is wicked and dangerous in the East, as they understand it.

But curiously, despite these horrors, the impression the novel makes is not one of bitterness. The wonderfully drawn Mrs. Pickering, both eccentric and competent, and equally a victim of prejudice through her sharing her life with Srinivas, holds a promise of hope, of reconciliation, with neither condescension nor sentimentality. At the end, when Mrs. Glass, mother of the murderous racist, offers nugatory consolation, she does not weep.

> "Don't take it too hard," said Mrs. Glass, nervously.
> Is that possible? wondered Mrs. Pickering, whose mind was crammed with images, of the fallen weak and helpless, and of their sons, and sons' sons, who would not be content as Srinivas had been but could be trusted to raise Cain—if Cain had not in fact already been raised.
> "You mustn't blame yourself," said Mrs. Glass, sweating.
> "Blame myself," said Mrs. Pickering. "Why should I? I cared for him."
> And, indeed, that seemed to her to be the core of it.[20]

At one point in her ninth and possibly best novel, *The Golden Honeycomb* (1972), Markandaya refers to it as a history. It does at times suggest an eighteenth-century novel: the family history, upbringing, and education of a young man who enjoys a few near-picaresque adventures on the road. It is also a historical novel in the true sense of the word: into her story of the fictional princely state of Devapur, Markandaya weaves appropriate references to contemporary history and has her characters become involved in actual events and their development changed by them—the Grand Durbar in Delhi in 1903, World War I, the beginning of the mill workers' agitation. There is, in distinction, very little "story" or plot; suspense does not figure; the reflective and sometimes lyrical development of the themes is all. The narration begins in 1870, when the British put Bawajiraj II on the throne of Devapur, a considerable state of some 20,000 square miles. The main body of the book consists of the recounting of the early life of Rabindranath, the illegitimate son of Bawajiraj III but nevertheless heir to the throne. The main events of his life are seen through the prism of his growing awareness of India and of the varieties and problems of human nature in general. His first great trauma comes at the Delhi Durbar when he is eight years old. Brought up (one thinks of Scott's William Conway) with an untroubled conviction of his father's absolute authority, he is shocked and ashamed when

he sees his father, like all the other maharajas and nawabs, bow
before the Viceroy.

Sees him pause and speak and bow, three low bows. Watches him retire.
Sees the shining warrior-king retreat, walking backwards. Backing away
like a lackey, like one of his own subjects at one of his own durbars.
  The Maharajah is mighty no longer. He is a subject. The sovereign is
this man on the Dais called the Viceroy. He is like a sun, dazzling, and
the whole of this Durbar, all of it to the last gold cupola, is there to do
him honour. And his father in the face of this sun has been frizzled up
into nothing. A vassal, that is the reality of it, who has to bow and scrape
and back away from the Presence. The vassal that his mother and grandmother have proclaimed, and he has never believed, the Maharajah to
be.[21]

Even more significant in Rabindranath's evolution is his visit
with his father to Bombay, when a mill workers' agitation disrupts
the princely program. Rabi gets caught up in the crowd and sees
city slum life for the first time. He is injured and helped by a girl
of the slums, who also claims his virginity. All this constitutes a
kind of awakening, the result of which we can only guess at. With
the conclusion of the novel, sometime after the end of World War
I, agitation by the poor has reached Devapur, and Bawajiraj III is
obliged to make some concessions to them. Whether Rabi will
later become a force for reform in his state or take part in the drive
for Independence is left to speculation.
  The novel is notable for the subtle and careful way relations
between English and Indians are delineated. At the author's command are an objectivity possessed only by Scott among the other
novelists I have considered and a knowledge of both British and
Indian psychology not matched by Jhabvala. The novel's style
marks a further development in the ironic but compassionate detachment of *The Nowhere Man*. The illusion of historical reality is
strengthened by many passages recounted in the historical present, like the lines quoted above. Everyone is eventually allowed
to have his say, his point of view represented: prince and laborer,
Brahmin and British Resident, and even horses, squirrels, and the
hunted boar. Unlike virtually all the fiction treating of Indo-British
relationships, *The Golden Honeycomb* is narrated without bitterness,
and, in the mostly untroubled life of the future ruler of Devapur,
perhaps the abiding impression we take away is his delicately
studied friendship with Sophie, the daughter of Sir Arthur Cope-
land, the British Resident. Neither the British nor the Indians

commit any violence on one another—which is not to say that Markandaya views the situation in the first quarter of this century as rosy; but she prefers to prick with a dart, not poisoned, instead of wielding the usual sledgehammer. Early in the novel the Brahmin Dewan, or minister, of Devapur rejects the crude *bania* (merchant) the British Agent has chosen for the throne.

"Not of the ruling class, Excellency," he murmurs. He selects the word *class* with care, meaning it to fall, with reverberations, within the vocabulary of the Agent. The Englishman understands. It has come to be like a duel between them, to which he is not averse. He believes he is never averse to playing a game when the odds are evenly balanced.
"I think, perhaps, Minister, you mean *caste*," he says, allowing his hand to fall, to reveal the curl of a disdainful lip.
"As you wish, Excellency," the Brahmin rejoins. . . . The Agent wishes. He cannot conceive that the foul connotations of *caste* can possibly attach to *class*. He believes in the latter, though he will never be crass enough to say so; the importance of the former he concedes only because he does not want a revolution on his hands.[22]

The most bitter conversation between the dewan (the son of the Brahmin minister in the dialogue just quoted) and the agent's replacement, Sir Arthur, takes place only in their imaginations. The dewan is outraged at the Resident's habit of shooting squirrels.

Chasms yawned between him and Sir Arthur. Dialogues, unspoken, but no need to suppose meanings not taken.
"Assassin."
"Bloody Hindu hypocrite."
"Kill, as soon as look."
"Wouldn't put a decent end to anything, every damn objection to a clean bullet."
"Christian arrogance."
"Sentimental nonsense. Impractical sentimentalist."
The two men, products of not dissimilar processes, eye to eye on so many issues, as near to glaring as polish permitted. Abyss there, all right. Fundamental distance.[23]

But the friendship, with all their reservations, between the dewan and the Resident is convincing, and Sir Arthur's feeling for India, as he is about to leave for home, is eloquently conveyed.

Though, really, this was one's country too, bone of one's bone, not to mention certain incursions of the spirit. Somehow it entered. Grain by grain, and before you knew where you were a part of you was Indian. Not literally, of course. There was the gap, and, yes, fences. One put them up, it was essential to maintain a separate and distinct identity, not to say poise; the Indians themselves were the first to despise those unbalanced Europeans who aped them. Sound instinct, that; though a little give on their side did nothing but good, one didn't relish battling through out-and-out Indian thickets. But, no question about it, a land to which one had devoted oneself, given half a lifetime of dedicated service and—why deny it—come to love.[24]

In contrast, Sir Arthur's replacement, Alfred Buckridge, of a less concessive temperament, one day writes in his journal, "There is something about the Indian Mind that is Absolutely Unintelligible," and later substitutes "Hindoo" for "Indian."[25] But the gap continues to narrow. Personifying the two peoples as "Residency" and "Palace," Markandaya writes: "They glared at each other, these two utterly different and utterly magnificent structures, over the stretches of Native and British terrain, over the decades, until passion could not be sustained at this devouring pitch and the glare became neutral, if slashed with suspicion. Suspicion could never be laid to rest, not while folk memories persisted and English bones had yet to crumble to dust in Indian graveyards (centuries still to go); but people and eras change, and in these urbane later years the glances exchanged were mostly tolerant, and not without touches of civilized emotion."[26]

The Golden Honeycomb is a highly original approach to the question of Indo-British relations. Its scope and subtlety are such that one is not surprised to learn that Paul Scott admired it.

The polarities that dominate Markandaya's fiction, particularly her later work, are by this time well defined: Britain and India, rich and poor, material and spiritual—all obviously related and sometimes interchangeable. In her fantasias on these themes, the note of reconciliation reaches a triumphant pitch in *Shalimar* (1982, published in Britain as *Pleasure City*). In this most recent of her novels, Markandaya refines to its limit the elliptical and oblique style of the preceding novels. Conventional plot all but disappears, to be replaced by a series of often only loosely related episodes. Continuity, more musical than dramatic, is produced through the structured repetition of images, colors, impressions, allusions, or sometimes only a single word. Thus, regarding some caves:

"Best ask—" Heblekar, he was about to say: perceptions there of a high elegance and calibre, a sounding-board of chaste distinctions; but finely controlled and struck through lacquer.[27]

The caves woke him. They were echoing as they had done for Heblekar—perhaps a thought more insistently, for the lacquer was thinner.[28]

Such story as there is tells of the building of a luxury hotel near
a remote fishing village on the coast of one of India's southern
states. Tully, grandson of Sir Arthur Copeland-Tully, the urbane
and humane British Resident in *The Golden Honeycomb* (indeed,
Tully's "tree went back to Clive") oversees the construction of
the hotel. The other protagonist is a remarkable sixteen-year-old
fisher-boy called Rikki (a Forsterian echo?) who, thanks to British
missionaries, speaks near-perfect English. Just as Tully is haunted
by echoes of the Raj, Rikki constantly communes with the long-
dead missionaries who educated him and awoke in him curiosity
and perceptiveness completely new in his village world. The true
subject of the novel is the friendship of Tully with Rikki; unlike
the friendship of Caroline with both Valmiki and Anasuya in *Possession,* which is tainted by envy, lust, possessiveness, and even
hatred—England and India together at their worst—this friendship
is characterized by a rare purity, innocence, and respect that may
be termed love without any fear of either sentimentality or em-
barrassed snickers. Tully's wife, like so many Western wives in
Anglo-Indian fiction, loses her husband to India, though not before she has introduced the sport of surfing, at which Rikki becomes an expert. Running throughout the book like a musical
countersubject is the friendship of Tully and Heblekar, who represents the new Indian Administrative Service; he is, it turns out,
the grandnephew of Sir Arthur's friend and sometime antagonist,
the Dewan of Devapur.

The building of Shalimar, an artificial and suspect Eden, takes
many months and disrupts forever the traditional life of the nearby
fishing village, bringing new prosperity to some, confusion and
alienation to others like Apu, Rikki's foster father. The hotel attracts tourists, artists, anthropologists, and photographers, some
irredeemably blind to India (which is to say reality), others, such
as Mrs. Pearl, who stumble, as it were, onto salvation. Set against
Shalimar is Avalon, a name that suggests an English and equally
chimerical paradise, Tully's grandfather's home on a height above
the beach. Rikki, along with his perhaps allegorical duties of life-
guard and bartender at Shalimar, constructs a magnificent mosaic
around the pool at Avalon, where Tully himself has placed his

own creation, a sculpture of a boy. Like the statue, the mosaic is never quite completed; when Tully leaves Shalimar, Rikki destroys the unfinished mosaic.

In a central episode, the English and Westernized Indian population of Shalimar go on a picnic to caves where, amid erotic sculptures and talk of Forster, an abandoned child is discovered. Happily bridging East and West, naïve, absurd Mrs. Pearl, who is goodness personified and who loves Rikki, adopts the girl and decides to linger on forever in Eden-India, for her the impossible seacoast in Bohemia made real, with her Perdita. No doubt Markandaya intends this episode to be, to some extent at least, an ironic commentary on Forster's Marabar Caves; her caves, not empty, not annihilating, not generative of illusions, are on the contrary filled with art celebrating human sexuality and offer a gift of the child, redeeming both the gift and the receiver.

The slender material of *Shalimar* provides the elements for an extraordinarily rich structure, full of refractions and resonances not so much Forsterian as Shakespearean. This is, after the manner of Shakespeare's late romances, a poem of reconciliation and the triumph of loving relationships. The families that are brought together—orphaned Rikki and his foster parents, Rikki and Tully, Mrs. Pearl and Rikki, Mrs. Pearl and the child—unlike those in *The Tempest* or *Pericles*, are families that never were, linkings of a generous, loving humanity that can bridge the widest gulfs, even that separating India and England. The divine order implied is beyond all conventional religions; as in late Shakespeare the mythology invoked is ancient Greek and Roman, with occasional references to various other religions of both East and West. The characters, as one expects in Shakespearean romance, are idealized, not complex, but never abstract. They are presented with such sympathetic irony that even foolish Mrs. Contractor or anti-Indian Boyle emerges as believably and likably human. Only Mrs. Lovat, the silly American novelist, who plans to "put" Rikki in a book, appears irredeemable.

Whereas in *The Coffer Dams* Markandaya had described the bitter tensions among British, city Indians, and tribals engaged in a different kind of construction project, in *Shalimar* she portrays a happier cooperation in which sensibilities and attitudes are changed, exchanged, and fused. The old bitterness is not ignored or forgotten (one vignette describes the exile of the last Mughal emperor, for example) but it is made bearable, reduced to a just proportion.

In thinking with gratitude of what India has given him, Tully recalls a conversation years before with his grandfather. " 'Subtle country, my boy. The minx knows—' over a shoulder busy with a rod, 'what she's given, and how to give back, in exact proportion.' And, as Tully perceived, the mix being returned was befittingly adroit. He could not for his life have sorted out the aloes from the honey."[29]

Once mixed, neither culture can ever be the same. Tully cannot be content with the old life he shared with his wife; Rikki cannot go back to being a fisherman but must continue at Shalimar, knowing as he does its deficiencies, shams, and dangers, and the saddeningly shallow experience of the region and all India of most of its guests. But whereas such a conclusion, gently though it may be conceived, would torment Ruth Jhabvala and send her into the deepest gloom, Markandaya seems to be proffering it as sufficient for life, for the lives of her characters. Like Iris Murdoch, she glories in the world's contingencies and rejects the existential despair of so many who are overwhelmed by India. She is unique among both British and Indian novelists in her serene and just contemplation of Indo-British relations and her ability to create convincing characters from both cultures. In her later novels she composes a fitting descant for the more massive and troubling symphonies of Paul Scott. They are works that may be considered as providing a fitting and consoling epilogue to the long and voluminous series of unhappy, violent works with which the English have tried to describe and define their troubled relations with India.

Afterword

I have concluded this study of Anglo-Indian novels with Kamala Markandaya not because she gives us the "other side of the coin"—for in fact she does not, but rather presents both sides with equal fairness and insight—but because her work, unlike that of the so-called Indo-Anglian novelists, is in the mainstream of British fiction and initiates a new stage in its development. By mainstream I mean the novel of manners in which the significance of both characters and events is found in the careful observation, with ideal (that is, loving) attention, of the interplay of social convention, personal motivation, and the author's genuine "conviction of our fellow-men's existence," as Conrad puts it, or Murdoch's "display of tolerance" for a "plurality of real persons" who "have a separate mode of being which is important and interesting to themselves." Many of the Indo-Anglian writers have used their novels as propaganda platforms (Anand) or philosophical treatises (Raja Rao) or write, as in the case of R. K. Narayan in his wonderful comedies of life in Malgudi, from a point of view so imbued with Indian attitudes that their work may be said to constitute a special genre. In their later novels Anita Desai and Nayantara Sahgal also have moved toward a more objective approach akin to Markandaya's social comedy, although they show far less concern with the theme of conflict and misunderstanding between Indians and British. Perhaps what marks Markandaya off from the other novelists of both British and Indian traditions is the fact that, for her, India is a reality unqualified before it is a problem, rather than the reverse. For Scott, India is a problem not because of his own attitudes or any limitations in his vision but simply because his subject is, precisely, the historical circumstances of the end of the Raj. For Jhabvala, India in her later work is a problem because, for whatever reason, she has peopled it with refugees, beings whom she has created not only without a country or a secure footing in any culture, but even without a sense of self, floating lives that must remain irrelevances in post-Independence India, skimmers over the surface without a goal or any inkling of the depths above which they dart. Other novelists I have surveyed find India a problem simply because for them it apparently was that and nothing else; that is, they have attempted to portray India chiefly as the appropriate theater for their private catastrophes, nervous breakdowns, marital conflicts, career failures, and the like, as though India were personally and malevolently responsible. Still other writers have hit upon India as an ideal avenue of escape into a past that is preferable because in that past there was no question of Indian equality, no question of British wrongdoing, and no question of the impermanence of this highly satisfactory order of things. In a recent article in the *New York Times Magazine*,[1] R. K. Narayan laments that all the numerous films then being made in India are directed toward resuscitating this past, focusing exclusively on the British experience of India before 1947 (he cites *Kim*, *A Passage to India*, *Heat and Dust*, *The Far Pavilions*) and wonders when foreign filmmakers will turn their attention to India itself. But the British (and for that matter the American) filmmakers, like the novelists, are not likely to interest themselves in what they can perceive only as a land with overwhelming and depressing problems, a land whose people have a fundamentally alien mind-set that appears to Westerners, always excepting a few eccentric antisocial types, as utterly manic. This view is not confined to Western observers, but, as I have mentioned earlier, it is widely trumpeted by Indian intellectuals and journalists as well. The generally negative attitude toward contemporary India is even reflected in the tourist trade statistics, for India, with its virtually uncountable marvels of art, architecture, and landscape, has not yet attracted a million tourists in any given year, while the city of Bangkok alone in the same period of time can boast of two to three times that many visitors to its smog and traffic jams.

Rather curiously, many American writers who deal with India reflect various aspects of the British tradition. Some novelists, such as Edison Marshall in *Bengal Tiger* (1952), recreate the terror and excitement of the Mutiny. Others see India and Indians as sinister, violent, or destructive, for example, McCloskey in *The Mallore Affair* (1967) or Towers in *The Necklace of Kali* (1961), or simply as irrational and ridiculous, for example, Vidal in *Kalki* (1978), where the derision is accompanied by misinformation and imprecise observation, failings found as well in journalistic works such as Theroux's *Great Railway Bazaar* (1975). This is surprising, if only because America's involvement with India is nonhistorical and thus uncomplicated by questions of national pride or national interests. But Americans visiting and writing about India often appear to accept the stereotyped responses of the Anglo-Indian tradition at its worst—that is, racist, whether unconsciously so or openly sneering—and proceed to reproduce it in their fiction. But it is outside the scope of this study to discuss the already sizable bibliography of American novels that deal with India, a subject that deserves an extensive investigation in its own right.

One can only speculate how long the various types of fiction that compose the Anglo-Indian tradition will continue to be written and achieve popularity. Probably indefinitely. The romantic imagination paints India as glamorous, mysterious, and dangerously seductive, paradoxically most dangerous and most seductive to those who feel superior to it, as a century and a half of fiction has taught us to expect. This India appears able to survive any amount of bad publicity in the country's post-Independence era. Even the problems of free India—bureaucratic snafus, missed connections, heat, dust, and dysentery—seem to be accorded an exotic, even fascinatingly demonological dimension by some foreigners visiting or living there.

The present situation regarding the best British fiction about India since 1947 may be summarized by pointing to the work of Scott, Farrell, and Markandaya. Paul Scott's novels mark an apogee in the development of the serious fiction that attempts to explore and interpret fairly the troubled and complex events immediately preceding Indian Independence. J. G. Farrell, with the brilliant searchlight of his irony, once and for all dispels the romantic notions about the Mutiny as a British triumph and the justification for the British mission. And Kamala Markandaya initiates a new era of imaginative literature about the subcontinent in which old ghosts are laid and the mind is freed to turn to a new and vastly different but equally problematical, complex, and baffling India.

Notes

Preface *(pp. ix–xi)*

1. Joseph Conrad, *A Personal Record*, p. 15, in *The Mirror of the Sea and* *A Personal Record* (London: Dent, 1950).

Introduction (pp. 1–6)

1. Rudyard Kipling and Wolcott Balestier, *The Naulakha* (New York: Doubleday & McClure, 1899), pp. 121–22.

2. Paul Scott, *The Corrida at San Feliu* (London: Granada, 1979), p. 153.

3. The theme of East-West incompatibility or problems in understanding provides the substance for many novels by Indian novelists writing in English during the last fifty years, such as Raja Rao's *The Serpent and the Rope*, Malgonkar's *Combat of Shadows*, Anand's *Two Leaves and a Bud*, and Rajan's *Too Long in the West*. Younger Indo-Anglian writers, Anita Desai and Salman Rushdie, for example, have shown far less interest in this theme. Indian fiction in Hindi, to take the most widely spoken of the vernaculars, scarcely ever considers East-West problems. From Premchand and Jai-nendra Kumar to Krishnā Sobti, Mohan Rakesh, and Shrilal Shukla, Hindi novels rarely even introduce non-Indian characters. Britain and Europe seem to have remained important chiefly for Indians such as Raja Rao and Rajan, who live and work abroad.

4. Quoted in Benita Parry, *Delusions and Discoveries: Studies on India in the British Imagination, 1880–1930* (Berkeley & Los Angeles: University of California Press, 1972), p. 43.

5. Susanne Howe, *Novels of Empire* (New York: Columbia University Press, 1949).

6. Allen J. Greenberger, *The British Image of India: A Study in the Literature of Imperialism, 1880–1960* (London: Oxford University Press, 1969).

7. Ibid., p. 1.

8. Ibid., pp. 6–7.

1 Anglo-Indian Fiction Before 1947 (pp. 7–24)

1. J. R. Ackerley, *Hindoo Holiday* (New York: Viking, 1932), p. 30.

2. William Buchan, *Kumari* (New York: Morrow, 1955), pp. 48–49.

3. Beverley Nichols, *Verdict on India* (London: Jonathan Cape, 1944), p. 136.

4. Ibid., p. 127.

5. Ibid., p. 157.

6. Ibid., p. 219.

7. Ibid., p. 64.

8. In *India: A Wounded Civilization* (Harmondsworth, England: Penguin, 1979), Naipaul writes, ''The crisis of India is not only political or economic. The larger crisis is of a wounded

old civilization that has at last become aware of its inadequacies and is without the intellectual means to move ahead" (p. 9).

9. Rumer Godden, *Breakfast with the Nikolides* (New York: Viking, 1964).

10. Paul Scott, *The Jewel in the Crown*, p. 72, in *The Raj Quartet* (London: Heinemann, 1978).

11. I do not think this is the case with Scott; despite this carelessness, an examination of his work quickly dispels any uneasiness about racism.

12. Jawaharlal Nehru, *Toward Freedom: The Autobiography of Jawaharlal Nehru* (Boston: Beacon, 1967), p. 272. This quotation also offers an interesting early instance of the metaphor of rape to describe Indo-British relations, of which Scott was to make such brilliant use in *The Raj Quartet*.

13. Ainslie T. Embree, "Imagining India: English-Language Fiction Set in Post-Independence India," in press.

14. Howe, *Novels of Empire*, p. 33.

15. Greenberger, *The British Image of India*, p. 204.

16. For a very different, and doubtless more accurate, view of the British in India, their daily lives and their relations with Indians of various backgrounds and rank, it is interesting to compare nonfiction accounts, like Ackerley's *Hindoo Holiday*, Forster's *Hill of Devi*, and particularly the oral histories recorded in Charles Allen's *Plain Tales From the Raj* (New York: St. Martin's Press, 1975). There one finds humor, appreciation of the absurd nature of many of the misunderstandings between ruler and ruled, and an indisputable pleasure in the Indian scene, as well as affection for the Indians themselves.

17. See Percival Spear, *The Nabobs: A Study of the Social Life of the English in Eighteenth Century India* (London: Oxford University Press, 1963), pp. 126–45, 195–99.

18. Mary Martha Sherwood, *The Works of Mrs. Sherwood* (New York: Harper & Brothers, 1860), 8:127.

19. Ibid., p. 129.

20. Ibid., 3:9.

21. Ibid., 4:26.

22. Sir Arthur Conan Doyle, *The Sign of Four*, in *The Annotated Sherlock Holmes*, ed. William S. Baring-Gould (New York: Clarkson N. Potter, 1967), p. 674.

23. In a Columbia University Ph. D. dissertation (1978), *Form in the Novels of Iris Murdoch*, David Beams reveals the complex Vedantic basis for the central allegory of Murdoch's *Bruno's Dream*.

24. For a detailed discussion of Steel and the other Anglo-Indian women novelists, see the chapters devoted to them in Parry, *Delusions and Discoveries*.

25. G. T. Garratt, "Indo-British Civilization," in *The Legacy of India*, ed. G. T. Garratt (Oxford: Clarendon Press, 1937), p. 416.

26. It is interesting to compare *Kim* in terms of both morality and plot structure with Twain's *Huckleberry Finn*, which surely must have had a strong influence on Kipling. There are many basic parallels: Huck and Kim, the Lama and Nigger Jim, the Mississippi and the Grand Trunk Road. But Huck, unlike Kim, being more morally mature and having experienced a loving relationship untouched with fuzzy Tibetan metaphysics, does not allow himself to be recaptured by a corrupt civilization and strikes out for the territory. A wit once observed that Kim is really Huckleberry Fink.

27. Rudyard Kipling, *Plain Tales from the Hills* (New York: A. L. Burt Co., n.d.), p. 79.

28. Ibid., p. 81.

29. Ibid., p. 85.

30. Ibid., p. 84.

31. Ibid., p. 85.

32. Ibid., p. 43.

33. Rudyard Kipling, *Life's Handicap* (London: Macmillan, 1891), p. 239.

34. N. C. Chaudhuri, "Passage to and from India," in *Twentieth Century Interpretations of a "A Passage to India,"* ed. Andrew Rutherford (Englewood Cliffs, N.J.: Prentice-Hall, 1970), pp. 68–77. After teaching *A Passage to India* to M.A. Final classes in an Indian

university, I can testify to the general antipathy Indians feel toward the novel; no amount of argument could convince students that Forster's view of India and Indians was anything but condescending and at heart hypocritical.

35. E. M. Forster, *A Passage to India* (New York: Harcourt, Brace & World, 1924), p. 51.

36. It is difficult to agree with Benita Parry when she writes: "Forster's mediation of those evanescent but intensely living experiences when man's imagination breaks through the crust of automatic perceptions to comprehend as a revelation his own essential being as identical with the One, be it humanity, the universe or a divinity, restores to them that reality which modern civilization would deny" (Parry, *Delusions and Discoveries*, p. 320). Parry understands this as being "Indian," but the very acceptance of "humanity" as identical with "the One" is at variance with what Indian metaphysicians have meant by the latter. Forster is compassionate and aware of the limitations of a liberal, rationalistic attitude that is superficial and untried, as he shows in the case of Miss Quested, but his fable remains, as Robin Lewis points out, a social comedy of failed relationships and defective communication ("Paul Scott's *The Raj Quartet*: A Post-Forsterian Vision," paper delivered at the Seventh Annual Wisconsin Conference on South Asia, University of Wisconsin, Madison, 4 November 1978). Atmosphere apart, with his negative or ambivalent characterizations of Indians and his principal attention devoted to the meanness and vulgarities of the Chandrapore English, Forster has little to say about India itself—its culture, its philosophy, or its struggle for independence.

37. Paul Scott, "India: A Post-Forsterian View," in *Essays by Divers Hands*. Transactions of the Royal Society of Literature, vol. 36 (London: Oxford University Press, 1970), pp. 113–32.

38. Forster, *Passage*, p. 254.

39. E. M. Forster, *The Hill of Devi* (London: Edward Arnold, 1953). See particularly p. 19 for the description of the "Gilbert and Sullivan" aspect of an Indian state; p. 33 for a "typical" Indian character; p. 87 for the absence of beauty; pp. 118–19 for a description of Gokul Ashtami much less serious than the corresponding scene in *Passage;* and p. 139 for a slightly facetious description of Dassehra. *The Hill of Devi* is more candid than *Passage* in its frequent condescension to its Indian subject.

40. Soon after finding himself unable to continue with *Passage*, in 1913 Forster began his novel of homosexual love, *Maurice*. Is it possible that all that keeps Aziz and Fielding apart at the end of *Passage* is Forster's unwillingness, in a novel meant for publication in his lifetime, to allow them to love one another? Whether Forster's diffidence and lack of candor about sexual problems seriously diminishes the quality of his fiction is a thorny question but outside the purview of this study.

41. "Was it wise that our betterclass women should be so scrupulously sheltered from rigours that Indian women endured year after year? Women with children, yes. . . . But the women who make such 'society' as India can manage to produce, and whose idle shallow opinions presently drift into the corresponding stratum of thought in England? He wondered how much of the poisoning of the world's thinking comes from the idleness and ease of sheltered women, especially young women." Edward Thompson, *An Indian Day* (Harmondsworth, England: Penguin, 1940), p. 145.

42. Ibid., p. 125.

43. Ibid., p. 169.

44. Ibid., p. 163.

45. See Greenberger, *The British Image of India*, passim, for further comment on their work.

46. F. Yeats-Brown, *Bengal Lancer* (London: Victor Gollancz, 1931), p. 286.

47. Greenberger, *The British Image of India*, pp. 138–39.

48. British racist attitudes were of course not confined to Indians; consider the portraits of Jews in English fiction of this century, e.g., Hirsch in Conrad's *Nostromo* (1904); the "Child," a usurer, in Percival Wren's *Beau Geste* (1924); Loerke in Lawrence's *Women in Love* (1920)—"He lives like a rat in the river of corruption, just where it falls over into the bottomless pit. . . . I expect he is a Jew—or part Jewish" (New York: Viking, Compass Books, 1964), pp. 418–19; or Ambrose Silk in Waugh's *Put Out More Flags* (1942). Equally unsavory Jews are found in Anglo-Indian fiction as well, e.g., Donald Macgregor, M.P., in Gordon Casserly's *Elephant God* (1920), and the Communists Markovitch and Weissberg in Steel's *The Law of the Threshold* (1924). Nehru quotes the saying that for the British, "les nègres commencent à Calais" (*Toward Freedom*, p. 308).

49. Yeats-Brown, *Bengal Lancer*, p. 8.

2 Four Modes of Indian Romance (pp. 25–63)

1. John Masters, *Coromandel!* (New York: Viking, 1955), pp. 18–19.

2. Quoted in Vincent Smith, *The Oxford History of India*, 2d ed., rev. and cont. to 1921 by S. M. Edwardes (Oxford: Clarendon Press, 1923), p. 725.

3. F. S. Roberts (Lord Roberts of Kandahar), *Forty-One Years in India* (London: Longmans, Green, 1902), p. viii.

4. *The History and Culture of the Indian People*, vol. 9, *British Paramountcy and Indian Renaissance*, part 1, ed. R. C. Majumdar, A. K. Majumdar, and D. K. Ghose (Bombay: Bharatiya Vidya Bhavan, 1963), p. 473.

5. Ibid., p. 613.

6. Paul Scott, *The Birds of Paradise* (London: Granada, 1982), p. 28.

7. Greenberger, *The British Image of India*, pp. 58–59.

8. M. M. Kaye, *Shadow of the Moon* (Harmondsworth, England: Penguin, 1979), p. 298.

9. John Masters, *Nightrunners of Bengal* (New York: Viking, 1951), p. 87.

10. Kaye, *Shadow*, p. 153.

11. Ibid., p. 313.

12. Forster, *Passage*, p. 27.

13. Kaye, *Shadow*, p. 298.

14. Ibid., p. 300.

15. For a re-evaluation of some of the Mutiny personalities see Michael Edwardes, *Bound to Exile: The Victorians in India* (London: Sidgwick & Jackson, 1969), passim.

16. As so often, E. J. Thompson is a happy exception; he was lecturer in Bengali at Cambridge and translated Tagore and other Bengali writers. John Masters appears to be competent in Nepali—the language of the troops he commanded—but from the transliterations and notes in his glossaries one learns that he was ignorant of any Indian script. See his notes on *haji* and *thuggee* in the glossary for *The Deceivers* (New York: Viking, 1952).

17. Valerie Fitzgerald, *Zemindar* (New York: Bantam, 1983), p. 143.

18. Similarly, in *The Deceivers*, William Savage finds it impossible to awaken his superiors to the danger of thuggee. His ability to pass for an Indian will be discussed later.

19. Fitzgerald, *Zemindar*, p. 98.

20. Masters, *Nightrunners*, p. 222. Note the climactic emphasis on "humiliation."

21. Ibid., p. viii.

22. Kipling, whose Hindi is no better than M. M. Kaye's, probably means *Sitabai*. Though *bhai*, "brother," is often used as a term of endearment for women, it would never form part of a woman's name; *bai* is a common suffix for women's names, particularly in Western India and often, though by no means exclusively, indicates women of a dubious profession.

23. See Greenberger, *The British Image of India*, pp. 19–22.

24. J. G. Farrell, *The Siege of Krishnapur* (Harmondsworth, England: Penguin, 1979), p. 13.

25. Ibid., p. 240.

26. Ibid., pp. 271–72.

27. Ibid., p. 159.

28. Ibid., p. 249.

29. Ibid., p. 345.

30. Ibid., p. 344.

31. Ibid., p. 177.

32. Ibid., p. 345.

33. Ibid., p. 232.

34. Ibid., p. 314.

35. Ibid., p. 35.

36. Ibid., pp. 167–68.

37. Ibid., p. 255.

38. Ibid., p. 90.

39. Ibid., p. 141.

40. Ibid., p. 215.

41. Ibid., pp. 96–97.

42. Ibid., p. 98.

43. Ibid., p. 267.

44. Ibid., p. 177.

45. Ibid., p. 263.

46. Ibid., p. 191.

47. A. E. W. Mason, *The Broken Road* (London: Hodder & Stoughton, 1929), p. 126.

48. Rudyard Kipling, *Kim* (New York: Doubleday, 1924), p. 1.

49. M. M. Kaye, *The Far Pavilions* (New York: St. Martin's Press, 1978), p. 949.

50. Ibid., p. 950.

51. Ibid., p. 357.

52. Ibid., p. 949.

53. Masters, *The Deceivers*, p. 32.

54. Ibid., p. 19.

55. Christine Weston, *Indigo* (New York: Charles Scribner's, 1943), pp. 157–58.

56. Ibid., p. 47.

57. Rabindranath Tagore, *Gora*, English translator unnamed (London: Macmillan, 1966), p. 406. *Gora*, in both Bengali and Hindi, means "white, pale, European" and was sometimes applied pejoratively to British soldiers.

58. John Masters, *Bhowani Junction* (New York: Viking, 1954), p. 21.

59. Ibid., p. 353.

60. W. Somerset Maugham, *The Razor's Edge* (New York: Doubleday, Doran, 1944), p. 286.

61. E. J. Thompson, *An Indian Day*, pp. 118–19.

62. Maugham, *The Razor's Edge*, p. 297.

63. For further discussion of these writers' links with Vedanta, see William York Tindall, *Forces in Modern British Literature* (New York: Knopf, 1947).

64. Consider this for dullness of style: "The decreased demand on the life force within Christopher thrust forward the question of action." Lidchi is also very often inaccurate—she has amoebic dysentery produced by a bacillus, uses *Protean* to describe the regenerative powers of the Hydra, and seems to believe that "Ol' Man River" is from *Porgy and Bess*.

65. Beams, "Form in the Novels of Iris Murdoch."

66. Iris Murdoch, *Bruno's Dream* (New York: Viking, 1969), p. 7.

67. Ibid., p. 57.

68. Ibid., p. 237.

69. Ibid., p. 99.

70. Ibid., p. 86.

71. Ibid., p. 102.

72. See William Hall, "*Bruno's Dream*: Technique and Meaning in the Novels of Iris Murdoch," *Modern Fiction Studies* 15, no. 3 (Autumn 1969): 429–44.

73. Murdoch, *Bruno's Dream*, p. 85.

74. Ibid., p. 237.

75. Ibid., pp. 78–79.

76. Ruth Prawer Jhabvala, "Moonlight, Jasmine and Rickets," *New York Times*, 22 April 1975.

77. Paul Scott, "*The Continent of Circe* by Nirad C. Chaudhuri," *Times Literary Supplement*, 2 December 1965, p. 1093.

78. Geraldine Halls, *The Cats of Benares* (New York: Harper & Row, 1967), pp. 199–200.

79. Masters, *The Deceivers*, p. 77.

80. Ibid., p. 179.

81. Ibid., p. 183.

82. Halls, *The Cats of Benares*, p. 38.

83. Ibid., p. 13.

84. Ibid., pp. 114–15.
85. Ibid., pp. 93–94.
86. Ibid., p. 48.
87. Janette Turner Hospital, *The Ivory Swing* (Toronto: McClelland & Stewart, 1982), p. 99.

88. Ibid., p. 47.
89. Ibid., p. 97.
90. Ibid., p. 203.
91. Ibid., p. 35.
92. Ibid., p. 46.
93. See Forster, *Passage*, p. 191.

3 The Mythology of India and Sex (pp. 64–75)

1. Kamala Markandaya, *Shalimar* (New York: Harper & Row, 1982), pp. 189–90.
2. Parry, *Delusions and Discoveries*, chapters 2 and 3.
3. Ruth Prawer Jhabvala, *Heat and Dust* (New York: Harper & Row, 1975), p. 170.
4. Louis Bromfield, *The Rains Came* (New York: Grosset & Dunlap, 1937), p. 472.
5. Halls, *The Cats of Benares*, p. 87.
6. Ibid., p. 86.
7. Ibid., p. 89.
8. Deborah Moggach, *Hot Water Man* (London: Jonathan Cape, 1982), p. 200.
9. Ruth Prawer Jhabvala, *An Experience of India* (New York: Norton, 1972), p. 115.

10. Ibid., p. 112.
11. Ruth Prawer Jhabvala, *A Stronger Climate* (London: John Murray, 1968), p. 163.
12. Ibid., p. 171.
13. Ibid., p. 17.
14. Ibid., p. 52.
15. Ruth Prawer Jhabvala, *In Search of Love and Beauty* (New York: Morrow, 1983), p. 26.
16. Jhabvala, *An Experience of India*, p. 192.
17. Ibid., p. 191.
18. Ibid., p. 220.
19. Ruth Prawer Jhabvala, *How I Became a Holy Mother* (New York: Harper & Row, 1976), p. 166.
20. Ibid., p. 168.
21. Ibid., p. 190.

4 Ruth Jhabvala (pp. 76–102)

1. Jhabvala, *An Experience of India*, p. 16.
2. Klaus Steinvorth, *The Indo-English Novel: The Impact of the West on Literature in a Developing Country* (Wiesbaden: Franz Steiner Verlag, 1975), p. 55.
3. Ibid., p. 54. Manohar Malgonkar's best-known novels, apart from his thrillers, are *The Princes* (New York: Viking, 1963) and *A Bend in the Ganges* (Delhi: Orient Paperbacks, 1964).
4. Ramlal Agarwal, "An Interview with Ruth Prawer Jhabvala," *Quest* 91 (September–October 1974), p. 36.
5. Quoted in *Contemporary Novelists* (New York: St. Martin's Press, 1976), p. 270.
6. Steinvorth, *The Indo-English Novel*, pp. 57–62.

7. Ruth Prawer Jhabvala, *Amrita* (New York: Norton, 1956), pp. 40–41.
8. Ruth Prawer Jhabvala, *The Nature of Passion* (New York: Norton, 1957), p. 17.
9. Ibid., p. 229.
10. Ibid., p. 119.
11. Ibid., p. 52.
12. Ibid., p. 170.
13. Haydn Moore Williams, *The Fiction of Ruth Prawer Jhabvala* (Calcutta: Writers Workshop, 1973), p. 28.
14. Even the two titles drawn from the Gita—"To Whom She Will" and "Get Ready for Battle"—appear ironic.
15. Jhabvala, *The Nature of Passion*, p. 243.
16. Ibid.
17. See Steinvorth, *The Indo-English Novel*, pp. 1–2.

18. See Mohan Rakesh, *Lingering Shadows* (trans. of *Andhere Band Kamre Mē*) (Delhi: Orient Paperback, n.d.); Agyeya (Sachchidananda Vatsyayana), *Nadi ke Dvip* (Islands in the stream) (Varanasi: Sarasvati Press, 1951); and Krishnā Sobti, *Surajmukhi Andhere Ke* (Sunflowers of darkness) (Delhi: Rajkamal Prakashan, 1972).

19. Ruth Prawer Jhabvala, *Esmond in India* (Harmondsworth, England: Penguin, 1982), p. 32ff.

20. Ibid., p. 39.

21. Jhabvala, *An Experience of India,* p. 10.

22. Vasant A. Shahane, *Ruth Prawer Jhabvala* (London: Arnold-Heinemann, 1976), p. 102.

23. Ruth Prawer Jhabvala, *The Householder* (New York: Norton, 1960), p. 159.

24. Ibid., p. 187.

25. The superficiality of Jhabvala's conception of this swami, along with the others who appear in her work, is apparent when one compares him (and his rather futile functioning) with, say, the complex and passionate involvement of the married couple and the swami in Kamala Markandaya's *Silence of Desire* (1960).

26. Williams, *The Fiction of Jhabvala,* p. 37.

27. *Bhua,* for the correct *Bua,* "Auntie."

28. Ruth Prawer Jhabvala, *A Backward Place* (London: John Murray, 1965), p. 255.

29. Ibid., p. 58.

30. Ibid., p. 108.

31. Ibid., p. 150.

32. Ibid., p. 235.

33. V. S. Pritchett, "Books," *The New Yorker,* 16 June 1973, p. 106.

34. Jhabvala, *A Backward Place,* p. 65.

35. Ibid., p. 187.

36. Quoted in Yasmine Gooneratne, *Silence, Exile and Cunning: The Fiction of Ruth Prawer Jhabvala* (London: Sangam, 1983), p. 1.

37. Pritchett, "Books," p. 107.

38. Ibid.

39. Williams, *The Fiction of Jhabvala,* p. 10.

40. Jhabvala, *An Experience of India,* pp. 12–13.

41. Ibid., p. 10.

42. For the most complete of N. C. Chaudhuri's many violent attacks on every aspect of Indian civilization, see his *Continent of Circe: An Essay on the Peoples of India* (London: Chatto & Windus, 1965).

43. Jhabvala, *Heat and Dust,* p. 65.

44. The film's talented cast, aided by splendid Indian settings, seems even less believable than the characters in the book, perhaps because their all too powerful physical reality belies the paralyzing melancholia and rigidity of the author's vision.

45. Jhabvala, *An Experience of India,* p. 8.

46. Ibid.

47. *Contemporary Novelists,* 3d ed. (Byfleet, England: Macmillan, 1982), p. 346.

48. Jhabvala, *In Search of Love and Beauty,* p. 128.

49. Ibid., p. 222.

5 The Early Novels of Paul Scott (pp. 103–119)

1. Quoted in *World Authors* (New York: H. W. Wilson, 1975), p. 1271.

2. Paul Scott, *The Alien Sky* (London: Granada, 1979), p. 208.

3. Paul Scott, *The Chinese Love Pavilion* (London: Granada, 1980), p. 15.

4. Marapore becomes the Mayapore of the *Quartet.* Scott presumably changed the name because he liked the idea of *maya* ("illusion") in the name of the town that is the setting for the Bibighar affair, though *Mara,* from a Sanskrit root meaning "to die, to kill," would have been richly evocative in its own way, since it is cognate with Latin *mors* and English *mar* and is also the name of Buddha's great deluding tempter, identified with *Kama,* or Eros.

5. Scott, *The Alien Sky*, p. 142. Note the reference to "individual kindness"—a swipe, perhaps, at one of Forster's favorite ideas.

6. Patrick Swinden, in *Paul Scott: Images of India* (New York: St. Martin's Press, 1980) is mistaken when he says that Vidyasagar reappears in the *Quartet* (p. 84). Apart from obvious differences in character, the Vidyasagar of *The Alien Sky* is sixteen in June 1947 whereas the Vidyasagar of the *Quartet* is a practicing journalist in his mid-twenties in August 1942.

7. Bromfield's *The Rains Came* also combines characters with American, English, and Indian backgrounds and draws on the distinctions among them for much of its plot and characterization.

8. Scott, *The Alien Sky*, pp. 50–51.

9. In *The Chinese Love Pavilion*, Teena Chang is half-Chinese, a quarter French and a quarter Dutch; she has alternating "European" and "Chinese moods," but her racial background does not seem to be problematical for her. In her Chinese mood she is conscious of mutability, mortality; in her European mood she is practical, possessive. She moves between the two moods without any apparent problem.

10. Scott, *The Alien Sky*, p. 102.

11. Ibid., p. 205.

12. Ibid., p. 152.

13. Swinden, *Paul Scott*, p. 22.

14. Paul Scott, *The Corrida at San Feliu*, p. 209.

15. Ibid., pp. 212–13.

16. Paul Scott, *The Bender* (London: Granada, 1982), p. 78.

17. In his childhood games, William Conway darkens his skin and dresses like an Indian, while Krishi, his Indian friend, becomes a god (Paul Scott, *The Birds of Paradise*, p. 78).

18. Paul Scott, *The Birds of Paradise*, p. 29.

19. Ibid.

20. The name *Tradura* hints at *traduce*.

21. Scott, *The Birds of Paradise*, p. 225.

22. Ibid., pp. 63–64.

23. Iris Murdoch, "The Sublime and the Beautiful Revisited," *Yale Review* 49 (December 1959):257.

24. Scott, *The Birds of Paradise*, p. 58.

25. Ibid., p. 117.

26. Ibid., p. 148.

27. Ibid., p. 160.

28. Ibid., p. 163.

29. Ibid., p. 220.

30. Ibid., p. 183.

31. Ibid., p. 232.

32. Ibid., p. 233.

33. Ibid., p. 220.

34. Ibid., p. 227.

35. Ibid., p. 19.

36. Ibid., p. 199.

37. Ibid., p. 187.

38. Ibid., pp. 234–35.

6 The Raj Quartet (pp. 120–156)

1. Paul Scott, *The Jewel in the Crown*, in *The Raj Quartet* (London: Heinemann, 1978). (All subsequent references will be to this one-volume edition; each novel will be designated as follows: *The Jewel in the Crown*—1; *The Day of the Scorpion*—2; *The Towers of Silence*—3; *A Division of the Spoils*—4.) The kinship of this counsel with (as well as its difference from) Stein's famous dictum in Conrad's *Lord Jim*—"The way is to the destructive element submit yourself. . . . In the de-structive element immerse"—is immediately apparent.

2. Ibid., 3:38.

3. Note particularly Swinden, *Paul Scott*.

4. Scott, *Quartet*, 1:1.

5. Ibid.

6. Swinden, *Paul Scott*, p. 71.

7. Chaudhuri is not even nominally a Christian, as Swinden maintains (ibid.); this is important, for it emphasizes the gulf between him and Miss Crane, which both succeed in bridg-

ing in the catastrophe on the road to Mayapore. See *Quartet,* 1:39.

8. Scott, *Quartet,* 1:58.

9. Ibid., p. 64.

10. Ibid., p. 439.

11. Not younger, as given by Swinden (*Paul Scott,* p. 70).

12. In the only astrological reference in the work, Scott points out that Sarah is an Aries (as he himself was), and Susan a Scorpio (*Quartet,* 2:54).

13. Mabel is actually Sarah's father's stepmother but is referred to as "Aunt Mabel."

14. Scott, *Quartet,* 3:369.

15. Ibid., p. 387.

16. Ibid., p. 210.

17. Ibid., p. 392.

18. Scott, *Quartet,* 4:206.

19. Ibid., p. 571.

20. Ibid., p. 205.

21. Ibid., p. 208.

22. Ibid., p. 536.

23. Part of the charm of Forster is of course the delicacy, even fastidiousness, with which his story of repressed violence is told, but there is also a price to pay for this in the occasional haziness that surrounds so much of what happens, the constant invocation of mystery and insoluble riddle. Even granting the difference in convention between the twenties and the sixties in regard to explicitness about sexual relations, one must concede that the characterization of Miss Quested, like that of Fielding, remains incomplete.

24. Scott, *Quartet,* 1:387.

25. Ibid., p. 400.

26. Ibid.

27. Ibid., p. 61.

28. Ibid., p. 400.

29. Ibid., p. 401.

30. Ibid., 4:337.

31. Ibid.

32. Ibid., 3:23.

33. Ibid., p. 27.

34. Ibid., 4:134.

35. Ibid., 3:312.

36. Ibid., 4:105.

37. Ibid., 2:331.

38. Ibid., p. 341.

39. Ibid., 3:255.

40. Ibid., p. 387.

41. Ibid., p. 161.

42. Ibid., pp. 236–37.

43. Ibid., pp. 220–21.

44. Ibid., 1:121.

45. Ibid., p. 131.

46. Ibid., p. 144.

47. Ibid., p. 136.

48. Ibid., 2:2–3.

49. Ibid., 1:425.

50. Ibid., 2:298–99.

51. Ibid., p. 141.

52. Ibid., p. 305.

53. Ibid., 4:113.

54. In a review of Jack Reading's *Chinese Opium Wars,* Scott wrote, "One of our sillier pretences is that trade followed the flag. Surely it was the other way round?" "Trade Before the Flag," *Country Life,* 5 June 1975, p. 1503.

55. Scott, *Quartet,* 1:431.

56. Ibid., 4:306.

57. Ibid., p. 301.

58. Ibid., p. 136.

59. Ibid., 2:321.

60. Ibid., 1:137–38.

61. Ibid., p. 119.

62. Swinden, *Paul Scott,* p. 98.

63. Scott, *Quartet,* 3:68.

64. Ibid.

65. Ibid.

66. Ibid., p. 67.

67. Ibid., p. 178.

68. Ibid., p. 69.

69. Ibid., 4:302.

70. Ibid., p. 207.

71. Ibid., p. 208.

72. Ibid., p. 222.

73. Ibid., p. 84.

74. See above, "Escape into the Past," chapter 2.

75. Conrad, *A Personal Record,* p. 92.

76. Marcel Proust, *A la recherche du temps perdu* (Paris: Gallimard, 1954), 3:1031 (my translation).

77. Scott, *Quartet,* 1:450.

78. Ibid., p. 451.

79. Ibid., p. 207.

80. Paul Scott, *Staying On* (New Delhi: Allied Publishers, 1978), p. 79.

81. Ibid., p. 80.

82. Ibid., p. 81.
83. Ibid., p. 31.
84. Ibid., p. 91–92.
85. Ibid., p. 216.
86. Ibid.

87. Paul Scott, "An Idealist in Action" (review of *Indira Gandhi* by Zareer Masani), *Country Life,* 19 June 1975, p. 1643.

7 Kamala Markandaya and the Novel of Reconciliation (pp. 157–171)

1. Kamala Markandaya, *The Nowhere Man* (New York: John Day, 1972), p. 84.

2. Kamala Markandaya, *The Golden Honeycomb* (New York: Crowell, 1977), p. 453.

3. "But America was literally and compellingly a new world, bold, virile, rich red blood in its throbbing veins and healthily free of that whiff of decadence that overhangs the over-civilized. Yet it was restless, brutal with the impatient brutality that comes from no-time-to-think, distracted and distracting, obsessed and preferring to be obsessed more by machines than by that most intricate and mysterious of machines, the mind. Which had been, of course, Valmiki's foundations." Kamala Markandaya, *Possession* (New York: John Day, 1963), p. 173.

4. Ibid., p. 82.
5. Ibid., p. 249.
6. Ibid., p. 17.
7. Ibid., pp. 157–58.

8. Ibid., pp. 105–6.

9. Kamala Markandaya, *The Coffer Dams* (New York: John Day, 1969), p. 138.

10. Ibid., p. 60.
11. Ibid., p. 165.
12. Ibid., pp. 68–69.
13. Ibid., p. 22.
14. Ibid., p. 211.
15. Markandaya, *The Nowhere Man,* p. 122.
16. Ibid., p. 139.
17. Ibid., p. 140.
18. Ibid., p. 142.
19. Ibid., p. 33.
20. Ibid., p. 312.
21. Markandaya, *The Golden Honeycomb,* p. 161.
22. Ibid., p. 4.
23. Ibid., p. 296.
24. Ibid., p. 302.
25. Ibid., p. 348.
26. Ibid., p. 349.
27. Markandaya, *Shalimar,* p. 191.
28. Ibid., p. 204.
29. Ibid., p. 338.

Afterword (pp. 172–174)

1. *New York Times Magazine,* 16 September 1984, pp. 94–95.

Bibliography

This bibliography lists only those books quoted or referred to in the text, and in addition, in the general section, reference works that were of particular value in preparing this study.

For a good bibliography of fiction in English that is concerned with India, see Brijen K. Gupta's *India in English Fiction*. This listing of over 2,200 titles, with brief annotations for many of them, also includes novels by Americans and Indians, along with a few translated from European and Indian languages.

Fiction

Anand, Mulk Raj. *Two Leaves and a Bud*. Bombay: Kutub-Popular, 1951.

Arnold, William Delafield. *Oakfield, or fellowship in the East*. New York: Humanities Press, 1973.

Bromfield, Louis. *The Rains Came*. New York: Grosset & Dunlap, 1937.

Buchan, William. *Kumari*. New York: Morrow, 1955.

Burgess, Anthony. *Earthly Powers*. New York: Simon & Schuster, 1980.

———. *The Long Day Wanes: A Malayan Trilogy (Time for a Tiger, The Enemy in the Blanket, Beds in the East)*. New York: W. W. Norton, 1964.

Candler, Edmund. *Abdication*. London: Constable, 1922.

———. *Siri Ram*. London: Constable, 1922.

Cary, Joyce. *An American Visitor*. London: M. Joseph, 1952.

Casserly, Gordon. *The Elephant God*. London: P. Allan, 1920.

Conrad, Joseph. *Lord Jim*. New York: Modern Library, 1931.

———. *Nostromo*. New York: New American Library, 1960.

Doyle, Sir Arthur Conan. *The Sign of Four*, in *The Annotated Sherlock Holmes*, ed. William S. Baring-Gould. New York: Clarkson N. Potter, 1967.

Farrell, J. G. *The Hill Station: An Unfinished Novel and An Indian Diary*. New Delhi: Vikas, 1981. Contains "Two Appreciations," by John Spurling and Margaret Drabble, and a "Personal Memoir" by Malcolm Dean.

———. *The Siege of Krishnapur*. Harmondsworth, England: Penguin, 1979.

Fitzgerald, Valerie. *Zemindar*. New York: Bantam, 1983.

Forster, E. M. *A Passage to India*. New York: Harcourt, Brace & World, 1924.

Godden, Jon. *The City and the Wave*. London: M. Joseph, 1954.

———. *The Peacock*. London: M. Joseph, 1950.

Godden, Rumer. *Black Narcissus*. Boston: Little, Brown, 1939.
———. *Breakfast with the Nikolides*. New York: Viking, 1964.
———. *Kingfishers Catch Fire*. London: Reprint Society, 1955.
———. *The Lady and the Unicorn*. London: Peter Davies, 1937.
———. *The River*. New York: Viking, 1946.
Halls, Geraldine. *The Cats of Benares*. New York: Harper & Row, 1967.
Han Suyin. *The Mountain Is Young*. London: Jonathan Cape, 1958.
Henty, George Albert. *At the Point of the Bayonet: A Tale of the Mahratta War*. London: Blackie & Son, 1902.
Hospital, Janette Turner. *The Ivory Swing*. Toronto: McClellan & Stewart, 1982.
Jhabvala, Ruth Prawer. *Amrita*. New York: Norton, 1956.
———. *A Backward Place*. London: John Murray, 1965.
———. *Esmond in India*. Harmondsworth, England: Penguin, 1982.
———. *An Experience of India*. New York: Norton, 1972.
———. *Get Ready for Battle*. Harmondsworth: Penguin, 1983.
———. *Heat and Dust*. New York: Harper & Row, 1975.
———. *The Householder*. New York: Norton, 1960.
———. *How I Became a Holy Mother*. New York: Harper & Row, 1976.
———. *In Search of Love and Beauty*. New York: Morrow, 1983.
———. *Like Birds, Like Fishes*. London: John Murray, 1963.
———. *The Nature of Passion*. New York: Norton, 1957.
———. *A Stronger Climate*. London: John Murray, 1968.
———. *Travelers (A New Dominion)*. New York: Harper & Row, 1973.
Kaye, M. M. *The Far Pavilions*. New York: St. Martin's Press, 1978.
———. *Shadow of the Moon*. Harmondsworth, England: Penguin, 1979.
Kincaid, Dennis. *Their Ways Divide*. London: Chatto & Windus, 1936.
Kipling, Rudyard. *Kim*. New York: Doubleday, 1924.
———. *Life's Handicap*. London: Macmillan, 1891.
———. *Plain Tales from the Hills*. New York: A. L. Burt Co., n.d.
Kipling, Rudyard, and Balestier, Wolcott. *The Naulakha*. New York: Doubleday & McClure, 1899.
Lawrence, D. H. *Women in Love*. New York: Viking, Compass Books, 1960.
Lidchi, Maggi. *Man of Earth (Earth Man)*. New York: Morrow, 1968.
McCloskey, William. *The Mallore Affair*. London: Heinemann, 1967.
Malgonkar, Manohar. *A Bend in the Ganges*. New York: Viking, 1963.
———. *Combat of Shadows*. London: Hamish Hamilton, 1962.
———. *The Princes*. Delhi: Orient Paperbacks, 1964.
Markandaya, Kamala. *The Coffer Dams*. New York: John Day, 1969.
———. *The Golden Honeycomb*. New York: Crowell, 1977.
———. *Nectar in a Sieve*. New York: New American Library, 1954.
———. *The Nowhere Man*. New York: John Day, 1972.
———. *Possession*. New York: John Day, 1963.
———. *Shalimar*. New York: Harper & Row, 1982.
———. *A Silence of Desire*. New York: John Day, 1960.
———. *Some Inner Fury*. New York: John Day, 1956.
Marshall, Edison. *Bengal Tiger*. New York: Doubleday, 1952.
Mason, A. E. W. *The Broken Road*. London: Hodder & Stoughton, 1929.

————. *The Drum*. London: Hodder & Stoughton, 1937.

Masters, John. *Bhowani Junction*. New York: Viking, 1954.

————. *Coromandel!* New York: Viking, 1955.

————. *The Deceivers*. New York: Viking, 1952.

————. *The Lotus and the Wind*. New York: Viking, 1953.

————. *Nightrunners of Bengal*. New York: Viking, 1951.

Maugham, W. Somerset. *The Razor's Edge*. New York: Doubleday, Doran. 1944.

Merriman, Henry Seton (Hugh S. Scott). *Flotsam: The Study of a Life*. London: Longmans, 1896.

Moggach, Deborah. *Hot Water Man*. London: Jonathan Cape, 1982.

Murdoch, Iris. *The Black Prince*. New York: Viking, 1973.

————. *Bruno's Dream*. New York: Viking, 1969.

————. *The Italian Girl*. New York: Viking, 1964.

————. *The Sea, the Sea*. New York: Viking, 1978.

————. *An Unofficial Rose*. New York: Viking, 1962.

————. *A Word Child*. New York, Viking, 1975.

Prichard, Iltudus Thomas. *How To Manage It*. London: n.p., 1864.

Proust, Marcel. *A la recherche du temps perdu*. 3 vols. Paris: Gallimard, 1954.

Rajan, B. *Too Long in the West*. London: Heinemann, 1961.

Raja Rao. *The Serpent and the Rope*. London: John Murray, 1960.

Scott, Paul. *The Alien Sky*. London: Granada, 1979.

————. *The Bender*. London: Granada, 1982.

————. *The Birds of Paradise*. London: Granada, 1982.

————. *The Chinese Love Pavilion*. London: Granada, 1980.

————. *The Corrida at San Feliu*. London: Granada, 1979.

————. *Johnnie Sahib*. London: Granada, 1979.

————. *A Male Child*. London: Granada, 1974.

————. *The Mark of the Warrior*. London: Granada, 1979.

————. *The Raj Quartet (The Jewel in the Crown: The Day of the Scorpion; The Towers of Silence; A Division of the Spoils)*. London: Heinemann, 1978.

————. *Staying On*. New Delhi: Allied Publishers, 1978.

Sherwood, Mary Martha. *The Works of Mrs. Sherwood*. 15 vols. New York: Harper & Brothers, 1860.

Shute, Nevil (Nevil Shute Norway). *The Chequer Board*. New York: Morrow, 1947.

Steel, Flora Annie. *The Hosts of the Lord*. London: Heinemann, 1900.

————. *Indian Scene (Collected Short Stories)*. New York: Longmans, 1934.

————. *The Law of the Threshold*. London: Heinemann, 1924.

————. *On the Face of the Waters*. London: Heinemann, 1897.

Stoll, Dennis Gray. *The Dove Found No Rest*. London: Victor Gollancz, 1946.

Suyin, Han. See Han Suyin.

Tagore, Rabindranath. *Gora* (English translator unnamed). London: Macmillan, 1966.

Thompson, Edward. *An End of the Hours*. London: Macmillan, 1938.

————. *A Farewell to India*. London: Ernest Benn, 1930.

————. *An Indian Day*. Harmondsworth, England: Penguin, 1940.

Towers, Robert. *The Necklace of Kali*. New York: Random House, 1961.
Vidal, Gore. *Kalki*. New York: Random House, 1978.
Walker, Harry David. *Harry Black*. Boston: Houghton Mifflin, 1956.
Waugh, Evelyn. *Put Out More Flags*. London: Heinemann, Octopus, 1977.
Wentworth, Patricia. *The Devil's Wind*. London: Andrew Melrose, 1912.
Weston, Christine. *Indigo*. New York: Charles Scribner's, 1943.
Wren, P. C. *Beau Geste*. New York: Grosset & Dunlap, 1926.

General

Ackerley, J. R. *Hindoo Holiday*. New York: Viking, 1932.
Agarwal, Ramlal. "An Interview with Ruth Prawer Jhabvala." *Quest* 91 (September–October 1974): 33–36.
Allen, Charles. *Plain Tales from the Raj*. New York: St. Martin's Press, 1975.
Beams, David W. *Form in the Novels of Iris Murdoch*. Ph. D. dissertation, Columbia University 1978.
Chamberlain, M. E. *Britain and India*. Hamden, Conn.: Archon Books, 1974.
Chaudhuri, N. C. *The Continent of Circe: An Essay on the Peoples of India*. London: Chatto & Windus, 1965.
———. *Hinduism*. Oxford: Oxford University Press, 1979.
———. "Passage to and from India." In *Twentieth Century Interpretations of "A Passage to India,"* edited by Andrew Rutherford, pp. 68–77. Englewood Cliffs, N.J.: Prentice-Hall, 1970.
Cohen, Morton. *Rudyard Kipling to Rider Haggard: The Record of a Friendship*. London: Hutchinson & Co., 1965.
Conrad, Joseph. *The Mirror of the Sea and A Personal Record*. London: Dent, 1950.
Contemporary Novelists. New York: St. Martin's Press, 1976.
Contemporary Novelists. 3d ed. Byfleet, England: Macmillan, 1982.
Dhawan, R. K., ed. *Explorations in Modern Indo-English Fiction*. New Delhi: Bahri, 1982.
Edwardes, Michael. *Bound to Exile: The Victorians in India*. London: Sidgwick & Jackson, 1969.
Embree, Ainslie T. "Imagining India: English-Language Fiction Set in Post-Independence India." In press.
———. "Tradition and Modernization in India: Synthesis or Encapsulation?" In *Science and the Human Condition in India and Pakistan*, ed. Ward Morehouse, pp. 29–38. New York: Rockefeller University Press, 1968.
Forster, E. M. *Abinger Harvest*. London: E. Arnold & Co., 1936.
———. "Reflections in India: I—Too Late?" *The Nation and the Athenaeum* 30 (21 January 1922): 612–16.
———. *The Hill of Devi*. London: Edward Arnold, 1953.
Garratt, G. T., ed. *The Legacy of India*. Oxford: Clarendon Press, 1937.
Godden, Jon, and Rumer Godden. *Two Under the Indian Sun*. New York: Alfred A. Knopf and Viking Press, 1966.
Golant, William. *The Long Afternoon*. New York: St. Martins Press, 1975.

Gooneratne, Yasmine. *Silence, Exile and Cunning: The Fiction of Ruth Prawer Jhabvala*. London: Sangam, 1983.

Greenberger, Allen J. *The British Image of India: A Study in the Literature of Imperialism, 1880–1960*. London: Oxford University Press, 1969.

Gupta, Brijen K. *India in English Fiction*. Metuchen, N.J.: Scarecrow Press, 1970.

Hall, William. *"Bruno's Dream:* Technique and Meaning in the Novels of Iris Murdoch." *Modern Fiction Studies* 15, no. 3 (Autumn 1969): 429–44.

The History and Culture of the Indian People. Vol. 9, *British Paramountcy and Indian Renaissance*, part 1, edited by R. C. Majumdar, A. K. Majumdar, and D. K. Ghose. Bombay: Bharatiya Vidya Bhavan, 1963.

Howe, Susanne. *Novels of Empire*. New York: Columbia University Press, 1949.

Hutchins, Francis G. *The Illusion of Permanence: British Imperialism in India*. Princeton, N.J.: Princeton University Press, 1967.

Isaacs, Harold R. *Images of Asia: American Views of China and India*. New York: Capricorn Books, 1962.

Jhabvala, Ruth Prawer. "Moonlight, Jasmine and Rickets." *New York Times*, 22 April 1975.

Kabir, Humayun. *The Bengali Novel*. Calcutta: Firma K. L. Mukhopadhyay, 1968.

Kakar, Sudhir. *The Inner World: A Psychoanalytic Study of Childhood in India*. Delhi: Oxford University Press, 1978.

Koestler, Arthur. *The Lotus and the Robot*. New York: Macmillan, 1967.

Krishna Rao, A. V. *The Indo-Anglian Novel and the Changing Tradition: A Study of the Novels of Mulk Raj Anand, Kamala Markandaya, R. K. Narayan and Raja Rao, 1930–1964*. Mysore: Rao & Rhagavan, 1972.

Lewis, Robin Jared. *E. M. Forster's Passages to India*. New York: Columbia University Press, 1979.

———. "Orwell's *Burmese Days* and Forster's *A Passage to India:* Two Novels of Human Relations in the British Empire." *Massachusetts Studies in English* 4, no. 3 (Spring 1974): 1–36.

———. "Paul Scott's *The Raj Quartet:* A Post-Forsterian Vision." Paper delivered at the Seventh Annual Wisconsin Conference on South Asia, University of Wisconsin, Madison, 4 November 1978.

Masson, J. Moussaieff. *The Oceanic Feeling: The Origins of Religious Sentiment in Ancient India*. Boston: D. Reidel Publishing Co., 1980.

Masters, John. *Bugles and a Tiger*. New York: Viking, 1956.

———. *Pilgrim Son: A Personal Odyssey*. New York: Putnam, 1971.

Mayo, Katherine. *Mother India*. London: Jonathan Cape, 1927.

Mehta, Ved. *The New India*. New York: Viking, 1978.

———. *A Family Affair*. New York: Oxford University Press, 1982.

Mukherjee, Meenakshi. "An Interview with Yasmine Gooneratne." *Book Review*, March–April 1983, pp. 213–16.

———. *The Twice Born Fiction: Themes and Techniques of the Indian Novel in English*. New Delhi: Arnold-Heinemann, 1974.

Murdoch, Iris. "The Sublime and the Beautiful Revisited." *Yale Review* 49 (December 1959): 247–71.

Naipaul, V. S. *India: A Wounded Civilization*. Harmondsworth, England: Penguin, 1979.

Narayan, R. K. "When India Was A Colony." *New York Times*, 16 September 1984.

Nehru, Jawaharlal. *Toward Freedom: The Autobiography of Jawaharlal Nehru.* Boston: Beacon Press, 1967.

Nichols, Beverley. *Verdict on India.* London: Jonathan Cape, 1944.

Nobbe, Susanne Howe. See Howe, Susanne.

Nordon, Pierre. *Sir Arthur Conan Doyle.* Paris: Didier, 1964.

Parry, Benita. *Delusions and Discoveries: Studies on India in the British Imagination 1880–1930.* Berkeley & Los Angeles: University of California Press, 1972.

Pritchett, V. S. "Books." *The New Yorker*, 16 June 1973, pp. 106–7.

Radhakrishnan, S. *Eastern Religions and Western Thought.* New York: Oxford University Press, 1959.

Ramanujan, A. K. "Is There an Indian Way of Thinking?" Revised version of paper presented at the First Workshop of the "Person in South Asia" Project sponsored by the ACLS-SSRC Joint Committee on South Asia, Chicago, September 1980.

Rao, K. Bhaskara. *Paul Scott.* Boston: Twayne Publishers, 1980.

Roberts, F. S. (Lord Roberts of Kandahar). *Forty-One Years in India.* London: Longmans, Green, 1902.

Said, Edward. *Orientalism.* New York: Pantheon Books, 1978.

Sandahl, Stella. "India and its Critics." *Toronto South Asia Review* 2, no. 2 (1983): 59–74.

———. "To Psychoanalyse a Civilization." *Journal of Indian Philosophy* 10 (1982): 299–303.

Schweitzer, Albert. *Indian Thought and Its Development.* Boston: Beacon Press, 1957.

Scott, Paul. "*The Continent of Circe* by Nirad C. Chaudhuri." *Times Literary Supplement*, 2 December 1965, p. 1093.

———. "An Idealist in Action" (review of *Indira Gandhi* by Zareer Masani). *Country Life*, 19 June 1975, pp. 1643–44.

———. "India: A Post-Forsterian View." In *Essays by Divers Hands*, pp. 113–32. Transactions of the Royal Society of Literature, vol. 36. London: Oxford University Press, 1970.

———. "Trade Before the Flag" (review of *The Chinese Opium Wars* by Jack Reading). *Country Life*, 5 June 1975, pp. 1503–4.

Selbourne, David. *Through the Indian Looking-glass.* London: Zed Press, 1982.

Shahane, Vasant A. *Ruth Prawer Jhabvala.* London: Arnold-Heinemann, 1976.

Shamsul Islam. *Chronicles of the Raj: A Study of Literary Reaction to the Imperial Idea Towards the End of the Raj.* Totowa, N.J.: Rowman & Littlefield, 1979.

———. *Kipling's Law: A Study of His Philosophy of Life.* London: Macmillan, 1975.

Singh, Bhupal. *A Survey of Anglo-Indian Fiction.* London: Oxford University Press, 1934.

Smith, Vincent. *The Oxford History of India.* 2d ed., rev. and cont. to 1921 by S. M. Edwardes. Oxford: Clarendon Press, 1923.

Spear, Percival. *The Nabobs: A Study of the Social Life of the English in Eighteenth Century India*. London: Oxford University Press, 1963.

Steinvorth, Klaus. *The Indo-English Novel: The Impact of the West on Literature in a Developing Country*. Wiesbaden: Franz Steiner Verlag, 1975.

Stone, Wilfred. *The Cave and the Mountain: A Study of E. M. Forster*. Oxford: Oxford University Press, 1966.

Swinden, Patrick. *Paul Scott: Images of India*. New York: St. Martin's Press, 1980.

Theroux, Paul. *The Great Railway Bazaar*. Boston: Houghton Mifflin, 1975.

Tindall, William York. *Forces in Modern British Literature*. New York: Knopf, 1947.

Weinraub, Bernard. "The Artistry of Ruth Prawer Jhabvala." *New York Times*, 11 September 1983.

Who's Who of Indian Writers. New Delhi: Sahitya Akademi, 1961.

Williams, Haydn Moore. *The Fiction of Ruth Prawer Jhabvala*. Calcutta: Writers Workshop, 1973.

———. *Indo-Anglian Literature 1800–1970: A Survey*. Bombay: Orient Longmans, 1977.

World Authors. New York: H. W. Wilson, 1975.

Wurgaft, Lewis D. *The Imperial Imagination: Magic and Myth in Kipling's India*. Middletown, Conn.: Wesleyan University Press, 1983.

Yeats-Brown, F. *Bengal Lancer*. London: Victor Gollancz, 1931.

Index